Scrapbook

Tips & Techniques

Over 100 quick and easy ideas!

M

MEMORY MAKERS BOOKS

DENVER , COLORADO

Table of Contents

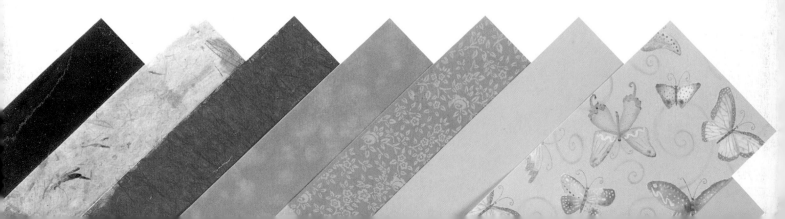

Children are God's way
of telling us that tomorrow
will be beautiful.

Aylssa - 4 1/2 years old

my big sister spent playing with me.

cheri age 12   erikia age 2   summer   1976 in brush, co.

Sisters

dog's
best
friend

matt, age 5
may 1972

We measure
Abby, not with
rulers, but with
lies & daisies.

You're

An introduction

If you're a die-hard scrapbooker, this book is for you. Inside you'll find four different sections, each detailing tons if techniques and showcasing pages for ideas and inspiration.

First, discover the amazing versatility of your scrapbook papers. Learn to squeeze every ounce of potential from each sheet. Watch your album pages blossom with new dimension, new texture and new patterns.

Next, learn how to use your scrapbook tools to their best and most creative advantage. If you've got the tools, Memory Makers has the tips and techniques for making the most of your investments. You'll find cutting-edge concepts for less-obvious and more innovative uses for popular tools you already own.

Then you can dress up your scrapbook pages with coordinating border, corner and title treatments to achieve a true designer look. You'll find great ideas for pulling together dynamic scrapbook pages that showcase the best of times, year round.

Lastly, you'll find favorite scrapbook lettering styles collected from the past few years of *Memory Makers* magazine, plus more than 20 new alphabets from the nation's top scrapbook lettering artists. With lettering styles ranging from elegantly classic to cutting-edge creative, there's sure to be an alphabet to suit each of your scrapbook pages perfectly.

What are you waiting for? Get started making the most of your scrapbook pages today!

CREATIVE
PAPER TECHNIQUES
for SCRAPBOOKS

More than 75 fresh paper craft ideas

MEMORY
MAKERS
BOOKS

Kylie

Brandi

Brittany

my girls have FUN!

This book belongs to

We dedicate this book to all of our *Memory Makers* contributors whose imaginative and delightful paper craft ideas are the inspiration behind this book.

TABLE OF CONTENTS

Sibling Revelry

Trying to take the perfect picture is an exercise in patience, and you have to have a lot of film!

Anna, Sasha and Daniel 2002

Sibling Revelry

INTRODUCTION

The colors, textures and patterns of paper continually stimulate our senses. You may love to look at paper, but, if you're like me, you also have to touch it. I like to feel the thickness, flexibility, and run my thumb across the surface texture. From my first fold-and-cut paper snowflakes made as a child, to the sophisticated folds in my scrapbooks today, paper's diversity simply fascinates me.

Paper and paper crafts have been around for thousands of years, across all cultures, and yet new paper crafts continue to emerge and find their way into our lives and into our scrapbooks. I am very excited about this book for many reasons.

This is a paper experience that will change forever the way you look at scrapbook papers! It features a wide array of easy-to-make paper craft projects that use simple, basic tools and supplies that you probably already own. No prior creative training is needed and the projects are well-suited for scrapbookers of all skill levels— so there's something for everyone!

Each project is accompanied by step-by-step illustrations. Most projects use specific patterned papers, templates and other basic supplies to teach the techniques. But our aim is to encourage individual experimentation. The true beauty of these paper craft techniques is that once you learn the basics, you can apply these techniques to your favorite scrapbook papers in colors that coordinate with your photos. We provide useful suggestions for helping you do just that! In addition, there are reproducible patterns and drawings to assist you in making these projects. The final *Gallery* section presents an array of gorgeous spinoffs of these techniques to further inspire you!

Who would've ever thought that a simple sheet of paper could be transformed into such a textural enhancement for your scrapbooks! I hope you will enjoy this book and will be inspired to experiment with your own scrapbook papers and these wonderful techniques. So go on, take a piece of paper and hold it. Turn it over in your hand. Fold it, cut it, tear it and create!

Michele

Michele Gerbrandt
Founding Editor
Memory Makers® magazine

PAPER 101

The economical prices and widespread availability of scrapbook papers—in hundreds of colors, patterns, textures and weights—make paper crafting all the more enjoyable. However, paper for scrapbooks should be both fun and functional. To be photo-safe, paper should be pH neutral (acid-free) and lignin-free. Many paper varieties are also buffered, which is preferable for scrapbooking projects. The paper techniques featured in this book use specific paper products, but each is easily adaptable to your favorite scrapbook paper types and patterns.

Be aware that while they are beautiful to look at, not all vellum, mulberry, metallic or handmade papers are of archival quality and as such, should not be allowed to directly touch photos and memorabilia. Have fun experimenting with a variety of different papers and you will soon see that contrast between the different paper types can greatly enhance the effect of a project.

Types of paper

Metallic Shiny, metallic papers—some holographic—are available in many colors. Use these for replicating page accents of metallic objects such as picture frames or when a little sparkle and sheen are desired.

Handmade Reminiscent of old-fashioned, rough-textured paper, its fibers, confetti and other elements add visual impact to paper art.

Mulberry Papers with a heavy look of wood fiber; useful for pages and paper projects calling for a natural, outdoorsy feel.

Suede A leathery-looking paper, available in a number of colors, which is useful for adding texture to paper crafts.

Vellum Transparent paper, either solid-colored or patterned, that is great for decorative elements where a sheer effect is desired.

Cardstock Sturdier paper, available in a multitude of colors and patterns, which is especially useful for backgrounds, matting photos and making paper photo frames.

Solid-colored paper Basic solid papers, available in hundreds of colors and a variety of weights, can be used alone or with any other paper type.

Patterned paper Multi-use, versatile paper that can support theme layouts and is available in hundreds of different designs and patterns.

Proper paper storage Protect your investment by treating your paper with care. Keep it out of the sun and away from moisture. Store the sheets flat if possible or upright in a container made specifically for storing paper, such as a Scrap-N-File™ (Caren's Crafts).

Selecting paper colors based on photos

Color affects our thoughts and emotions as well as the outcome of our scrapbook pages. Some colors (red) inspire energetic feelings while others (blue and green) are calming. When selecting paper colors for your scrapbook pages, choose shades that are consistent with the mood of your photos.

Another successful strategy is to draw colors and patterns from your photos. You may wish to pick up on the blue in the background sky, or the green of grass, the color or pattern of an outfit or the hue of a person's eyes. Once you determine a primary color, choose other colors that complement your primary choice.

If you aren't confident about choosing colors, consider buying papers in presorted packages. These packets come with corresponding, coordinating papers in color and theme variations. Prepackaged papers help take the guesswork out of paper selection.

Can't figure out what colors to use? Pick up a color wheel at your local art or craft store. A color wheel has a rotating dial that helps users choose colors that work together harmoniously. The wheel shows complementary colors (colors that fall directly opposite each other on the wheel, such as green and red) and other combinations. There are dozens of ways to use the color wheel when scrapbooking.

Determining paper grain All machine-made paper is easier to fold or tear in one direction than in the other because the paper consists of parallel fibers, called "the grain." Working against the grain can give uneven and ragged results, which is fine if that is the look you desire. For crisp folds and smoothly torn edges, go with the grain. Experiment with sample scraps from your scrapbook papers to learn how to identify the grain as we have done below. Then use this knowledge to your advantage when creating your paper art.

Tearing paper When paper—in this case vellum—is torn against the grain, it creates uneven and ragged tears as shown on the left. Likewise, when the same vellum is torn with the grain, the result is a predictable tear.

Folding paper The square of patterned paper at the top of the example above was folded against the grain, resulting in a rough fold. When the same paper is folded with the grain, a clean, crisp fold is created.

TOOLS & SUPPLIES

Use this list of tools and supplies to help you get started in these exciting and creative paper techniques. You'll find that you probably already have most of the "basic" tools listed. These are tools that you will need for most any paper craft project. The "optional" tools listed on the next page are tools used in various projects featured in this book. While it is not essential that you have these tools to make specific projects, they can certainly make the job easier. Tips and techniques for using tools follow on pages 16 through 18.

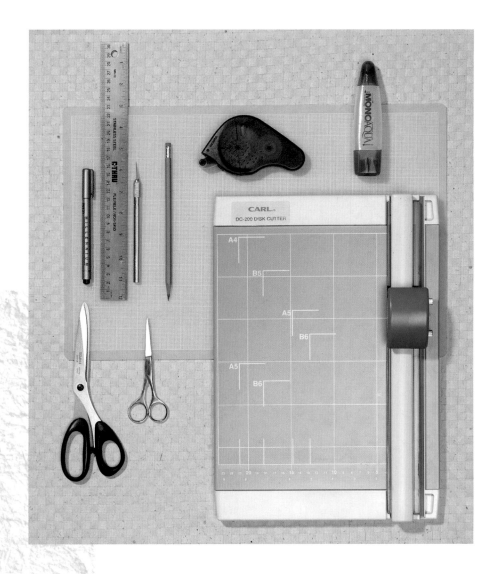

The Basics
- Craft knife
- Cutting mat
- Liquid adhesive
- Metal straightedge ruler
- Pencil
- Personal paper trimmer
- Pigment pens
- Regular scissors
- Small scissors
- Tape adhesive

Your workspace For successful paper crafting, keep your workspace clean and organized. Regularly remove any adhesive residue from your cutting mat and tools. Keep basic tools handy, as you will use them the most.

Optional tools

- Art Deckle™ ruler
- Bone folder
- Embellishments (beads, buttons, wire, etc.)
- Embossing stylus
- Graph paper
- Graphing ruler
- Letter templates
- Memorabilia keepers
- Metal flakes
- Nested templates
- Paper crimper
- Quilling needle, slotted quilling needle & paper strips
- Removable artist tape
- Rubber stamps & inkpad
- Shape punches
- Small paintbrush
- Spoon
- Tweezers
- Vellum adhesive

Mounting paper projects in scrapbooks

For longevity, we recommend the use of acid- and lignin-free albums and paper products, archival-quality adhesives, PVC-free plastics and pigment inks for journaling.

ILLUSTRATED TIPS & TECHNIQUES

These illustrated tips and techniques will help you achieve the best possible results from your paper, tools and supplies. Begin with a work surface that is clean and protected by a self-healing cutting mat. A self-healing cutting mat does not become pitted by craft knife cuts, ensuring that new paper cuts will always go where you put them. Make sure your tools are clean and dry. Replace any cutting blades and sharpen the edges of scissors on a whetstone, if needed, before you begin any paper craft project.

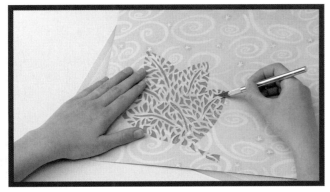

Cutting with a craft knife For straight cuts, hold the craft knife against the edge of a ruler. Use a craft knife to cut in tiny areas where scissors can't reach. Cut into cardstock at an angle to prevent white backing from showing through.

Cutting against a metal straightedge ruler When cutting straight lines, cut against a metal straightedge ruler with a nonskid backing instead of a plastic graphing ruler, which the knife will cut into. Hold paper and ruler firmly to prevent slipping.

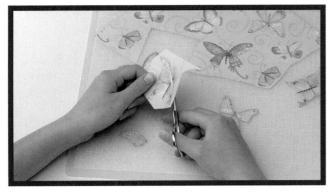

Cutting with scissors Scissors should be clean and sharp. For precision, small scissors work best when silhouette-cropping elements from paper. Use long strokes with larger scissors to ensure a smooth-cut line.

Cutting with a paper trimmer Paper trimmers are great for making perfectly straight cuts and for cutting your own quilling strips. Hold paper firmly in place with left hand, then lower or slide the blade down quickly and smoothly.

Anchoring a work in progress Hold artwork down while you are working on it, particularly when weaving on a loom, with low-tack, removable artist tape. The tape will remove easily without marring the paper surface or leaving residue behind.

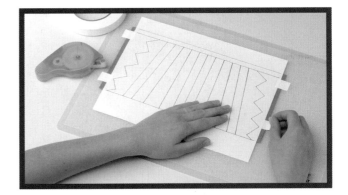

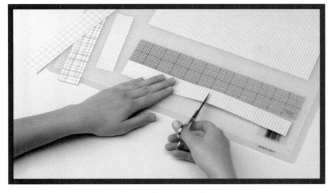

Measure twice, cut once When cutting paper strips or blocks for a project that requires evenly sized, accurate strips, follow the golden rule of carpentry and quilting: Measure twice and cut once.

Measuring with a graphing ruler A graphing ruler can be used with a pencil to mark grids or cutting lines on the back of paper. You can easily view the paper surface beneath the ruler's clear surface for accurate measuring when needed.

Marking placement guides Use a pencil and ruler to draw guidelines to help you accurately place vertical or horizontal paper strips for weaving, for evenly spaced punching, etc.

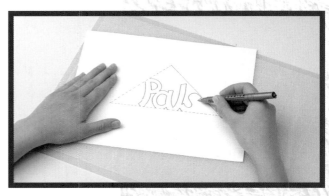

Making a pattern Make a freehand cut or template-traced pattern on cardstock. Strive for accuracy—a well-made pattern provides the best results. Label pattern with solid lines for cut lines and dotted lines for fold lines.

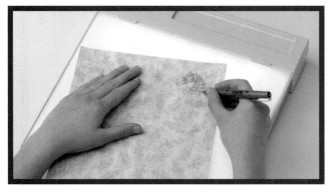

Transferring a pattern to paper Transfer patterns to paper directly from the source on a light box, with tracing paper or against a sunny window. To size a pattern to fit your page, use a photocopier; print the resized image directly on paper or transfer it by hand.

Scoring against a metal straightedge ruler When folding cardstock or mulberry paper, use a metal straightedge ruler and a bone folder to "score" the paper first where you will place the fold. This will make it easier to achieve a crisp fold.

Creating a crisp fold After scoring the paper with a bone folder—made of real bone or plastic—fold the paper on the score and then rub the bone folder along the length of the fold to flatten the crease into a crisp, finished fold.

Flattening a fold Turn your finished, folded art over and rub a spoon along all fold lines to flatten out the folds on the backside. This will give the front of your art a flat, smooth appearance.

Controlling a tear Different papers tear differently; some tear clean, others ragged. For greatest control, tear between the finger and thumbnails. Practice tearing a wide variety of papers to learn what to expect from each paper type.

Using a Deckle ruler for tearing For uniform and straight tears, try using tearing paper against the edge of a Deckle ruler, which works well for tearing soft papers such as mulberry and vellum.

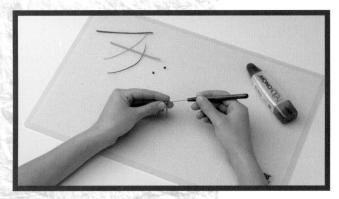

Using needle for tightly quilled centers A slotted needle is a quick-and-easy tool to use for quilling, but only a needle or hatpin will give you a very tightly coiled "peg." Dampen the end of paper strip to help it stick to the needle for rolling.

Tearing quilling strip ends Before rolling a quilling strip into a coil, tear one end. Insert the straight, untorn end into the slotted needle and coil. Apply adhesive to the torn end of the finished coil for a "seamless" finish.

1

CUTTING

When you lovingly cut cut your first valentine as a child, you ventured into the centuries-old craft of paper cutting. Paper cutting originated in China approximately 1500 years ago, and the art form has been passed on from generation to generation and across many cultures. Numerous forms of single- and multiple-layer paper cutting are apt and suitable techniques for scrapbook pages. In this section, you will discover how to:

- *Create pull-apart borders and backgrounds using decorative rulers, templates and freeform designs*
- *Cut apart and reassemble paper to create multidimensional designs*
- *Create free-form, pull-apart alphabets*
- *Add relief detail to template-cut shapes*
- *Cut multicolored, layered designs utilizing a single pattern*
- *Create intricate designs through silhouette cropping*

Paper cutting is the foundation of many other creative paper techniques. Master these basics and then combine them with the other amazing techniques featured in later chapters.

Single-Layer Cutting

Single-layer cutting is the very foundation of creative paper techniques. Cut a simple sheet of paper with scissors or a craft knife, and it is transformed into a versatile page embellishment. Create a variety of borders and backgrounds by experimenting with decorative rulers and templates. Or create freeform designs using just your imagination and creative muse for single-layer cut paper designs with lots of impact.

Cynthia Anning

Pull apart a shaped border

Add pizazz to a border using a decorative ruler to draw lines and then cut paper into strips in a variety of widths. Changing the design of the decorative ruler and placing your borders at the upper or lower edges of the page will give you a completely different look. Follow the steps on the next page to create border; mount on page. Single and double mat photos. Freehand cut waterdrop designs. Print title lettering on computer and then crop and mat.

What you will need

- Two sheets of coordinating, solid-colored papers
- Decorative ruler (Creative Memories)
- Computer front (Creating Keepsakes)

1 Draw two parallel lines ¼" apart using a decorative ruler to form the cutting guidelines.

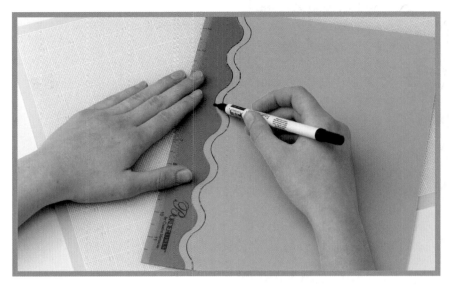

2 Cut along the drawn guidelines with a pair of scissors or use a craft knife (if the decorative ruler you use has a more linear pattern), forming two strips of paper.

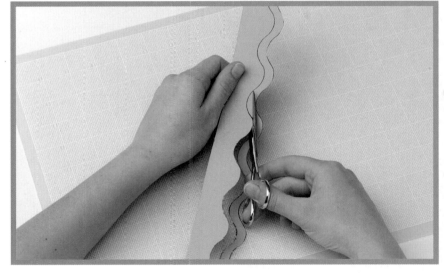

3 Mount strips onto background paper, pulling them apart to leave ¼" space between the two to allow background paper to show through.

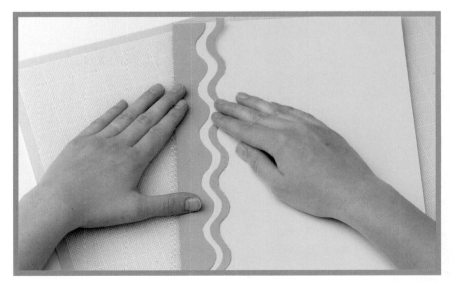

Use a template to create a pull-apart design

Create visual interest using a simple template design by cutting out the shape, pulling it apart, and then mounting all the segments on background paper, leaving space between each piece. Change the template shape to coordinate with your page and photo themes, if desired. Follow the steps on page 23 before triple matting design. Circle cut photos; mount on page. Add journaling at center and title phrase around edge of second matting.

Kelly Angard; Photos Torrey Miller

What you will need

- Two to four sheets of coordinating, solid-colored papers
- Leaf template (Fiskars)
- Circle shape cutter or circle template

1 On paper of choice, position and trace template shape; draw two parallel lines about ¼" apart, connecting the drawn shapes and forming continuous cutting lines.

2 Using small, sharp scissors, cut along drawn lines, making sure to use one continuous stroke of the scissors for a clean cut. Similar to silhouette cropping, have patience and move the paper in and out of the scissor blades instead of moving the blade around the shape.

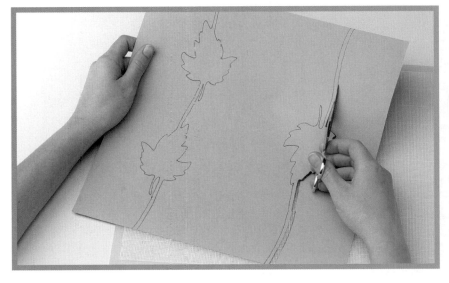

3 Place the five cut-apart segments in order on complementary-colored background paper, making sure to pull segments apart to allow background paper to show through. Adhere segments. Turn page over and trim off any overlap of the segmented pieces.

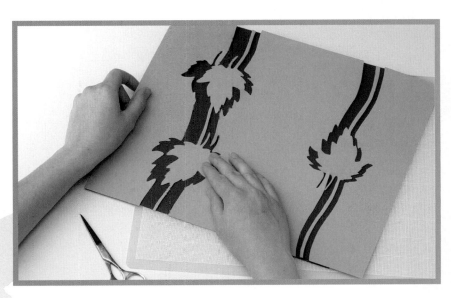

Pull apart a free-form background

Draw your own freehand design to be cut, pulled apart, and then reassembled to complement the theme of your photos. Follow the steps on the next page to create the animal-print background design shown here. Try this technique for creating zoo, flag, beach, landscape or rainbow backgrounds—or any theme where a wavy pattern is desired. Freehand draw and cut paw prints; crop photos to fit. Circle cut smaller photos and mat on black paper. Adhere sticker letters and paw-print stickers. Complete page with journaling.

Lorna Christensen

What you will need

- Two sheets of coordinating, solid-colored papers
- One sheet black paper
- White pencil
- Sticker letters (Provo Craft)
- Paw-print stickers (Creative Memories)

1 Freehand draw striped animal pattern on backside of solid-colored paper.

2 Photocopy drawn paper or number the stripes sequentially to make reassembly easier, if desired. Use scissors to cut along the drawn lines; set aside pieces in their proper order.

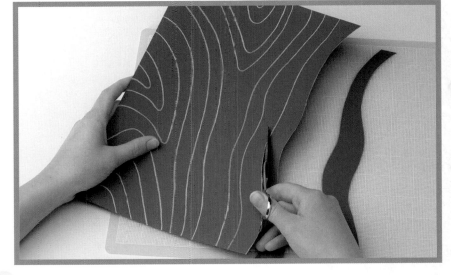

Reassemble pieces in order with front side showing (your pattern will be a reverse image of what you drew) onto complementary-colored background paper, making sure to leave space between each piece so the background paper shows through. You may not be able to use all of the outer stripes depending on how much space you leave between the stripes. Finally, trim off any overlap.

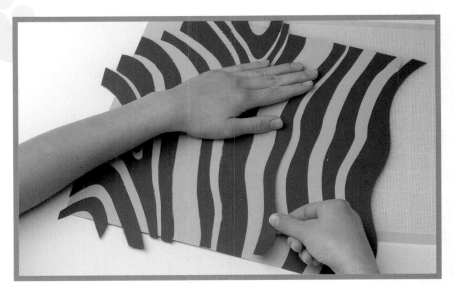

Add depth to patterned paper pull-aparts

Take patterned paper to a new dimension by slicing random segments and layering with self-adhesive foam spacers. Follow the steps on page 27 to create a background with depth. Double mat background design. Double mat photos; round corners and trim one with decorative scissors. Create title letters with template and patterned paper, mat and silhouette crop. Mount on vellum trimmed with decorative scissors and triple mat. Layer photos and title block on page, tucking corners under slices layered with foam spacers. Cut two 10" pieces of craft wire, twist a loop at one end with needle-nose pliers, add beads and twist second end to hold beads in place. Repeat process in random fashion, adding curves, loops and beads. Secure to page with flexible adhesive.

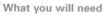

What you will need

- Two duplicate sheets of patterned paper (Creative Imaginations)

- Three sheets of coordinating, solid-colored papers

- Vellum (Strathmore)

- Decorative scissors (Fiskars)

- Corner rounder punch

- Self-adhesive foam spacers

- Lettering template (EK Success)

- Wire (Artistic™ Wire)

- Beads (Westrim)

- Needle-nose pliers

- Flexible adhesive (Glue Dots International)

Kelly Angard

1 Begin with two sheets of the same patterned paper. Slice one sheet along design lines; set the other aside.

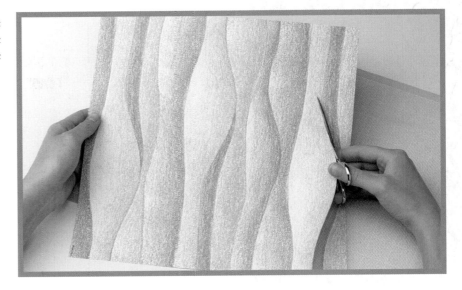

2 Reassemble slices onto solid-colored paper, leaving space between each slice so that the background shows through.

3 Slice selected segments from second sheet of patterned paper. Adhere onto first sheet of patterned paper atop same pattern lines with self-adhesive foam spacers.

Pull apart some title letters

Chopping-block title lettering gives your page a "woodsy" look—especially when cut from interesting patterned papers. Cut title letters from paper squares as shown on the next page. Adhere to background paper. Single and double mat photos. Add pen detail and journaling. Punch leaves; add to drawn vine and randomly scatter on page.

Joanna Navone

What you will need

- Scraps of coordinating solid-colored papers
- Pencil
- Leaf punches (Emagination Crafts)

1 Cut patterned paper into 1 x 1" squares. Freehand draw or trace letters lightly with a pencil, exaggerating some letters to make sure your pencil lines extend to the outside edges of the square. Cut on lines with scissors. Reassemble pieces on page, leaving space between to allow background paper to show through. Practice straight letters, such as E, L and Y before tackling rounded letters like B, R and S.

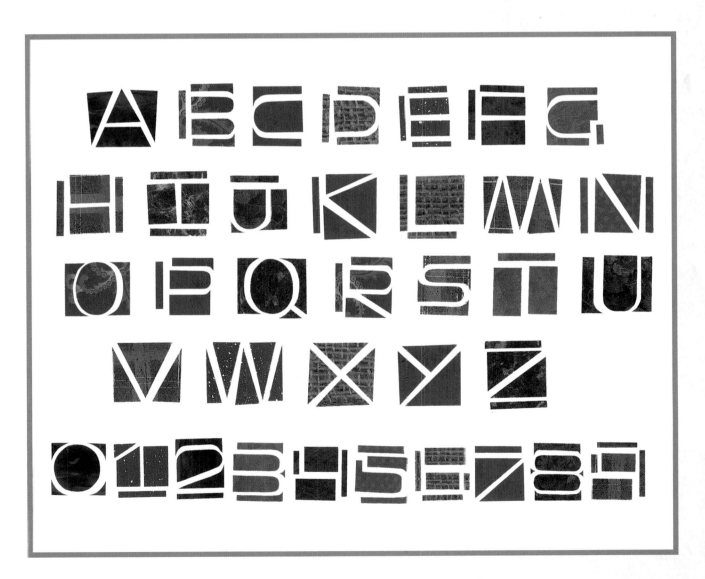

MULTIPLE-LAYER CUTTING

Cutting multiple layers of paper provides a myriad of ways to add shape, dimension and color to a scrapbook page. Each time you add a layer to your page, you add new possibilities to your design. Simple template shapes become more lifelike, and the designs in patterned paper almost seem to pop off the page. Each cut you make becomes an irresistible window offering a peek at the layers of paper below.

Jodi Amidei

What you will need

- Five to six sheets of coordinating, solid-colored papers
- Shape template (Provo Craft)
- Lettering template (Daisy Doodle)
- Pencil
- Small swirl punch (All Night Media)

Add detail to template shapes

Give template shapes dimension by cutting or punching details and designs before layering over complementary background paper. Follow the steps on page 31 to create unique template designs. Triple mat photo and add pen stroke detail. Tear solid-colored paper for earthen border; add pen stroke details. Layer photo and template shapes on page. Create title letters with template, mat and silhouette crop before adding pen stroke detail.

1 Select two solid-colored papers for each template shape to be used. Trace template shape on both sheets of paper and cut out. Select one of the two colored shapes for the top layer; set the other aside.

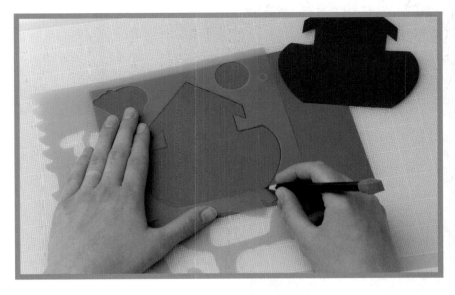

2 Use a metal straightedge ruler and a pencil to draw details on shape. A freehand design may also be drawn onto template shape as shown on the giraffe.

3 Use a craft knife to cut out drawn design. Another option to cutting a design with a craft knife is to punch a design, as shown on the sheep. Layer cut or punched shape over second shape previously set aside, with either flat adhesive or self-adhesive foam spacers for added dimension.

Cut details into layered design

A hand-cut and layered design is an exquisite feature that can complement the theme of your photos. Follow the steps on the next page to create the leaf design shown here. Use your own pattern or template shape to match your page theme. Crop photos into ovals, mat and layer on page. Create title block by double matting paper rectangles slightly askew. Adhere sticker letters and complete with journaling and pen detail.

'LEAF' IT TO US!

Like most kids, Cami & Evan love raking leaves in the fall! Of course, jumping into the big piles is the most fun!

Stacey Shigaya

What you will need

- One sheet of patterned paper (Paper Adventures)

- Two sheets of coordinating solid-colored papers (The Crafter's Workshop)

- Pattern on page 128

- Oval shape cutter or oval template

- Sticker letters (Making Memories)

1 Photocopy and size pattern provided onto regular white paper to fit your scrapbook page. Place pattern onto foreground paper of choice, positioning where you want the cut image to be. Tack paper down with removable artist tape to hold in place, if desired. Use a craft knife and steady hands to carefully cut out tiny shapes.

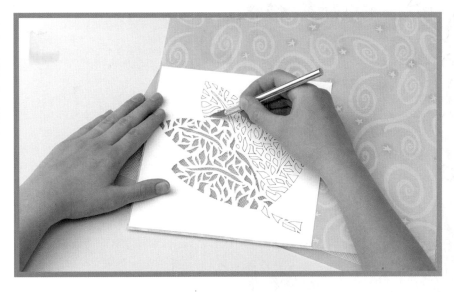

2 Select a sheet of solid-colored paper for the second layer; place it beneath cut foreground paper. Adhere together to prevent the paper from sliding when cutting. Using cut foreground paper as a pattern, carefully cut out shapes just a bit smaller than those cut on the foreground paper so that the second layer shows through the first.

3 Select a third sheet of solid-colored paper for the third and final background layer. To assemble, layer cut foreground and middle sheets atop background layer and adhere.

Cut peek-a-boo layers into patterned paper

Patterned papers provide a variety of options for cutting out details and layering for one-of-a-kind works of art. Follow the instructions below to create the layered border shown here. Then double mat smaller photos and mat large photo on patterned paper, torn and crumpled for texture, with self-adhesive foam spacers; mat again. Print title and journaling from computer; cut to size. Adhere fiber along top of page; mount title squares over fiber, leaving space for fiber to show through.

What you will need

- Two duplicate sheets of patterned paper in different colors (EK Success, Magenta)

- One sheet of coordinating-color, striped patterned paper (EK Success)

- Two sheets coordinating solid-colored papers

- Craft fiber (On the Surface)

- Self-adhesive foam spacers

- Computer font (Hallmark's Scrapbook Studio)

Brandi Ginn

1 Select two patterned papers in contrasting colors to cut designs from and layer with each other. Slice a 2½" strip from each sheet of paper for the border. Using a craft knife, cut along paper's natural design lines for first layer. Mount over second 2½" strip of paper in contrasting color; cut design into lower layer a little bit smaller than original cuts. Depending upon your eye, you may want to pencil in the design to cut on the second layer. Assemble and adhere the two cut layers with self-adhesive foam spacers atop a third border strip that is 2¾" wide. Mount completed border down side of background paper.

Cut and layer a self-framing background

Geometric designs on patterned paper provide perfect lines for cutting, layering and reassembling with foam spacers to create a self-framing background. Follow the steps on page 36 to create a layered background from a single sheet of paper. Insert fiber-accented photo, sliding it beneath the innermost layers, and adhere in place. Cut title letters from template and solid-colored paper; mount on title block and add journaling. Insert title block beneath innermost layers next to photo and adhere.

Pamela Frye; Photo Lois Duncan

What You Will Need

- One sheet of patterned paper (Memory Muse Designs)
- Two sheets of coordinating, solid-colored paper
- ⅛" and ¼" self-adhesive foam spacers
- Fiber
- Lettering template (C-Thru Ruler Co.)

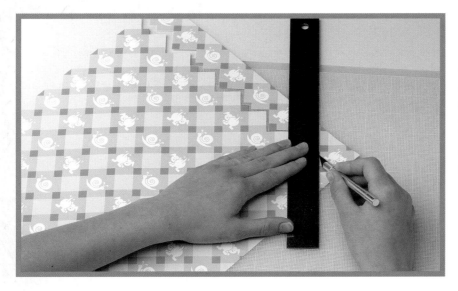

1 Use a craft knife and metal straightedge ruler to cut below the top row of diamond shapes, resulting in a border strip. Cut a second strip from the top of paper in the same manner. Repeat on the lower edge of the paper, resulting in four border strips. If your paper's design allows, you can also do this down the side edges to create side borders.

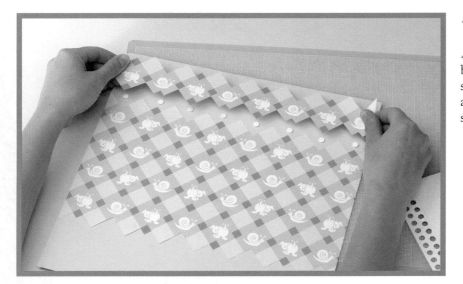

2 Adhere center section of diamond-shaped paper in the center of a sheet of solid-colored background paper. Use ⅛" self-adhesive foam spacers to reassemble and adhere one upper and one lower border strip next to the center section.

3 Use ¼" self-adhesive foam spacers to reassemble and adhere the remaining upper and lower border strips in place next to those adhered in Step 2.

Cut and layer an elegant title page

Create a stunning title page with elaborately patterned paper cut and layered three times for a multidimensional work of art. While this patterned paper has a very specific design, you can use this technique on any patterned paper with an elegant, baroque, old-world botanical or antique textile print. Follow the steps on page 38 to create this design. Freehand draw and cut title banners; outline with pen and write title. Mount with self-adhesive foam spacers.

Kelly Angard

What you will need

- Two duplicate sheets of patterned paper (NRN Designs)

- Two sheets of coordinating solid-colored papers

- Self-adhesive foam spacers

1 Trim dark gray border away from patterned paper in one continuous cut; set aside (not shown). Silhouette crop elements from the corners of the first sheet of patterned paper, following natural design lines. Using a craft knife, cut out a large design "medallion" from the center of the same sheet of patterned paper (not shown).

2 Adhere solid-colored papers behind the openings in detached corner pieces and center medallion of patterned paper. Trim off any excess overlap and set pieces aside.

3 One-eighth of an inch in from the edges of a solid-colored sheet of background paper, center and adhere the trimmed gray border from Step 1. Reassemble and layer cut and matted elements atop second sheet of patterned background paper, placing pieces over their original positions with self-adhesive foam spacers.

2

CUTTING & FOLDING

Picture the simple elegance of a Chinese paper fan, and you can easily understand the decorative impact that can be created by paper cutting and folding. Cutting and then folding paper adds depth and texture to a scrapbook page. Here you will learn to:

- *Turn folded paper strips into lovely, window-style "louvers"*
- *Piece together a number of varieties of bargello quilts*
- *Accent photos with a paper technique inspired by a camera lens' shutter opening—the iris fold*
- *Pinch paper to create pleats borrowed from the world of sewing*

Patience and creativity are all that's needed to master these simple but stunning techniques. With every cut and fold you make, you'll add a touch of elegance to your pages.

LOUVERS

Like the interior design accents from which this paper technique draws its inspiration, "louvers" are single-folded strips of paper that are used to fill in a cut-out "window" on your page. By varying the patterns, textures and directions of the paper strips, you can create a variety of showcases for your photos. Tuck the corners of photos, journaling blocks and memorabilia behind the strips for a truly unique scrapbook display.

Brandi Ginn

Create horizontal louvers to feature photos

The practical, linear design of a horizontal louver mat creates an interesting and useful display for photos. Patterned papers add visual impact. For a 12 x 12" page, start by trimming a 12 x 12" sheet of solid-colored cardstock down to 11¼" wide x 10¼" tall. Then cut out a 9¼" W x 8¼" T rectangular "window" opening to create a 1" wide frame; set frame aside. Follow the steps on page 41 to create cut-and-fold paper louvers. Mat photos; tuck under louvered strips and adhere. Print title and journaling on vellum; cut in blocks or to size, then mat and mount on page.

What you will need

- Two to five monochromatic, coordinating patterned papers (Making Memories)
- One sheet coordinating, solid-colored cardstock for frame
- Bone folder
- Vellum
- Computer fonts (*Boyz R Gross* downloaded from Internet; *LD Going Nuts* Inspire Graphics)

1 Begin by slicing sixteen 2" wide strips from different patterned papers. On the backside of each paper strip, use a metal straightedge ruler as a guide to run a bone folder down the center of each strip lengthwise to score a fold line (see page 17).

2 Fold each strip on the scored line with wrong sides pressed together, pressing along the fold with bone folder to form the louver strips.

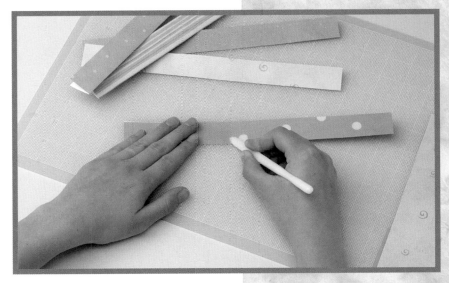

3 Apply adhesive to the inner edges of the back side of the frame. Mount folded louver strips horizontally across the frame's opening, overlapping strips about ½". Work from the top down and bottom up, keeping the folds pointed inward, toward the center of the frame. Continue until the frame opening is louvered.

Make a diagonal louver variation

Diagonal louvers, such as these within a stamped and embossed window frame, provide visual variation for nestling photos and memorabilia. For a 12 x 12" page, trim down one sheet of cardstock to 11¼ x 11¼"; cut a 8¾ x 8¾" opening to form frame. Stamp and emboss images on frame. Mat frame with second color of cardstock; cut out center opening, leaving ⅛" edge showing behind the top frame. Cut twenty 2" strips of white or cream-colored paper, then follow steps on page 41 to score and fold louvers. Apply adhesive to the inner edges of the backside of the frame. Mount louver strips on the diagonal, overlapping strips ½". Layer strips, beginning at the center and working out toward corners in both directions. Mat photos and journaling block; layer and tuck along with memorabilia beneath louvers. Cut title letters from template; punch holes for letter details. Double mat and layer with self-adhesive foam spacers.

Torrey Miller

What you will need

- Two sheets of coordinating, solid-colored cardstock for matted frame

- One to two sheets of white or cream-colored paper for louvers

- Rubber stamps (Hero Arts, Stampin' Up), embossing ink (Ranger), embossing powder (Stampendous)

- Bone folder

- Lettering template (Scrap Pagerz)

- Hole punch

- Self-adhesive foam spacers

Frame a photo with textured louvers

Crimped, patterned vellum, folded and mounted as louver strips on frame, provides a delicate, textured touch to portraits. Begin by mounting photo on background paper. Follow the instructions below to create the louvered layers. Cut two 1 x 8" strips of embossed card stock; mount horizontally above and below portrait. Print title on patterned paper; silhouette cut. Print journaling on vellum; layer over patterned paper and mount on page with eyelets.

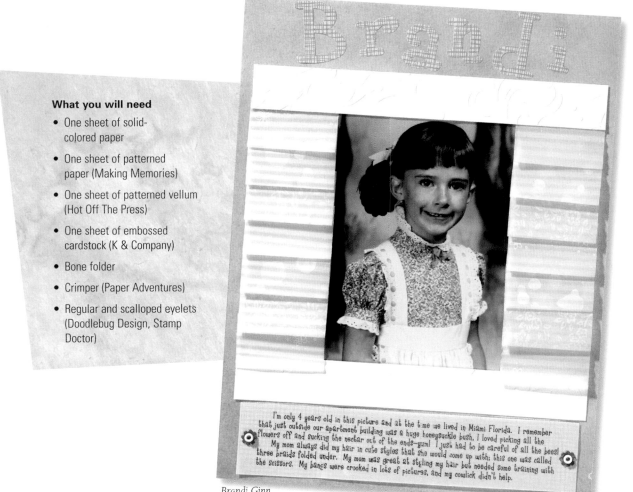

What you will need

- One sheet of solid-colored paper

- One sheet of patterned paper (Making Memories)

- One sheet of patterned vellum (Hot Off The Press)

- One sheet of embossed cardstock (K & Company)

- Bone folder

- Crimper (Paper Adventures)

- Regular and scalloped eyelets (Doodlebug Design, Stamp Doctor)

Brandi Ginn

1. Slice fourteen 2 x 2" patterned vellum squares; score at center with bone folder and fold in half lengthwise. Open folded strips; pass through crimper and refold strips carefully so as not to flatten out crimps. Layer horizontally on both sides of photo, with the folds pointing down, overlapping about one-fourth of an inch.

BARGELLOS

Like many contemporary paper techniques, "bargello" draws its inspiration from older crafts. Bargello was originally a needlework technique in which rows of color were used to create geometric shapes. Quilters and paper crafters then adapted it. Here, strips of paper are cut and folded to make abstract, yet traditional motifs—a perfect technique for the scrapbook page.

Erikia Ghumm

Layer a spectacular bargello background

Mix and match a variety of patterned papers for a stunning quilted background design. Experiment with the placement of the folded bargello strips and softer paper colors for an entirely different look. Follow the steps on pages 45 and 46 to create the bargello effect shown here. Double mat photo, leaving enough room on first mat for journaling. Freehand draw title letters. Outline letters in pen, silhouette crop, and mount on page with self-adhesive foam spacers.

What you will need

- Five to seven sheets of complementary-colored patterned papers (Hot Off The Press, Provo Craft, Scrapbook Wizard, Scrappin' Dreams)
- Bone folder
- Self-adhesive foam spacers

1 Cut numerous 1½" wide strips from a variety of complementary-colored patterned papers. The number of strips needed will vary depending on the size of your page and detail of the design.

2 With a bone folder and a metal straightedge ruler, score the backsides of all the strips lengthwise ¼" from the edge of each strip.

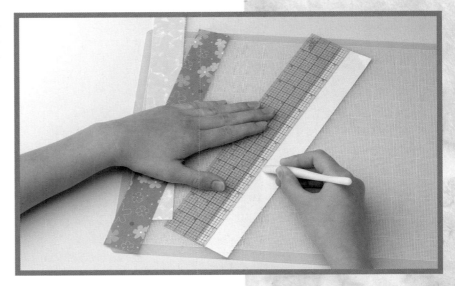

3 Fold the strips lengthwise on the scored lines, matching wrong sides together.

4 Use a pencil and a ruler to draw guidelines on solid-colored background paper where you want to begin adhering the folded strips. Alternate patterns and adhere folded strips diagonally starting in one corner and overlapping one over the other about ½", allowing the ends to hang off the page.

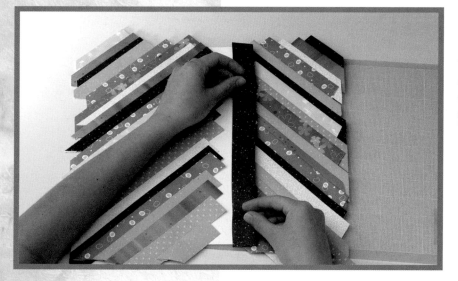

5 Continue alternating patterns and adhering strips diagonally to cover the second half of the background paper. When all diagonal strips are in place, mount vertical strips to hide diagonal strip ends and any pencil lines that may still be visible.

6 Turn the page over and use scissors to trim off any overlap, carefully cutting along the edges of the background paper.

Cut and fold a bargello mat

Layer folded strips of complementary-colored patterned papers into a textured mat perfect for highlighting a portrait. Rotate photo, mat or both in different angles for a varied effect. Start by slicing 1½" strips of patterned papers; score and fold lengthwise following steps on pages 45 and 46 to form folded strips that are ¾" wide. Layer onto an 8¼" square piece of paper, turn over and trim. Double mat bargello design. Quadruple mat portrait, mount on bargello mat design. Layer atop patterned background paper. Cut four ½" wide patterned paper strips; mat with solid-colored paper strips. Mount diagonally at each corner; turn page over and trim edges. Crop and journal matted title block; mount on page.

What you will need

- Four sheets of complementary-colored patterned papers (Colors by Design, Ever After, Frances Meyer, Karen Foster)

- Two sheets of coordinating, solid-colored papers

- Bone folder

Kelly Angard

IRISES Popular in Holland, this paper technique mimics the iris diaphragm—or metal blades—that form the aperture opening of a camera lens. Cut and folded strips of paper softly overlap each other while leaving an opening in the center through which precious photos are revealed. The technique is created on the back of your scrapbook page, providing a creative surprise when you are finished and you turn your page over to reveal a magnificent photo frame!

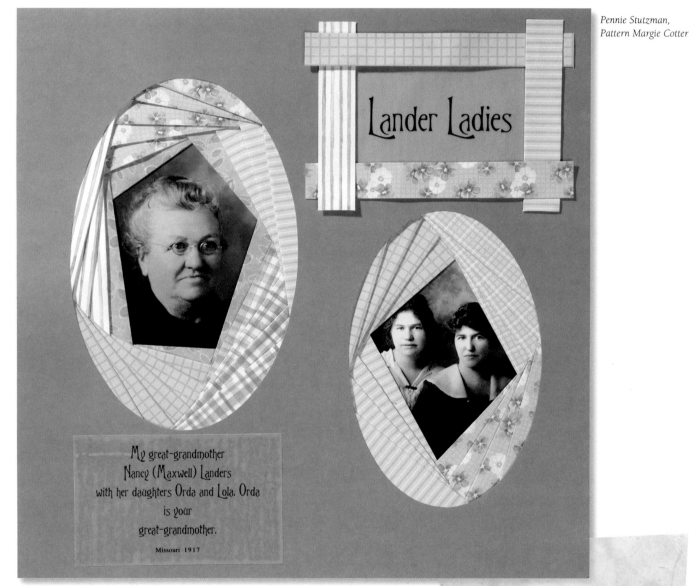

Pennie Stutzman,
Pattern Margie Cotter

Craft elegant oval iris frames

The surprising art of iris folding results in gorgeous photo frames. We provide patterns for oval and rectangular iris frames, but you can easily create your own pattern by using a different template shape and drawing your own placement lines. Follow the steps on pages 49 and 50 to create the oval frames shown here on a 12 x 12" page. Print title and journaling on vellum. Frame title with additional strips of folded, patterned paper.

What you will need

- Four to six complementary-colored sheets of patterned papers (Hot Off The Press, Karen Foster, Colorbök)

- One sheet of cardstock for background

- Pattern on page 128

- Removable artist tape

- Bone folder

1 Cut twenty-five 2 x 6" strips from patterned papers for the large oval iris frame. Cut sixteen 2 x 6" strips for the small oval iris frame.

2 Use a bone folder to score strips in half lengthwise, then use bone folder to fold strips with wrong sides facing together.

3 Photocopy and size patterns to fit scrapbook page. Position patterns on the front of your page where you want the oval frame openings to be; hold in place with removable artist tape, if desired. Use a craft knife to cut out the patterns' outer oval shapes only (don't cut on any of the pattern's interior placement lines; you'll need them for step 5). Or, use a graduated oval template or shape cutter that is the same size as your pattern to cut openings on scrapbook page.

4 Place pattern pieces face down over cut opening on the front of the page, centering so that the patterns' numbers and placement guidelines show on the back side of the page; adhere with removable artist tape.

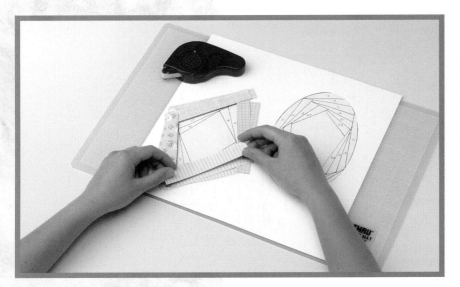

5 You will work from the patterns' outer edges inward to adhere folded strips of paper in numerical order following pattern numbers. Place the folded edges inward toward the center of the pattern, overlapping strips as you go, staying true to the patterns' placement guidelines.

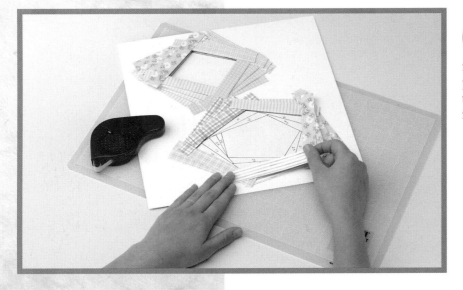

6 Continue adhering strips until the patterns are covered. Flip the page over and carefully remove the pattern so as not to tear page. Slip photos behind the patterned paper iris openings and mount in place.

Make a rectangular iris frame variation

The rectangular iris frame works great for horizontal photos. With either oval or rectangular frames, you can make the photo opening larger by not adding the last row of folded paper strips. Start with sixteen 2 x 7½" patterned paper strips. Then follow steps 2 through 5 on pages 49 and 50 to make the iris folded frame using pattern on page 128. Slip photo behind iris frame; mount in place on back of page. Cut title letters from patterned paper using template. Print journaling on vellum; mount on page with eyelets.

Sean and Cameron are Bob's boys alright! They sound, act and joke around just like him—they are "Bitty Bobs" for sure!

August 1999 Sean, age 7; Cameron, age 10

Pennie Stutzman, Pattern Margie Cotter

What you will need

- Patterned papers (Magenta, Provo Craft)
- Pattern on page 128
- Bone folder
- Lettering template (Cut-It-Up)
- Vellum
- Eyelets (Impress Rubber Stamps)

PLEATS

Like the freshly pressed dust ruffle over a box spring mattress, pleated photo mats and frames lend a smart, crisp look to your pages. The key to successful pleating, another paper craft adapted from sewing, is precise cutting and folding. Corners are then nipped and tucked by "mitering" them with a metal straightedge ruler and craft knife. Use pinch pleats for a soft, feminine look or try box pleats for a more rugged, masculine feel.

Lynn Morgan for Anna Griffin, Inc.

Combine box and pinch pleats for elegance

Add an elegant touch to your page by folding patterned papers into pleated frames. Paper may be pleated along one edge or diagonally, but pleating always entails folding in opposite directions at marked intervals. Follow the steps on the following pages to create the box pleat and pinch pleat frames. Mat photo on patterned paper framed with silhouette cropped and matted ribbon design. Mount with self-adhesive foam spacers. Silhouette crop roses to adorn the frame's corners. Mat again on green patterned papers. Print title journaling on vellum; layer over printed title strip. Mount on paper cut and folded to look like ribbon.

What you will need

- Four sheets of coordinating patterned papers (Anna Griffin)
- Title strip (Anna Griffin)
- Bone folder
- 45° triangle (optional)
- Double-sided adhesive
- Self-adhesive foam spacers

1 *BOX PLEAT* Using a pencil and straightedge ruler, draw parallel lines alternating at 1" and ⅜" intervals across the back of patterned paper. Score lines with a bone folder and metal straightedge ruler.

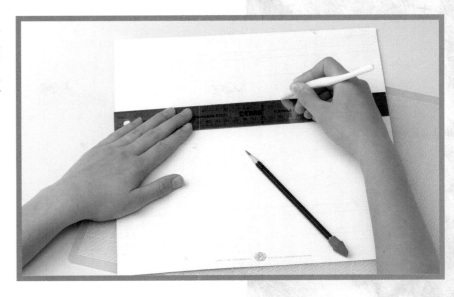

2 Start at one edge of the paper. Work your way across the paper pulling, pinching and pleating on scored lines, folding the ⅜" scores toward each other, alternating from front and back sides, until all folds are completed.

3 Cut pleats into ½" strips by holding all pleats down flat with a metal straightedge ruler on top of folded paper. Using a craft knife, slice down upon the folds, not up (see step 6 on page 130). Adhere double-sided adhesive across back of strips to hold pleats in place.

4 "Miter" corners with a metal straightedge ruler and craft knife, cutting at a 45° angle (use a 45° triangle if you have one), resulting in a clean, angled corner where border strips meet at page corners. Adhere pleated paper strips around page's outer edge. See steps 5 and 6 on page 130 for pinch pleat instructions to make the second row of pleats.

Torrey Miller; Photo Leslie Aldridge

What you will need

- Two sheets of coordinating patterned papers (Karen Foster, Scrap Ease)

- Two sheets of coordinating, solid-colored papers

- Bone folder

- Self-adhesive foam spacers

Create a raised box pleat variation

Add visual interest and dimension to a folded box pleat frame by layering patterned paper strips before folding and applying self-adhesive foam spacers to form peaks and valleys. Double mat photo and mount on matted background paper. Follow the steps on page 130 to create raised box pleat.

3

FOLDING & CUTTING

Think back to those childhood days when you made paper doll chains and snowflakes. Folding paper first and then cutting it provides a completely different spectrum of design possibilities than simply cutting paper or cutting and then folding it. In this section you will learn to:

- *Create paper chains, borders and frames using patterns or templates*
- *Embellish paper chains with stickers*
- *Fold and cut a multi-window "kirigami" frame*
- *Use decorative rulers and punches to create folded frames*
- *Transform a simple napkin fold into a poinsettia and snowflake*
- *Use a lettering template to create a personalized cut-out frame*

A few simple folds and some creative cuts will provide you with an endless supply of unique embellishments for your pages, no matter what their theme.

PAPER CHAINS

Remember when you opened your first chain of paper dolls? Like magic, the paper unfurled to reveal a line of little figures all linked together and holding hands. Experience the same sense of wonder by customizing paper chains to fit your scrapbook page themes for one-of-a-kind photo frames and page borders. With paper chains, your creative options are limitless.

Jodi Amidei

Fold and cut a paper chain

A folded and cut paper chain can serve not only as a border design, but also as the perfect resting-place for title letters. Experiment with any freehand-drawn shape or template shape to make quick-and-easy paper chains to match your page theme. Follow the steps on page 57 to craft the mitten paper chain shown here. Embellish mittens with pen details, snowflake punch and yarn or felt. Double mat photos; layer on page. Tear patterned paper; layer over matted background paper at bottom of page. Mount large mitten chain over torn paper for border. Stamp title letters on small mitten paper chain; mount across top of pages.

What you will need

- One sheet of patterned paper (Westrim)

- Three to four sheets of coordinating, solid-colored papers

- Patterns on page 128

- Small snowflake punch

- Letter stamps (Plaid Enterprises)

- Yarn (Lion Brand Yarn)

- Felt

1 Photocopy and size mitten patterns; cut out patterns. Fold paper—that is the same length as your page width—accordion style, making sure pattern fits the width of the folds.

2 Trace patterns onto folded paper, placing patterns' fold marks on the papers' folds.

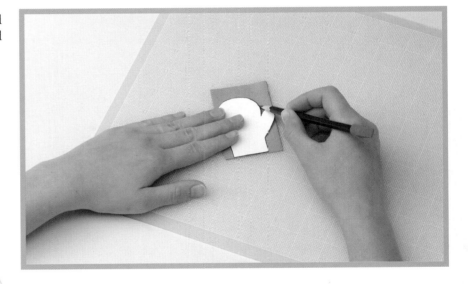

3 Cut out traced shape, being careful not to cut on the folds. Open the resulting paper chains and embellish as desired.

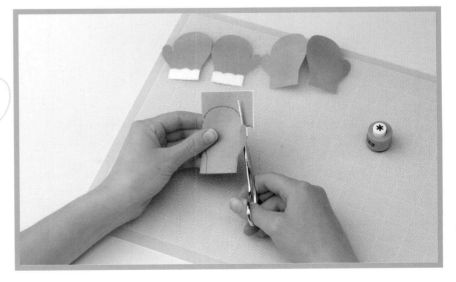

Lorna Christensen

Create a customized paper chain frame

It is easy to make a thematic paper chain by freehand drawing your design or tracing template shapes—joined by fold lines—onto theme papers. The freehand-drawn paper chain shown here is made up of snowman, snowflake and igloo shapes, and cut from embellished patterned papers. Follow the steps on page 59 to make the seasonal paper chain. Mat large photo; mount paper chain pieces around photo. Add pen detail to paper chain. Circle cut photos; mount on page and add pen detail around photos. Cut snowman shape from template; adhere title sticker letters. Mount second paper chain border along bottom of page.

What you will need

- Two sheets of coordinating patterned papers (Me & My Big Ideas)

- One sheet of coordinating solid paper

- Pattern on page 128

- Snowflake stickers (Mrs. Grossman's)

- Sticker letters (Creative Memories)

1 Embellish dot patterned paper strip with snowflake stickers for page border.

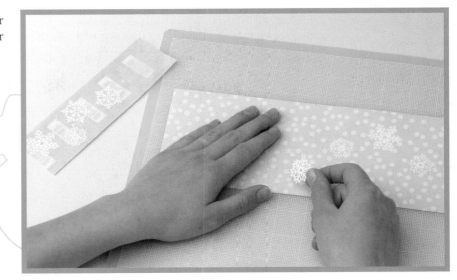

2 Fold both patterned papers in half lengthwise, with right sides facing in. Photocopy and size pattern twice—once for page border and again, smaller, for photo frame. Trace patterns onto embellished and patterned papers, making sure to connect the three designs together as shown.

3 Cut out around outer edges of design with scissors. Unfold paper chains and mount on page and around matted photo.

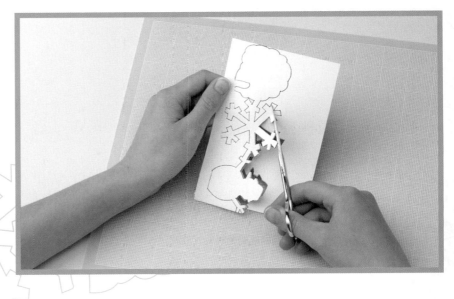

KIRIGAMI

The term "kirigami" comes from the Japanese words "kiri" and "kami" which mean "cut" and "paper" respectively. It is a traditional craft in which paper is folded and cut into decorative objects and designs. Kirigami is a versatile technique that can be used to give scrapbook pages a multicultural feel. Many traditional kirigami motifs are inspired by nature and can be adapted to fit themes ranging from romance to Christmas.

Ann Kitayama

Fold and cut kirigami windows

Create windows for photos to peek through with a simple fold-and-cut technique. Choose a template shape, or create one of your own that works with the theme of your photos. Follow the steps on page 61 to create the window pattern shown here. Crop photos to fit behind selected openings; mount to backside of windows. Layer and mount over solid-colored background paper. Complete page with title and journaling.

What you will need

- One sheet of patterned paper (Rocky Mountain Scrapbook Company)

- Pattern on page 128

- One sheet of coordinating, solid-colored paper

60

1   Four fold an 8½ x 11" sheet of patterned paper lengthwise at 2⅛" intervals (see page 130 for fold instructions).

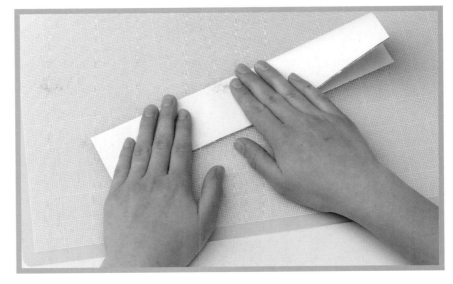

2   Photocopy and size pattern. Trace pattern or template shape of choice onto folded paper. Trace partial shapes over the folds of paper as shown in illustration on page 130 to create the all-over background pattern.

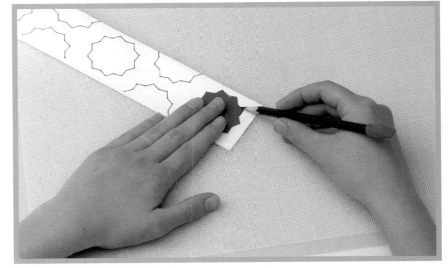

3   Cut out all traced lines with a craft knife and scissors. When all cuts are completed, open the folded paper and flatten the folds with a spoon (see page 18 for tips) or slightly warm iron (no steam or water!), if needed.

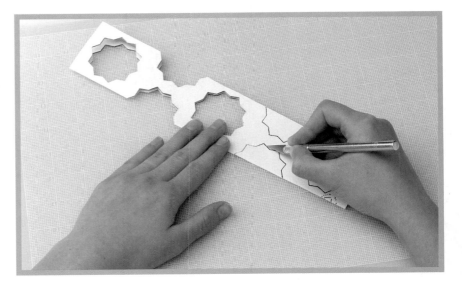

Punch a thematic kirigami frame

Highlight a beautiful holiday portrait with a paper-cut and punched kirigami frame. Alternatively, create your own theme frame with a different punch and vary the frame's inner edge with a different decorative ruler or with decorative scissors. Follow the steps on the next page to create the frame. Adhere photo behind frame. Mat framed photo on patterned paper; mount on page. Print title and journaling; cut to size and trim using decorative ruler. Attach vellum to page with eyelets. Mat smaller photo; mount on page over vellum. Cut two ⅛" strips of paper; mount on left side of page for accent.

Pamela Frye; Photo Jennifer Benedict

What you will need

- One sheet of patterned paper (Sandylion)
- Three sheets of coordinating, solid-colored papers
- Decorative border ruler (Cut-It-Up)
- Vellum (Karen Foster)
- Small tree punch (EK Success)
- Eyelets (Impress Rubber Stamps)

1 Double-fold a sheet of paper to be used as photo frame (see page 130 for illustrations for page 64 to create folds). Use a metal straight-edge ruler to draw two guidelines—one parallel and one perpendicular to the folds—to mark the opening of the frame. Trace decorative ruler design just inside drawn guidelines.

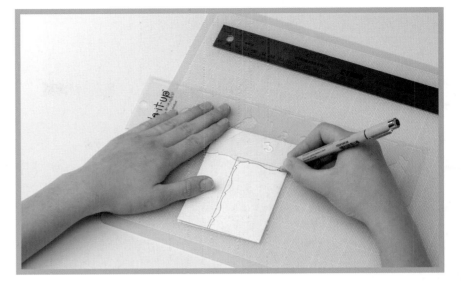

2 Draw punch placement guidelines at ¾" intervals around outer edges of folded paper, using a ruler and a pencil. Punch small trees atop the evenly spaced guidelines.

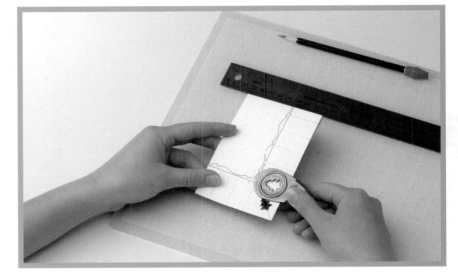

3 Cut the decorative lines to form the frame's opening with scissors. Unfold and flatten the folds' creases (see page 18).

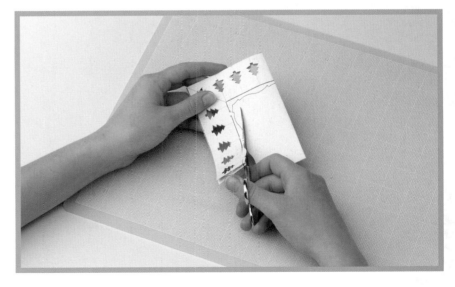

Fold and cut a kirigami heart frame

Enhance a treasured photograph with an elegant, symmetrical border-cut frame accented by hearts. Try making your unique version by freehand drawing or tracing cut lines with decorative rulers, adding a thematic shape for accent. First, cut a 4⅝" W x 5⅛" T window opening in an 8½ x 11" sheet of patterned paper, centered and 2" from upper edge of paper. Slip the photo behind window, center and adhere. Follow the instructions below (see page 130 for folding illustrations) to create the double-folded and cut suede paper frame. Mount over patterned paper. Cut title block, mat with suede paper trimmed with decorative ruler and scissors; adhere. Pen title and date.

Ann Kitayama

What you will need

- Two different sheets of monochromatic-colored patterned papers (Handmade Paper)

- Suede paper (Wintech)

- Pattern on page 129

- Decorative ruler (Westrim Crafts)

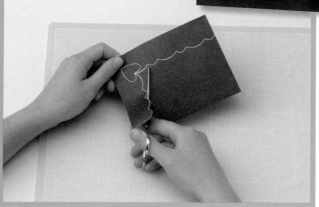

1 Photocopy and size the pattern on page 129 to fit photo or page size. Double-fold suede paper following instructions on page 130, folding with right sides together. Transfer pattern to paper (see page 17), matching up fold lines. Cut on lines with scissors. Unfold and flatten creases (see page 18).

Napkin-fold and cut kirigami poinsettias

Take the art of kirigami to an exciting level with napkin-folded flowers cut from delicate mulberry paper. Once you master the napkin fold, experiment with your own freehand-drawn patterns for unique kirigami embellishments. Follow the steps on the next page to create the poinsettia flowers and leaves in sizes that fit your page. Mount finished flowers and leaves over patterned background paper. Punch small circles for flower centers and adhere. Double mat photo. Cut title and journaling block; mat on solid-colored paper. Pen title and journaling.

Sharon Moore

What you will need

- One sheet of patterned paper (Bo-Bunny Press)
- One sheet each of red and green mulberry paper (Bazzill Basics)
- Two sheets of coordinating, solid-colored papers
- Poinsettia and leaf patterns on page 129
- 36° triangle pattern on page 129
- ¼" round hand punch

1 For the red poinsettia petals, begin with an 8½" square sheet of red mulberry paper. Fold the paper squares into a napkin fold (see page 130 for folding illustrations).

2 Photocopy and size flower petal pattern. Place cut pattern on folded paper, matching up the pattern's fold lines. Trace around the pattern's edges with a pencil.

3 Cut along the traced lines and unfold the poinsettia. Flatten out the fold creases (see page 18). Repeat the above steps to make the green poinsettia leaves.

Create symmetrical kirigami snowflakes

Symmetrical paper-cut designs, made from a napkin-folded paper pattern, dangle on a festive, winter theme page. Make the two snowflakes shown here using our patterns or draw and use your own snowflake pattern. Follow the steps below to create either snowflake. Mount snowflakes on solid-colored cardstock squares; chalk edges before matting. Double mat photos; mount on patterned background paper matted with solid-colored paper. Print title and journaling; cut to size and mat. Attach eyelets to title, journaling and snowflake blocks. Tie together with embroidery floss.

What you will need

- One sheet of patterned paper (Scrap Ease)

- Three to four sheets of coordinating, solid-colored papers (Bazzill Basics, Doodlebug Design, Robin's Nest)

- Patterns on page 129

- Eyelets (Doodlebug Design)

- Embroidery Floss (DMC)

- Chalk (Craf-T Products)

Sharon Moore

1 For the larger snowflake, begin with a 4" square of thin white paper. Note: It may be difficult to find acid-free white paper thin enough for kirigami. Consider using the white back side of a solid-colored or patterned paper. Fold paper into a napkin fold (see page 130 for folding illustrations). Photocopy and size snowflake patterns; cut out. Trace around pattern edges with pencil. Cut detailed design with a craft knife. Unfold and flatten out fold creases (see page 18).

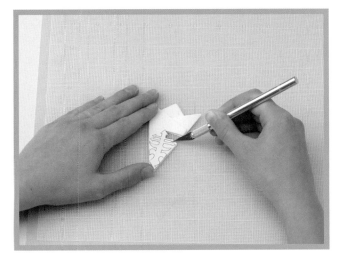

Personalize a kirigami design

Incorporate a name, monogram or title into a symmetrical, personalized paper-cut design that can also serve as a frame for a photo. Use our pattern or create your own with template letters. Simply ensure that the first letter reaches both upper and lower edges of the folded paper triangle. Use upper- or lowercase letters; however, all letters must touch the lower fold of the triangle. Follow the steps below to cut the word "pals" into a symmetrical design. Cut word from two colors of paper; trim one word in second color. Layer over one section to highlight word. Mount photo at center of patterned paper; layer paper-cut design over photo and adhere. Fold and cut a freehand border design; mount around outside edges of background paper. Cut and pen title square.

What you will need

- Four sheets of complementary-colored patterned papers (Frances Meyer, Hot Off The Press)

- One sheet of coordinating, solid-colored paper

- Pattern on page 129

Pamela Frye; Photos Cristana Campbell

1 Transfer pattern to folded paper (see page 130 for folding illustrations). Cut outer edges of lettering with scissors, making certain not to cut through fold lines. Use a craft knife to cut out details at the center of letters.

4

LAYERING

Remember cutting and pasting images with wild abandon as a child,
without even knowing you were creating your first collage? Layering involves
adhering paper cutouts onto a page to create a picture or pattern.
Pre-existing paper patterns, photos and memorabilia are cut out and
reassembled to create a visual display whose sum is greater than
the total of its parts. In this chapter, you will discover how to:

• Create "paper tole" using patterned papers

• Emboss and curl die cuts to give them a three-dimensional look

• Create Victorian-style pages using patterned paper collage

• Make an assemblage of complementary page elements

• Silhouette-crop photos and other design elements

• Tear paper to create an artistic montage

These easy paper techniques will add yet another "layer" of creative
dimension to your scrapbook page design skills.

PAPER TOLE
Derived from the art of decoupage, "paper tole" involves shaping and layering several copies of an individual design element over a base print to create a three-dimensional effect. Paper tole provides the perfect way to highlight a favorite paper pattern or die cut in your album while accenting your photos.

What you will need
- Three duplicate sheets of patterned paper (Paper Adventures)
- One sheet of coordinating patterned paper (All My Memories) for mats
- Two sheets of coordinating, solid-colored papers
- One sheet of vellum (DMD Industries)
- Eyelets (Doodlebug Design)
- Flat sheet of craft foam
- Embossing stylus
- Bone folder
- ⅛" thick self-adhesive foam spacers

Kelly Angard

Paper tole with patterned paper

Turn flat images cut from patterned paper into fabulously layered, three-dimensional designs with a simple cut here and a few curls there. This technique works well with any patterned paper that has medium to large design elements. For this simple variation of our cover page, mat one sheet of trimmed, 12 x 12" patterned paper. Follow the steps on the next page to create paper tole elements; set elements aside. Add title and journaling to vellum, hand color and attach to page with eyelets along right border. Mat photos and arrange on page as shown. Mount paper tole elements atop their duplicate image on background paper, allowing some to overlap onto photos and title block.

1 Silhouette crop some randomly chosen design elements from the second and third sheets of patterned paper. Cut enough pieces to have two each of selected elements. Then, cut one each of the silhouette cropped elements into segments following natural cutting lines. You will have one whole butterfly and one pieced butterfly for each design element.

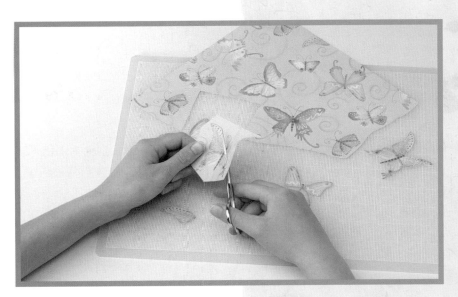

2 Lay each piece right-side-down on a soft surface such as a sheet of craft foam. Gently shape and curl each piece using a shaping tool such as an embossing stylus or bone folder. Repeat this step on all cropped and cut pieces.

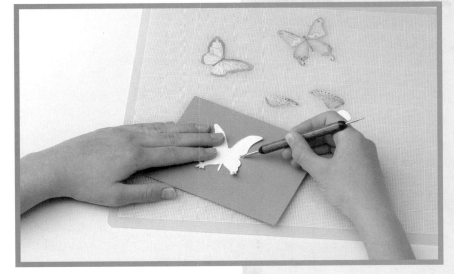

3 Then use the rounded tip of a bone folder to rub the butterflies and cut pieces in a circular motion to make the cut pieces curl. Rubbing too much can crumple the paper. Repeat this step on all cropped and cut pieces. Steps continue on page 130.

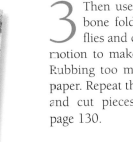

Curl die cuts for depth

Here's another quick recipe for paper tole dimension: Cut apart printed die cuts or "punch outs," curl each piece and layer over duplicate die cuts with self-adhesive foam spacers. First, follow the steps on the facing page to create the layered elements. Mat photos with paper and printed frame. Layer photos and dimensional die cuts on a solid background. For the window box, layer two identical pieces cut from a duplicate printed frame. Adhere letter stickers for title.

Lorna Christensen

What you will need

- One sheet each of coordinating plaid (Doodlebug Design) and gingham (Making Memories) patterned paper

- Two to three duplicate die cuts: frame (My Mind's Eye), flowers (Imaginations, Inc.), jar/bug (Doodlebug Design) and doll/dress/hair (EK Success)

- Embossing stylus or rounded bone folder

- Sheet of craft foam

- Self-adhesive foam spacers

- Letter stickers (Provo Craft)

1 For each dimensional design, obtain two copies of the same printed die cut. Lay the first die cut aside for the base or lower layer. Cut apart the duplicate die cut into its logical parts. For example, cut leaves apart from flowers and then cut additional slits between petals.

2 Lay each piece right-side-down on a soft surface such as a sheet of craft foam. Gently shape and curl each piece using a shaping tool such as an embossing stylus or bone folder. See Steps 2 and 3 on page 71.

3 Using self-adhesive foam spacers, layer shaped pieces over the base die cut in the same relative position. If desired, use additional layers for even more depth. For example, layer the bug die cuts on the jar die cuts.

COLLAGE

In collage, individually cut or torn items are arranged artistically on a page. There are many variations of this technique. In a Victorian-style collage like the one shown below, preprinted shapes are cut from patterned paper and rearranged to create a new background design. In an assemblage, both flat and three-dimensional items are combined. In a montage, the primary design element is your photos. Any collage style results in a memorable scrapbook page.

What you will need
- Three to four sheets of coordinating patterned papers (Anna Griffin)
- One sheet of coordinating, solid-colored paper
- Oval shape cutter or template
- Preprinted title strip (Anna Griffin)

Kelly Angard; Photo MaryJo Regier

Silhouette designs from patterned paper

Simple silhouetting is all it takes to create custom collage backgrounds and page elements. This cutting and layering technique works particularly well when you want to rearrange the designs on trimmed, patterned paper to better suit your layout. To enhance this heritage photo, Victorian flowers were layered to form a wreath-like frame. To create the floral background, follow the steps on the facing page. Double mat the oval photo. Use self-adhesive foam spacers to layer photo in page center with additional floral embellishments. Cut out and mat title strip.

1 Select patterned papers with large design elements that enhance the colors, theme or time period of your photos. For the matted background, select solid or tone-on-tone coordinating papers.

2 Using small, sharp scissors, silhouette crop each design element from patterned papers. Silhouetting is less fatiguing when you move the paper in and out of the scissor blades rather than moving the blade around the shape.

3 Arrange the silhouetted designs on the matted background. When you are satisfied with the arrangement, adhere each piece in place.

Assemble a visual story

Although collage means literally "to glue," most of us think of collage as a combination of layered paper images. In "assemblage," the collage is accented with three-dimensional items. There are no rigid rules for these paper techniques, but it helps to start with a theme and choose colors and objects to enhance it. For scrapbooks, select smooth, flat objects whenever possible. This whimsical assemblage combines patterned paper, ribbon, sewn-on vintage buttons, stickers, elements cut from magazines and hand-tinted, vintage photos. Refer to the steps on the following page for instructions. Incorporate a title and journaling into your design.

Sarah Fishburn

What you will need

- Four to five sheets of complementary-colored, thematic patterned papers (Colors by Design, The Paper Co., Sandylion)
- Assorted thematic stickers (Frances Meyer, Paper House Productions, Pressed Petals, Wordsworth Memories)
- Foreign postage-stamp reproductions (Art Accents)
- Flowers and butterfly images cropped from magazines
- Gingham ribbon
- Vintage buttons

76

1 Select a theme for your assembled collage based on your photos. Gather papers, photos and design additions to fit the theme, colors and style.

2 Select the background paper. Arrange the photos and other elements for visual appeal until you are satisfied with the design. This is a creative process that can take as little or as much time as you wish.

3 Silhouette crop photos and other paper items. Layer and mount elements in desired positions.

Tear a collage

There is something therapeutic about tearing paper. Perhaps it takes away the stress of a day! In any case, a layered montage with torn elements creates a soft and casual feeling. The key is to start with a photo as the focal point. Then layer torn paper shapes and design elements to complement the photo. Refer to the instructions below to arrange this school-theme layout. Mat the printed caption with torn green paper. For depth, mount the tassel die cut with self-adhesive foam spacers.

What you will need

- Three to four sheets of school-theme patterned papers (Colorbök, Colors by Design)

- One white or cream-colored sheet of cardstock for background

- Color photocopy of page from old nursery-rhyme or school book

- Children's art and writing

- Tassel die cut (Deluxe Cuts)

- Self-adhesive foam spacers

Torrey Miller; Photo Heidi Finger

1 Begin with a sheet of neutral cardstock as the background. Choose papers and other elements to complement the focal photo, colors and theme. Randomly tear paper strips and shapes. Layer elements alongside photo on the background, overlapping edges. When you are satisfied with the arrangement, adhere all design elements. Then flip the page over and trim away any overlapping edges with scissors.

5

TEARING

Tearing paper offers a decorative "edge" that softens the look of a page. Tearing also provides surprising and spontaneous results depending upon: The paper's texture and thickness; the direction of the tear; the speed with which you tear; and how you guide the paper with your hand. Here you will learn to:

- *Use a pattern to piece together a torn-paper design*
- *Alternate positive- and negative-torn "space" to create a page border*
- *Design a free-form page embellishment*
- *Make a mosaic utilizing torn tiles of colored paper*
- *Create translucent vellum backgrounds and overlays*
- *Incorporate lettering into a torn scene*
- *Use beads to mimic water on torn vellum*
- *Gild the edges of torn mulberry paper*

The act of tearing paper is as satisfying as the gorgeous results that torn paper provides. Try these techniques, and you won't be able to rip yourself away from tearing paper!

TEARING SHAPES

Paper piecing, borders and other embellishments take on a whole new form when shapes are torn instead of cut. Designs can look rugged, soft or whimsical—perfect for outdoorsy or playful layouts. The beauty of this technique comes from its imperfections; don't be afraid of making mistakes. Each tear lends character to your page.

What you will need

- Five to six sheets of earth-toned (see colors in caption), solid-colored papers
- Pattern on page 129
- Removable artist's tape
- Embossing stylus or bone folder (optional)
- Yellow pressed flower
- Clear photo corners (Canson)

Linda Strauss

Tear out paper patterns

A paper pattern makes it easy to achieve the torn look without having to do it all freehand.
Coloring books and clip art make great patterns for tearing. For this pocket title page, start with a dark sage background. Tear (see tearing tips on pages 13 and 18) the top edge of a light sage square to resemble a mountain range; adhere to background along left, lower and right edges to form pocket. Refer to the steps on the facing page to create the moose. Mount travel postcard with clear photo corners. For the title, cut a 2" speckled sage strip and tear thin brown strips for letter parts. Write letters with black pen and insert travel memorabilia.

1 Photocopy and enlarge the moose pattern on page 129 to fit your layout design. Cut out each pattern piece and mark the front sides.

2 Use removable artist's tape to temporarily attach each pattern piece to the appropriate colored paper. If you don't have removable adhesive, place the front of each pattern piece on the back side of the appropriate colored paper and trace. Carefully tear out each piece along the pattern edges. If the paper does not tear easily, try scoring the tearing lines with an embossing stylus or bone folder.

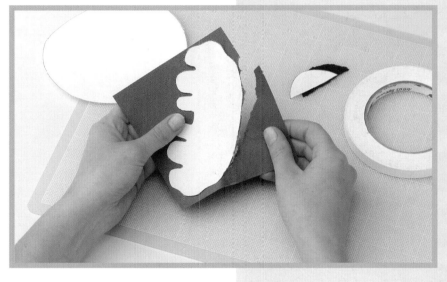

3 Arrange the moose pieces on the page background atop pocket. Mount in place. Add pressed flower to mouth. Use a black pen to outline the brown and white pieces.

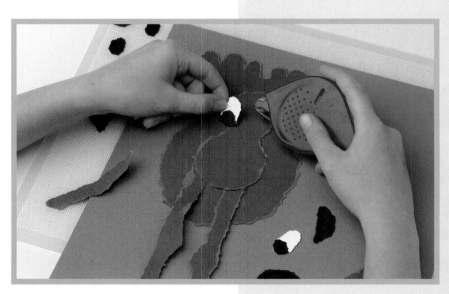

Contrast positive and negative shapes

Try this tearing technique with other designs such as stars, fish, flowers, leaves, letters or numbers. For the background, mount patterned tissue paper on white cardstock. Tear the left edge of a 7 x 12" brown rectangle and mount along right side of page. Mat photo with metallic gold. Print and tear out title and caption; outline with black pen. Follow the instructions below to tear out positive and negative brown hearts. Embellish layout with butterfly, flower and phrase torn from patterned tissue paper.

What you will need
- One sheet each of brown, white and metallic gold solid-colored papers
- Patterned tissue paper (source unknown)
- Gold metallic thread and sewing needle

A dream is a wish your heart makes

We're just a little BEHIND in our garden here. We had just moved to our new home and the yard didn't have a lawn yet. Mario escaped from the house to play in the water, June 1996.

Paradise

Linda Strauss

1 Start by tearing two 4" brown squares. Fold each square in half like a card. Tear out one half of a heart shape along the folded edge. If you'd rather not fold the paper, tear the heart shape directly into the paper leaving a seam at the lower edge, leaving the frame intact. Sew gold thread around the edges of one torn heart. Use both positive and negative torn shapes on page.

Shape natural elements

Use torn shapes to recreate objects from nature and add an impressionistic style to seasonal layouts. For the foldout summer page, tear and layer colored shapes to form clouds, cherry tree, hills and bees on a matted panel and attach to page with artist's tape. Accent with punched microdot red cherries. Layer matted photos, caption, title letters cut from template, triangles and squares on an aqua background. Tear leaves and cut and punch cherries for accent.

For the winter page, layer torn shapes to create snow, tree, rabbit and bird for border. Layer torn pieces for trees and snow atop light blue letters cut from template, trimming edges as needed. Accent matted photo with corner triangles embellished with birds torn from red and yellow paper. Draw details with black pen.

What you will need

- One sheet each of white, brown, lime green, dark green and yellow, solid-colored papers
- Two sheets each of red, aqua and light blue solid-colored paper
- Circle shape cutter or circle template
- Lettering templates (EK Success, Frances Meyer)
- Microdot and ⅜" circle punches

Alex Bishop

TEARING SCENES
Give your pages a change of scenery with torn-paper backgrounds made from tiny, tile-sized pieces of colored paper, strips of torn vellum and torn-paper shapes. For added impact, tear your page titles as well!

Shannon Taylor

Piece a mosaic backdrop

Round up the kids and put them to work. They will have a blast tearing normally off-limits scrapbook papers into small mosaic pieces. They can even help design the scene! Follow the steps on the facing page to create the background scene. Cut title letters from lettering template; detail with pen. Double mat photos, tearing edges of outer mats. Mat printed vellum caption with paper frame. Join caption to photo using eyelets and jute. Mount clovers on 2" paper square and slip into memorabilia pocket.

What you will need
- One sheet each of white, light blue, aqua, tan, brown, sage green and dark green solid-colored papers
- Gray chalk (Craf-T Products)
- Lettering template (EK Success)
- Vellum
- Eyelets
- Natural jute
- Pressed clovers
- 2 x 2" Memorabilia Pocket (3L)

1 Use a pencil to freehand draw outline for background scene. Keep the design simple with fairly large sections. If you find a design in a book or magazine that you want to use as a starting point, first turn it into a simple line drawing using tracing paper. Then transfer the drawing onto the layout.

2 Choose paper colors that best represent each element of the scene. Try patterned papers for added texture. For example, you might try "sand" patterned paper for a beach scene. Tear each paper color into small scraps no larger than ¾". Keep the colors separated and organized in plastic sandwich bags. Add dimension to the white pieces by shading the edges with gray chalk.

3 Glue the torn paper pieces in the appropriate sections of the scene, starting with the background elements and finishing with the foreground elements. Overlap edges as needed to cover the entire layout.

Create movement with torn vellum

If you remember the scene but forgot to take a picture, you can re-create it with multiple layers of colored and vellum paper. For this page, start with a sage background. Tear and layer vellum clouds and green mountains, shading mountains with black ink. Color-photocopy and enlarge printed pine trees, if desired. Silhouette-crop trees; mount with self-adhesive foam spacers. For the rocks, freehand tear and layer strips of colored vellum; top with silhouette-cropped photos. Use the computer font to make a pattern for the title letters. Adhere letters to the clip art frame.

Donna McMurry

What you will need

- One sheet each of sage and green solid-colored papers

- One sheet each of white and earth-toned colored vellum papers (The Paper Company)

- Black stamping ink

- Preprinted pine tree die cuts (The Beary Patch)

- Clip art frame (Carolee's Creations)

- Self-adhesive foam spacers

- Computer font (Microsoft)

Layer a vellum landscape

When torn, vellum has a soft white edge that adds subtle detail to this landscape scene. The natural elements further capture the beauty of the scenic photos. Begin with white cardstock as the page base and work from the top down. For the sky, layer white vellum over blue vellum. Tear and layer various shades of blue and green vellum for mountains, hills and journaling blocks. Mount photos and tuck in pressed ferns. Accent with pressed flowers.

What you will need

- One sheet of white cardstock for background

- One sheet each of white, light blue, dark blue, purple, green and goldenrod vellum papers (Strathmore)

- Vellum adhesive (3M)

- Pressed ferns and flowers (Nature's Pressed)

Linda Strauss

HAPPINESS IS IN THE JOURNEY

Here Joel and friends, Monica, Denis and Emily Fajardo, rent bikes to do some sightseeing in Jackson Hole, Wyoming.

1 Experiment with the placement of torn vellum landscape strips prior to adhering on background with vellum adhesive. When finished, turn page over and trim away any excess overlap with scissors.

Incorporate torn lettering

Blending these large title letters into the torn pond water prevents them from overwhelming this colorful fishing layout. For the background, layer tan on speckled blue paper. Crop and mat photos using corner rounder punch. Follow the steps on the next page to create pond water with title letters. Freehand cut pattern for green and tan grass. Mount grass beneath pond water title. Stamp and heat emboss fish using blue ink on light gray paper. Punch frogs and dragonflies, using white vellum for dragonfly wings. Draw details and write captions with white pen.

Debra McDonald

What you will need

- Two sheets each of light blue speckled patterned paper

- One sheet each of tan, light green, dark green, olive, aqua, blue and navy solid-colored paper

- One sheet of white vellum (DMD Industries)

- Corner rounder punch

- Small frog, dragonfly and egg punches (Carl, Family Treasures, McGill)

- Lettering template (C-Thru Ruler Co.)

- Bass stamp (Stampa Rosa)

- Blue stamping ink

- Clear embossing powder

- Self-adhesive foam spacers

1 First tear and layer paper to create the pond water that stretches across the bottom of the layout. Use the lettering template to lightly trace each letter in the desired position.

2 Use a craft knife to cut out each letter, through all torn paper layers. Use egg-shaped punch to punch holes out of the letters B and A. Mat letters with navy blue paper, leaving a thin border around the letters.

3 Mount letters so that they completely cover the cut-out openings.

TORN EDGE ACCENTS
Add polish to torn edges by accenting a title block with a vellum overlay and tiny beads to mimic water bubbles. Or line a page background with the rich look of torn mulberry gilded with metal flakes.

What you will need
- Two sheets of duplicate patterned paper (Paper Adventures)
- One sheet each of light blue, dark blue and aqua solid-colored papers
- One sheet each of green and patterned vellum (Autumn Leaves)
- Lettering template (Scrap Pagerz)
- Diamond dust paper for letters (Paper Adventures)
- Vellum adhesive (3M)
- Liquid adhesive
- Clear seed beads (Westrim)

Chris Peters

Imitate bubbly water

Torn vellum creates the perfect watery look, and now it's available in a patterned version that resembles water. The small seed beads mimic bubbles. Start with patterned bubble paper for the background. Crop and double mat photos and arrange as desired. Follow the steps on the facing page to create the title and caption. Write caption with blue pen.

1 Cut out the title letters using a lettering template. Mount letters on torn aqua square. Mat title with straight blue square and torn green vellum square. Use the water-patterned vellum for the title overlay. Freehand tear the upper edge of the vellum in a wavy pattern so it covers the lower two-thirds of the title block.

2 Mimic water bubbles by using tweezers and a liquid adhesive to mount clear seed beads along the upper edge of the vellum overlay. Allow to dry thoroughly.

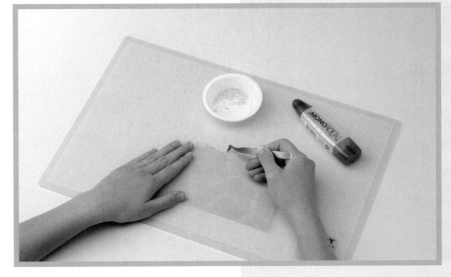

3 Use torn strips of vellum adhesive to attach the vellum overlay to the title block at the sides and lower edges only. For the caption, create a similar vellum overlay for a 1½" matted blue strip.

Gild the edges of torn mulberry

Mulberry paper is the secret to beautiful feathery edges. One way to tear mulberry is to wet the line you want to tear, using water and small paintbrush. Then gently tear along the damp line. For straighter edges, try tearing dampened mulberry paper against the edge of a Deckle ruler as shown on page 18. For this wedding layout, tear multiple strips of colored mulberry and gild the edges as shown below. Layer the mulberry strips on a white background. Use blue paper and white mulberry to mat the photo and create the caption.

What you will need

- One sheet each of royal blue, peach, pink, light blue and white mulberry paper (PrintWorks)

- One sheet of coordinating, solid-colored paper

- Multicolored gold leaf flake (Amy's Magic)

- Gold leaf adhesive (Amy's Magic)

- Small paintbrush

- Tweezers

Kelly Angard

1 Carefully brush gold leaf adhesive on the feathery edges of each mulberry strip. Use tweezers to carefully apply the gold leaf to the wet areas. Keep your hands as dry as possible to prevent the gold leaf from sticking to them. Cover gilded paper strips with a clean sheet of paper and blot. Using a dry brush, dust away excess leaf and save for future use.

6

WEAVING

Paper weaving lends a rich textile look to your pages. And, like the fabrics that inspired them, woven paper designs vary in style from homespun to ethnic to elegant. Woven into this chapter are instructions on how to:

- *Make a tightly woven background out of straight paper strips*
- *Create a loose weave that makes the most of both positive and negative space*
- *Weave a random, wavy pattern or a randomly torn woven design*
- *Use a pattern to create a paper loom*
- *Cut a randomly curved loom*
- *Utilize a nested template to make a loom*
- *Create a woven, laced border with a Dutch feel*

Paper weaving is a much easier technique to accomplish than it may look. Master these simple techniques, and you will be ready to weave some scrapbook magic of your own.

WEAVING STRIPS

Paper strips are the basic materials used in paper weaving. Vary their thickness and spacing to create a variety of effects. Tight weaves look like a crisp placemat, whereas a loose weave gives an open, airy feeling. Wavy or torn strips are perfect for pages with rustic, outdoorsy themes.

Haley fell instantly in love with our new kitten who she affectionately named Oreo. The kitten was a stray at our neighbors farm and in need of a good home. It didn't take much convincing when they brought her over and Haley got a hold of her. They've been inseparable ever since. New friends, now friends for life.

Jodi Amidei

Craft a tightly woven mat

The under/over weave produces striking results when combined with solid and patterned papers. For this backdrop, cut 9½" long by ½" wide paper strips in the following quantities: 10 blue, 9 lavender, 18 patterned purple. Weave the strips following the steps on the next page. Double mat the weaving with purple, then blue paper. Mount diagonally on a plum background and trim corners. Arrange matted photos and caption. Use lettering template to cut out and mat title.

What you will need

- Two sheets of different purple patterned papers (Colorbök, Paper Adventures)
- Two sheets each of lavender and blue solid-colored papers
- One sheet of purple solid-colored paper
- Lettering template and computer font (Provo Craft)

1 Start with a ½" blue strip. With the blue strip on top, mount a ½" purple patterned strip perpendicular to the blue strip at the corner; adhere.

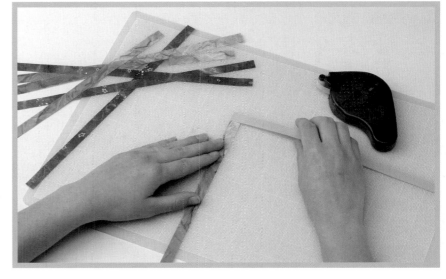

2 Mount a second purple patterned strip next the first, this time with the purple strip on top of the blue strip; adhere. Continue mounting purple strips across the width of the blue strip, alternating above and below.

3 Weave a ½" lavender strip under and over the patterned purple strips. Push snugly next to the first blue strip. Weave the next row over and under with a blue strip. Repeat this step until you have completed the weaving, alternating lavender and blue strips. When you have finished, trim the ends of each row if needed and use artist's tape to secure the strips in place on the backside of the weaving.

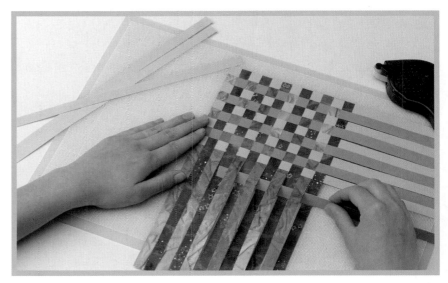

Weave a loose lattice

This variation of the under/over technique gives the illusion that the background color is actually woven into the design. The lattice works particularly well for this layout because the patterned strips reflect the colors of the sunset photo while the contrasting gray background tones down the overall effect. Begin with a black page. To weave the lattice, follow the steps on the facing page. Mat photo with black and mount on lattice. Freehand outline title on patterned paper using the template as a guide. Cut out title and mat with black. Write caption with black pen.

What you will need

- One sheet of sunset patterned paper (Wübie)
- One sheet of gray paper
- White pencil
- Lettering template (EK Success)

Sun over Zambia   August 28, 2000

Nancy Korf

96

1 Start with an 11½" square of gray paper. Use a ruler and white pencil to mark the placement for the weaving strips, starting ⅝" in from the upper left corner. Make two "tick marks" ¼" apart for each strip. Allow ¾" spacing between each strip. Mark all four sides of the gray square in the same manner.

2 Cut 22 patterned strips ¼" wide by 11½" long. Place 11 strips vertically on the gray square, positioning them on the tick marks. Adhere the upper ends in place.

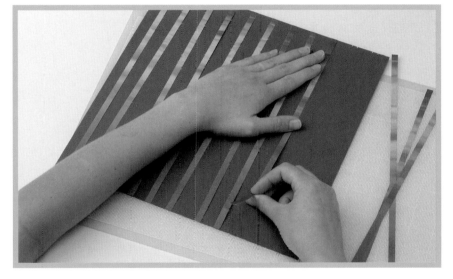

3 Weave the first horizontal strip over and under. Adhere the ends so they cover the tick marks. Weave the second horizontal strip under and over, securing the ends in place. Continue weaving until you have completed the lattice. When you have finished, adhere the lower ends of the vertical strips in place. Mat the entire lattice with a 12" black square.

Cut random wavy strips

Add a casual look to a loose under/over weave by using wavy, free-form strips in bright colors. Integrate the photos into the design by layering them beneath some of the strips. When you're pleased with the arrangement, mount the elements on a tan background. Write captions on vellum with blue pen. Highlight each letter with a light blue pen. Cut out each caption with wavy edges to mimic the weaving strips.

ON THE SEA SHORE

JACOB, DAVID, ISAIAH
SUNSET STATE BEACH
AUGUST 1998

PLAY ON THE SEA SHORE
AND GATHER UP SHELLS, KNEEL
IN THE DAMP SAND DIGGING WELLS.
RUN ON THE ROCKS WHERE THE
SEAWEED SLIPS, WATCH THE WAVES
AND THE BEAUTIFUL SHIPS.
— MARY BRITTON MILLER

Pamela Frye; Photo Sandra Escobedo

What you will need

- One sheet each of tan, brown, orange and blue cardstock

- One sheet of white vellum (DMD Industries)

Tear colored vellum

Give the edges of your weaving a finished look by folding the ends to the backside of the background paper. The torn vellum strips further soften this basic over/under weave for a light, airy look. To create the woven background, follow the instructions below. Double mat both the weaving and the photos. Print, cut out and mat the caption. Fill the title letters with colored pencils. Punch ferns from colored vellum.

What you will need

- One sheet each of rust, goldenrod, cream and light green vellum (Paper Adventures)

- One sheet each of rust, goldenrod and cream solid-colored papers (Club Scrap)

- *Agent Orange* font (downloaded from Internet)

- Colored pencils

- Fern leaf punch (The Punch Bunch)

Jodi Amidei

1 Tear colored vellum strips approximately ¾" to 1" in width. Arrange eight vellum strips vertically on a cream background. Fold the ends over the top and bottom edges and secure on the back. Flip the page over and weave in the horizontal strips. Fold and secure the ends in the same manner.

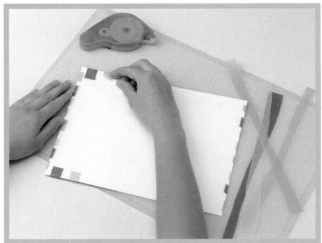

WEAVING ON A LOOM

A loom provides a framework within which paper strips can be woven. You can make a loom by using a pattern, tracing the edges of a decorative ruler, or cutting along the grooves of a nested template. The loom provides a basic structure to your design that allows you to experiment with paper strips of varying shapes and widths.

Kelly Angard; Photos Helena Schwartz

Cut a symmetrical loom

This seemingly complex background is created from a symmetrical loom made by cutting slits in a folded sheet of paper. Simply follow the steps on the facing page to re-create the look. Triple-mat the photos. Cut the patterned title letters using the template. Mount each letter beneath a vellum rectangle and outline with black pen. Adhere letter stickers for the smaller words. Write the caption on a separate vellum rectangle using a letter sticker for the first letter. Weave ¼" aqua strips through vertical slits cut in both the title and caption.

What you will need

- One sheet of 12 x 12" purple solid-colored paper for loom
- One sheet each of yellow, aqua and orange solid-colored paper
- One sheet of patterned paper (Colors by Design)
- One sheet of translucent white vellum
- Pattern on page 129
- Removable artist tape
- Lettering template (Frances Meyer)
- Letter stickers (Provo Craft)

1 Photocopy and size the pattern to fit one-half of a 12 x 12" scrapbook page. Fold purple paper in half. Attach the pattern to the folded paper using removable artist's tape, taking care to match the fold lines. Secure both the pattern and paper to a cutting mat with removable artist tape or tape to paper and cut with scissors.

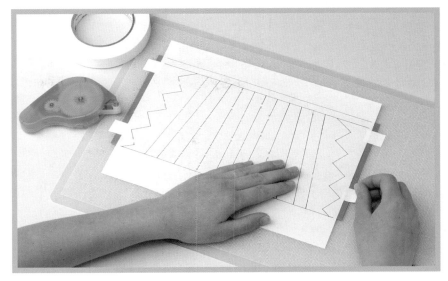

2 Use a metal straightedge ruler and craft knife to cut the pattern lines through all layers. Take care to start and stop the cuts according to the pattern. Remove the pattern and unfold the purple paper.

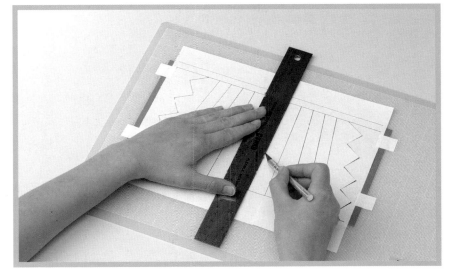

3 Cut yellow, aqua and orange strips of various widths. Loosely weave the strips into the purple loom. Start at the top and work your way down, alternating colors with each row. Secure the ends of each strip and trim away any excess.

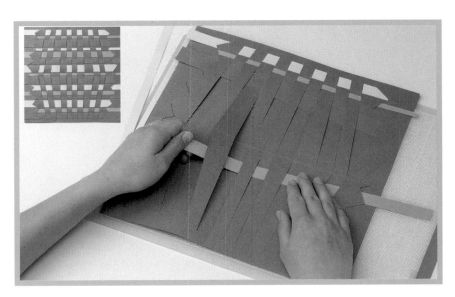

Try asymmetrical woven waves

Cutting wavy slits in a patterned background creates an asymmetrical loom that is woven with coordinating solid strips. Use our wavy line pattern or create your own lines with a decorative ruler. Follow the steps on the next page to weave the loom. Crop, mat and layer the photos with star die cuts. Use the wavy ruler you created in step 2 to cut and mat a banner strip for the title. Cut the title letters using the template. For the caption, mount white paper beneath a star die cut. Write the caption with blue pen.

Kelly Angard; Photos Cynthia Anning

What you will need

- Two duplicate sheets of patterned paper (Making Memories)

- Three sheets each of black and red solid-colored papers

- One sheet of white solid-colored paper

- Pattern on page 129

- Star die cuts (Ellison)

- Lettering template (The Crafter's Workshop)

1 Cut red, white and black strips in various widths ranging from ⅛" to ½".

2 Photocopy the wavy line pattern on page 129 and transfer to white cardstock to create a decorative ruler. Place the ruler edge about ½" from the top edge of the patterned paper and trace the wavy line with a pencil. Move the ruler down 1" and draw another wavy line. Repeat every inch down the paper until you reach the bottom. Carefully cut each wavy line with a craft knife, taking care not to cut through the left and right edges of the page. Repeat for a second loom.

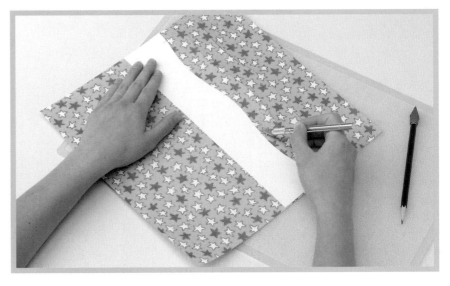

3 Randomly weave colored strips into the looms working from left to right. Secure the ends in place and trim excess. Double mat both weavings to complete the backgrounds.

Make a graduated template loom

A circle-cutting graduated template makes it easy to create a circular loom. The design gives a strong sense of movement to this superhero page. Try other shapes of graduated templates to make a varied loom. To re-create this look, mat the patterned background with navy paper. Mount a red rectangle in the page center. Create the circle weaving following the steps on the facing page. Mount the weaving as shown and trim the right side. Crop and mat the photos and write a caption. Adhere letter stickers for the title.

What you will need

- One sheet of patterned paper (Stamping Station)

- One sheet each of navy, blue, yellow, red and white solid-colored paper

- Coluzzle® Nested™ Circle Template (Provo Craft)

- Foam cutting mat

- Swivel cutting knife

- Letter stickers (Provo Craft)

Kelly Angard

1 Cut eighteen ¼" wide strips from solid-colored papers in quantities of: 6 red, 6 blue and 6 yellow.

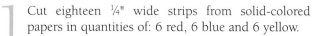

2 Place the nested circle template over white paper on a foam cutting mat. Insert the swivel knife into a template-cutting channel and make the cut. Repeat until all template channels are cut. Remove the template and complete the cut on the outermost channel to allow the circle loom to fall away from the rectangular frame.

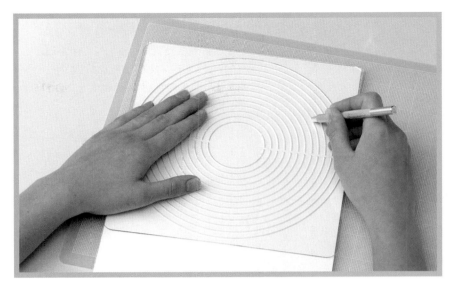

3 Weave four strips into the center of the loom to hold the loom together. Use a craft knife to complete the channel cuts, forming full circles.

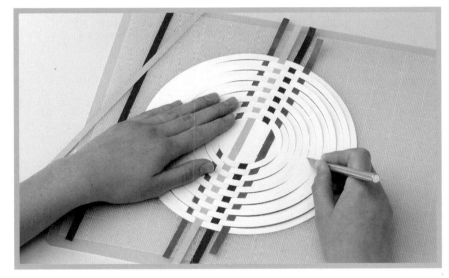

4 Weave remaining strips vertically into the loom, alternating colors as you go. Trim the end of each strip leaving a ⅛" overhang. Insert a ½" red strip horizontally through the center to cover the uncut center portion of the loom. Trim ends.

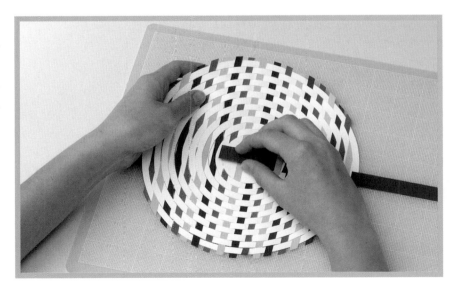

DUTCH-INSPIRED WEAVING

The laced weaving patterns on these pages look like the delicate embroidery of a Dutch girl's bonnet. Weaving thin strips of paper through cut slits in cardstock creates the traditional laced border and heart and flower motifs. These patterns give a finishing touch to baby, springtime or valentine layouts.

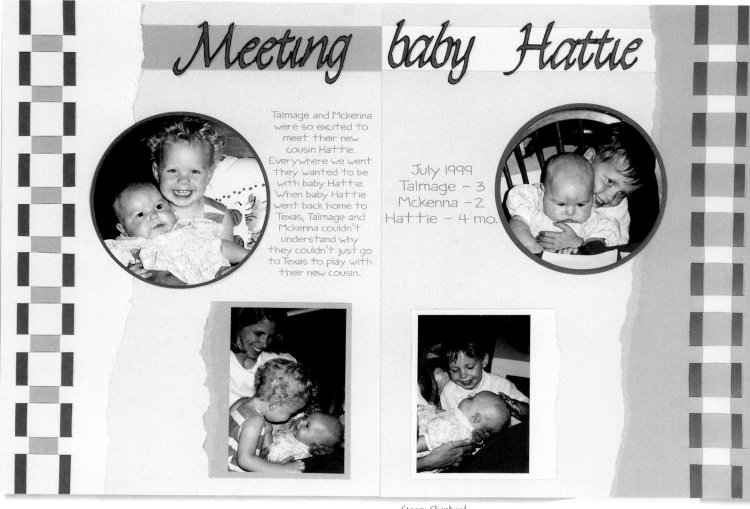

Stacey Shepherd

Lace a delicate border

Laced borders are the ideal choice if you like the woven look but want to save a little time. Start by printing a caption on one side of a pale sage background. Mount 1" blue and yellow strips across the top. Print and silhouette-crop title letters. Follow the steps on the facing page to lace the woven borders. Mount the borders as shown on the layout. Crop and mat photos, tearing mat edges as desired. Add journaling.

What you will need

- Three sheets of sage solid-colored paper
- One sheet each blue and teal solid-colored paper
- One sheet of yellow, mini corrugated paper (DMD Industries)
- Pattern on page 129
- Computer font (Provo Craft)
- Circle shape cutter or circle template
- Removable artist's tape (optional)

1 Tear the inside edges of each border strip so that the finished width is between 2" and 3". Starting ¼" from the left straight edge and ¾" from the top edge, use a pencil and clear ruler to lightly draw a horizontal cutting line 1¼" long on the back of the paper. Draw a second cutting line ⅜" below the first. Draw a third cutting line ¾" below the second. Continue drawing lines, alternating the spacing between ⅜" and ¾'. If you prefer, photocopy the pattern on page 129 and secure it to the border strip using removable artist's tape and cut through pattern and paper on cutting lines.

2 Use a craft knife to cut through each penciled line. If you are using a pattern, cut the lines through both the pattern and the border strip.

3 Cut two ½" strips and four ¼" strips. Weave three strips into each border, one wide and two narrow.

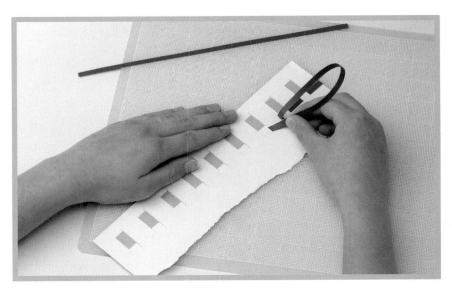

Laced hearts and flowers

These miniature weavings add form and texture without adding a lot of bulk. Once you understand the basic technique, you can easily create custom designs. To create the heart borders and flower accents, follow the steps on the next two pages. Start with a textured lavender background for the layout. Write the title with purple pen using the font as a pattern. Outline each letter with black pen. Mat and arrange all page elements.

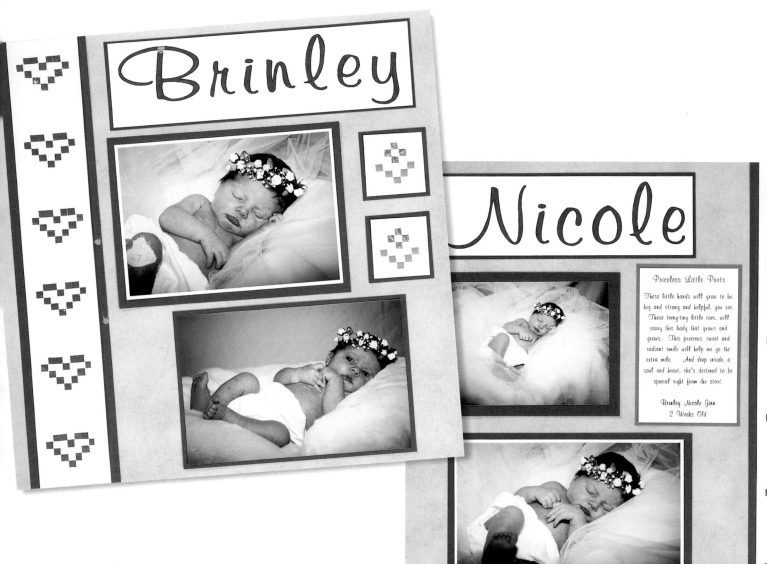

Brandi Ginn

What you will need

- Two sheets of lavender patterned paper (Making Memories)
- Two sheets of purple solid-colored paper
- One sheet each of white, red and green solid-colored paper
- One sheet of purple vellum paper (Paper Adventures)
- Patterns on page 129
- Computer font (downloaded from Internet)
- Poem from *The Scrapbooker's Best Friend, Volume II* (EK Success)

1 *HEARTS* For each heart border cut seven red strips ⅛" wide and 12" long. For easier lacing, use papers that are lighter weight than cardstock. For variety, you can also use paper quilling strips, satin ribbon or strips of fabric. To make the lacing easier, cut one end of each strip at an angle.

2 Photocopy and size the pattern to fit the page and place over a 2 x 12" white border strip. Use a metal straightedge ruler and craft knife to cut along the pattern lines, going through both the pattern and border strip. Remove the pattern. Using just the tip of the knife, slice through each cutting line again to help widen each slot so the paper will slide through more easily.

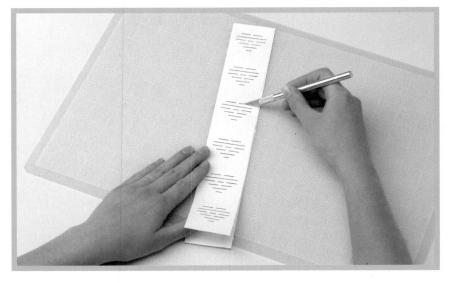

3 Starting at the lower left corner of the border, thread a strip through the back to the front and then down through the slot just above it. Working from the bottom up, continue lacing in and out all the way to the top of the border. Lace the remaining strips in the same manner, tucking each strip snugly against the previous one. Pull strips taut with each new weave, leaving a ¼" overhang on the backside. If a paper strip tears while you are weaving, simply trim it on the back and insert a new strip so that the seam does not show. Follow steps 2 and 3 on the next page to complete the heart border.

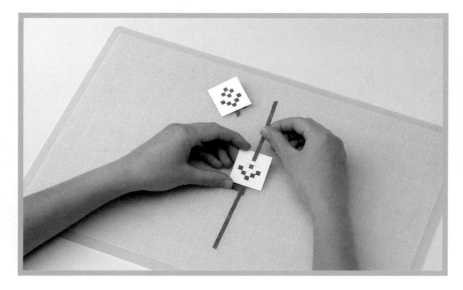

1 *FLOWERS* For each flower, cut one red patterned strip and one green strip, each ⅛" wide and 12" long. Using the pattern on page 125, lace the design in a manner similar to steps 2 and 3 on the previous page. Work from left to right, weaving all the green strips; trim the ends on the backside. Then weave the red strips from left to right.

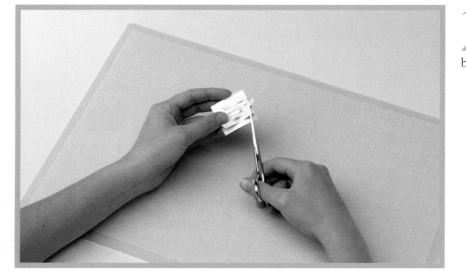

2 Turn the finished weaving over and trim excess extending beyond the edges of the white background.

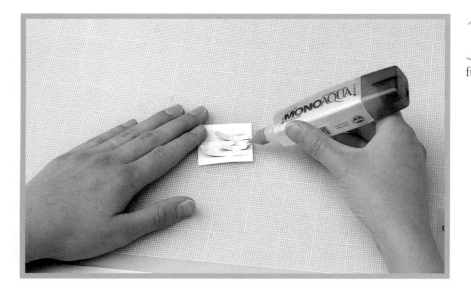

3 Use a liquid adhesive to lightly glue the ends of the laced strips in place. Mat each weaving to further secure the design.

7

QUILLING

Quilling is a craft in which thin strips of paper are coiled, shaped and adhered into and onto designs. The craft—which originated in Europe and spread to America during colonial times—got its name from the feather quills around which the paper was originally rolled. Nowadays special needles are available for use as quilling tools. The following pages will show you how to:

- *Make basic shapes out of quilling paper strips*
- *Apply just the right touch to skillfully shape coils*
- *Combine shapes to create freestyle designs*
- *Quill letters and numbers*
- *Add dimension to stamped or printed images*
- *Incorporate encapsulated quilling into your layouts*

Quilling is a relaxing and rewarding paper technique. While intricate designs do take time to create, there are also simpler quilling techniques for those with less patience. Learn how to quill, and you will become part of a beautiful paper craft tradition spanning many generations.

BASIC QUILLED SHAPES
With a squeeze here and a pinch there, coils of paper are transformed into beautiful shapes such as flower petals, teardrops, stars, holly leaves and tulips. The key to successful quilling is patience. With practice, you will learn how much tension is required to create each type of coil and how much pressure is necessary to alter its shape. The following quilling shapes are the most commonly used. They can be joined together in a multitude of ways to create new designs.

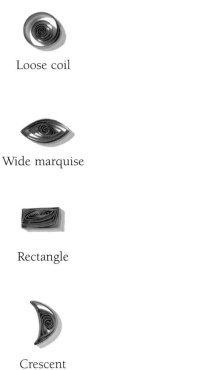

Loose coil

Petal

Teardrop

Wide marquise

Leaf

Star

Rectangle

Square

Triangle

Crescent

Narrow marquise

Tulip

Oval

Off-centered loose coil

Holly

Egg

Peg or tight coil

Loose coil

"S" shape

"V" shape

Heart

1 Most basic quilled shapes begin as a circle—coiled either loosely or tightly—and are then pinched into a more defined shape. To form a basic circle, insert one end of a strip of quilling paper into the tip of a slotted needle. Roll the handle of the tool with one hand as you let the paper coil between your thumb and fore finger of the other hand. You control how loosely or how tightly the coil is rolled.

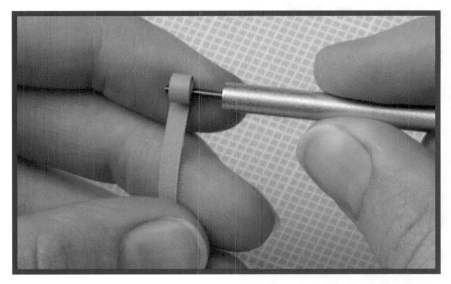

2 Once the coil is rolled, tear the end of the paper strip to provide a "seamless" seam for gluing. Apply a tiny drop of liquid adhesive to the inner side of the paper tail and press it against the roll. Allow quilled coil to dry.

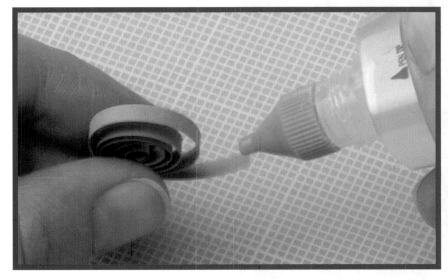

3 To create any of the shapes shown on the facing page, gently pinch the coiled circle between the thumb and forefingers of both hands, coaxing the circle into the desired shape. In the example shown, the circle is being pinched into a wide marquise shape.

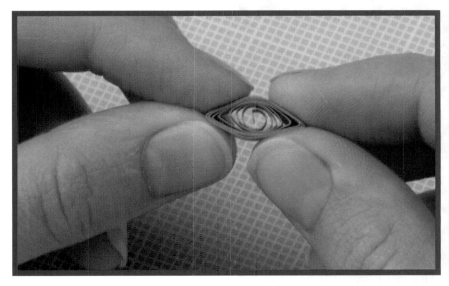

FREESTYLE QUILLING
Quilled shapes can be combined on your page to create elaborate designs. A circle and teardrops become a flower; elongated shapes such as the "S" are transformed into vines and tendrils. Try combining other shapes to create your own freestyle embellishments.

Ruth Mason

Design free-form floral accents

Learn to form basic quilling shapes and you will be off and running with this unique and striking paper technique. These floral arrangements create a dramatic frame for brightly colored summertime photos. Follow the steps on the facing page to create the quilled designs. Then crop and mat the photos using circle and oval cutters and a corner rounder punch. Trim selected mat edges with decorative scissors. Write captions on paper rectangles using a brown pen.

What you will need
- Two sheets of cream-colored cardstock
- One sheet each of yellow, green and pink solid-colored paper
- Assorted colors of 1/16" and 1/8" quilling papers (Lake City Craft)
- Small daisy, small oak leaf punches
- Jumbo grass clump punch (Nankong)
- Corner rounder punch
- Circle and oval shape cutters or templates
- Decorative scissors (Fiskars)

1 The floral corner accents are designed around a base of quilled tendrils. Create these tendrils using ⅛" green quilling paper, curving the strips and rolling the ends in loose coils. Mount the strips as shown in the areas in which you wish to create corner designs.

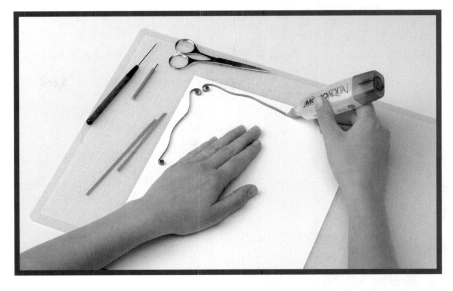

2 Quill the necessary shapes to create the floral design. The base tendrils are embellished with leaves and vines made with ⅛" paper coiled into heart shapes and "S" and "C" scrolls. Quill the larger colored flowers with ¹⁄₁₆" paper using tight coils for the centers and marquise shapes or loose, glued coils for the petals. Quill more petals of each color than you need so you can select the best for each flower. For the small daisies, curl the petals of punched daisies upward and glue tight coils in the centers. For the tiny orange flowers, fringe ⅛" orange strips and quill in a tight coil, pressing the fringe outward. Quill additional teardrop and marquise shapes to embellish the design.

3 Assemble the quilled shapes around the base tendrils, layering the flowers and leaves with punched oak leaves, trimmed strips for grass and punched grass clumps. Glue designs in place.

QUILLED LETTERS & NUMBERS Looking for a unique page title accent?

Try a quilled alphabet. As with other lettering techniques, your letters should be proportional to each other.

Try mounting your titles on letter blocks and embellishing them with quilled flowers and other decorations.

Ruth Mason

Sculpt a quilled title

Quilled letters add the finishing touch to this delightful garden of spring flowers. Self-adhesive foam spacers make the upper title words stand out while protecting the delicate letters from being crushed. First crop and mat photos. For the title, freehand cut rectangles and punch squares. Adhere letter stickers and quill letters as shown on the facing page. Embellish title with punched daisies. Stamp and cut out orange butterflies, curving wings as in paper tole. Quill flowers and leaves, cut stems and background grass. Assemble and mount design with grass dies cuts and punched flowers.

What you will need

- Assorted solid-colored papers
- Assorted colors of ¹⁄₁₆" and ⅛" quilling papers (Lake City Craft)
- Corner rounder punches
- Circle punches: ⅛" and ³⁄₁₆"
- ⅝" square punch (All Night Media)
- Medium flower punch

1 Use the letter and number samples below to quill letters. Use graph paper to keep the size of the letters consistent. Lay each letter on graph paper and adjust the size as necessary to fit the desired grid.

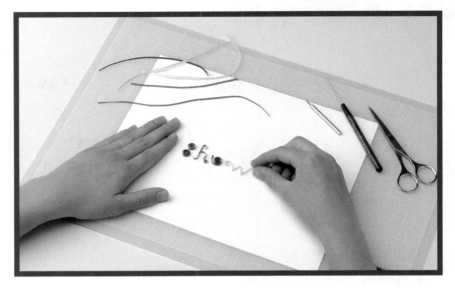

- Small daisy and mini sun and flower punches (Family Treasures, Fiskars)
- Letter stickers (Making Memories)
- Butterfly Stamps (All Night Media, Stampendous)
- Black stamping ink
- Grass border die cuts (source unknown)
- Self-adhesive foam spacers

QUILLED IMAGE ACCENTS
Add dimension to rubber-stamped images, clip art and patterned paper with quilled accents that echo shapes in the printed designs. Flowers seem to come alive, balloons appear ready to float away, and gum balls look good enough to eat!

What you will need

- One sheet of patterned paper (Sonburn)
- One sheet each of green and white solid-colored paper
- Corner rounder punch
- Bulb stamps (Stampin' Up!)
- Black stamping ink
- Colored markers
- Assorted colors of ¹⁄₁₆" quilling paper (Lake City Craft)

Jan Williams;
Photo MaryJo Regier

Embellish stamped images

Look no further than your stamping toolbox for quilling design ideas. There are thousands of stamp images available and most can be accented and enhanced with quilling. For the patterned paper background, mount a ¼" evergreen strip along the top. Crop and double mat the photo using a corner rounder punch and a printed caption. Stamp, color, punch and mat each flower. Quill the floral designs as explained below.

1 Choose quilling paper to match the color of each flower. Quill loose coils, glue the end and place each coil on the stamped image to determine the appropriate size. Pinch each coil to fit the outline of the stamped image. For the leaves, quill larger loose coils, glue ends and pinch into marquise shapes. Freehand cut flat leaves. Glue design in place, layering as necessary and adding fringed accents.

Fill in a stencil shape

Like stamps, stencil designs lend themselves well to quilling, as does clip art. The background paper inspired the seahorse motif on this poolside page. Follow the instructions below to quill the design. Use an oval cutter to crop the oval photos and mats for the title and caption. Adhere sticker letters and write caption. Crop and mat rectangular photo using a corner rounder. Silhouette-crop remaining photo. Cut a partial page frame from two shades of solid cardstock. Layer elements on the patterned background.

Jan Williams

What you will need

- Two sheets of seahorse patterned paper (Paper Adventures)

- Two sheets of coordinating, solid-colored papers

- Oval shape cutter or oval template

- Gold glitter sticker letters (C-Thru Ruler Co.)

- Corner rounder punch

- Pattern from *The Big Book of Nature Stencil Designs* (Dover Publications)

- Blue, aqua and sage green $\frac{1}{16}$" quilling papers (Lake City Craft)

1 Follow the directions on page 17 to transfer the seahorse pattern to the background paper. To make the seahorse, roll a tight aqua coil for the eye and loose coils for the remaining parts. Pinch the coils into squares, rectangles and other shapes to fit the pattern. For the seaweed, roll and pinch narrow marquise, leaf and teardrop shapes. Arrange the pieces to fit the pattern and glue in place.

Bring patterned paper to life

Look for designs in background papers that you can embellish with quilled shapes. Bright blue birds and fat balloons with spiral strings add both dimension and color to this picnic layout. Starting with a printed background design, select the elements that you want to embellish with quilled shapes. Roll and pinch the shapes to fit the objects and glue in place; add punched eyes to birds. Refer to the step below to roll a spiral. Crop the photos, mats and oval frame. Cut a slit in the background page along the lower edge of the design. Layer photos in page center, tucking lowest photo beneath slit in page. Write caption with blue pen.

Jan Williams

What you will need

- One sheet of patterned paper (Frances Meyer)

- One sheet of coordinating, solid-colored paper

- Blue, yellow, pink, purple, brown and black ⅟₁₆" quilling papers (Lake City Craft)

- ⅟₁₆" circle hand punch (Fiskars)

- Oval shape cutter or oval template

1 To make a spiral, wrap a quilling strip tightly around a sewing needle for small spirals or around a quilling needle for large spirals. Pull to loosen as necessary.

Encapsulate quilled designs

Plastic memorabilia holders protect quilled pieces and may also be utilized as an element in your page design. First quill the gum balls to fill the 3-D Keeper as shown on the facing page. Cut a circle in the blue background paper large enough for the 3-D Keeper and mount from the backside. Use the pattern on page 129 to cut out the gum-ball machine from red and black paper. Crop and mat photo and printed title. Embellish with additional quilled gum balls.

What you will need

- One sheet of patterned paper (Hot Off The Press)

- One sheet each of blue, red, black and white solid-colored papers

- Circle 3-D Keeper™ (C-Thru Ruler Co.)

- Assorted colors of ⅛" quilling paper (Lake City Craft)

- Pattern on page 129

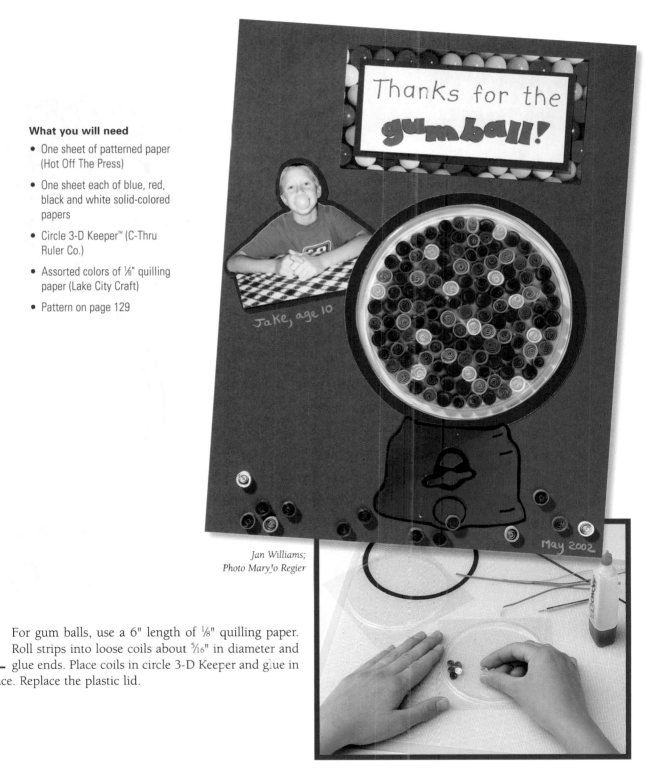

Jan Williams;
Photo Mary Jo Regier

1 For gum balls, use a 6" length of ⅛" quilling paper. Roll strips into loose coils about ⁵⁄₁₆" in diameter and glue ends. Place coils in circle 3-D Keeper and glue in place. Replace the plastic lid.

Quilled present

Try this design for a birthday or holiday page. Using 6" lengths of ⅛" quilling paper, roll loose coils and pinch into square shapes. Fill square 3-D Keeper with coils to create gift box design. Add punched bows and embellish with loosely rolled coils and teardrops rolled from ¹⁄₁₆" paper.

Jan Williams

Quilled heart

Quilled hearts arranged in a heart shape are an easy embellishment for any romantic layout. Using 4" lengths of ⅛" quilling paper, roll "S" coils with 1" at one end and 3" at the other. Glue two "S" coils together to form a heart shape.

Arrange hearts around the edge of the heart 3-D Keeper with the small ends toward the center. To complete the inner heart shape, roll 1" strips into loose glued coils and use for filler between small ends of hearts. Glue all shapes in place. Create the center heart in the same manner as the outside hearts using 6" lengths of quilling paper.

Jan Williams

GALLERY As you can see, paper—that most basic of scrapbooking supplies—is also the most versatile, taking on a different personality each time it is cut, folded, layered, torn, woven, laced or rolled. The scrapbook artists featured in this book have taken paper from flat to fabulous with simple creative paper techniques. We're sure that their art will inspire you to experiment with your own creative paper techniques. Be sure to send us a photograph of your masterpiece!

By a Nose louvers, Torrey Miller

Ryan in Nana's Garden
kirigami, Sharon Moore

KANDRA & NICOLE

What they talk about

Kandra and Nicole Silva have been best buddies since 2nd grade. Kandra was a new student at Sunset View Elementary and her teacher asked Nicole to be a friend to her and show her around. When they became 4th graders Nicole moved to northeast Provo but they still stick together and call each other all the time. And every week one of them sleeps overnight at the other's house. They talk about: Dragonball Z, Harry Potter, things on Cartoon Network, Ben our neighbor, pets, school, the plays they've been in together--The Wizard of Oz and Tikki Tikki Tembo, a Shakespearean workshop they took together.

— on Kandra's deck —

Kandra & Nicole shape tearing, Linda Strauss

I Love School multiple-layer die cuts, Kelly Angard

124

Batter Up! quilled image accents,
Jan Williams

Olivia freestyle quilling,
Jan Williams

Everafter shape tearing,
Linda Strauss

Heritage Wedding diamond
bargello frame, Kelly Angard

A Visit With Grandpa & Grandma
random bargello quilt,
Stacey Shigaya

The Key to Happiness
assemblage, Erikia Ghumm

Hunter single-layer cutting,
Erikia Ghumm

Bathing Beauty quilling over
stenciled design, Jan Williams

PATTERNS
Use these helpful patterns to complete scrapbook pages featured in this book. Enlarge by percentage shown and photocopy the patterns. When transferring patterns to your paper of choice (see page 17), be sure to note solid, continuous lines for cut lines and dotted lines for fold lines.

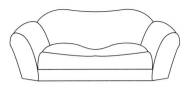

Page 10 Paper tole sofa (380%)

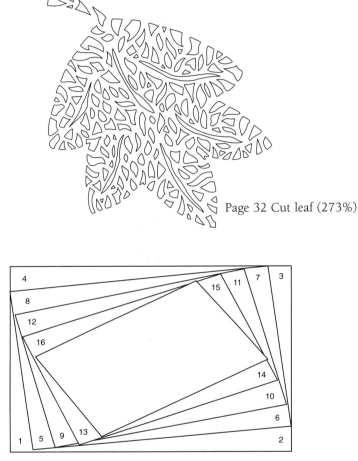

Page 32 Cut leaf (273%)

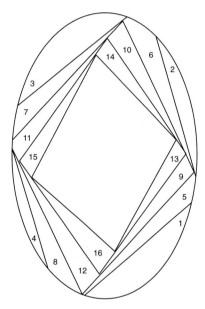

Page 48 Oval iris frame (210%)

Page 51 Rectangular iris frame (205%)

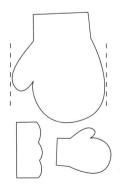

Page 56 Paper chain mittens (210%)

Page 58 Paper chain snowman
(181% for frame; 300% for border)

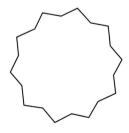

Page 60 Kirigami snowflake windows
(151%)

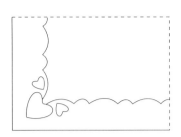

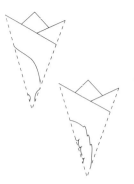

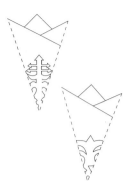

Page 64 Kirigami heart frame (338%)

Page 66 Kirigami poinsettia & leaf (588%)

Page 67 Kirigami snowflakes (588%)

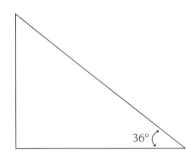

36°

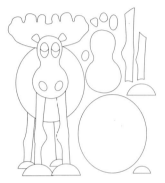

Pages 65-67
35° triangle for napkin fold (253%)

Page 68 Kirigami "Pals" (360%)

Page 80 Shape tearing moose (628%)

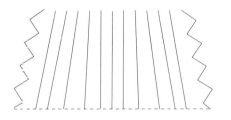

Page 100 Folded symmetrical loom (523%)

Page 102 Random curved loom (580%)

Page 106 Woven laced border (500%)

Page 108 Dutch-inspired flower (170%)

Page 108 Dutch-inspired hearts (230%)

Page 121 Quilling gum-ball machine (460%)

Additional instructions & credits

Sibling Revelry
This page features a louvered window with a paper-torn and wrapped frame and a paper tole sofa. Papers: Colors by Design, Magenta, Making Memories, PrintWorks. See pattern for sofa on page 128. Photos Brenda Martinez

Pinch pleat

5 *PINCH PLEAT* To form the second row of pleats on the page, use a pencil and metal straight-edge ruler to draw parallel lines, alternating at ⅝" and ⅜" intervals, across the back of patterned paper. Score lines with a bone folder and ruler. Use both hands to "pinch" paper, coaxing scored lines up into a peak that can be folded to resemble an accordion fold. Continue until entire page is pleated.

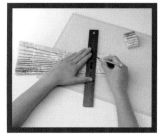

6 Cut 1" strips, vertically, using a craft knife and straightedge ruler, making sure to slice down upon the folds and not up against folds. Miter corners (see step 4 on page 54) and add tape adhesive to the back before mounting pleated strips on page atop box pleat border.

Raised box pleat

1 Follow steps 1 through 4 on pages 53 and 54 for making box pleat border strips. Instead of adhering tape adhesive to back of strips to keep pleats in place, apply self-adhesive foam spacers to the backside of border strip on alternating sections of folds as shown. Flip the border over and mount to outer edges of the page.

Patterned paper tole

4 Adhere curled pieces atop silhouetted butterflies, matching patterns and designs, with ⅛" self-adhesive foam spacers.

5 Mount paper tole elements atop their duplicate image on background paper with additional self-adhesive foam spacers, allowing some to overlap onto photos and title block.

Kirigami windows

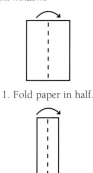

1. Fold paper in half.

2. Fold paper in half again.

3. Trace shapes randomly, overlapping partial shapes atop fold lines.

Kirigami heart frame

1. Start with 8½ x 11" paper.

2. Fold C and D to A and B, and crease.

3. Fold BD to AC, folding paper in half again.

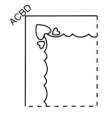

4. Transfer pattern (page 129) to folded paper, matching up fold lines; cut.

Kirigami poinsettias & snowflakes

1. Start with an 8½" square of paper. Fold D to A, folding in half to form triangle.

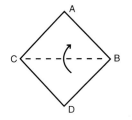

2. Fold B to C; just crease at lower, center point.

3. Photocopy and size 36° triangle pattern on page 129; transfer to cardstock and cut out. Place triangle on center point of folded paper triangle. Fold B toward AD along upper edge of 36° triangle; remove cardstock triangle.

4. Fold right edge of paper to edge of previous fold.

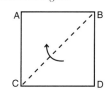

5. Flip folded paper over. Fold C over to line up with left edge fold.

Personalized kirigami

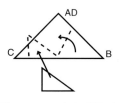

1. Start with a 12" square of paper. Fold D to A diagonally to form a triangle.

2. Fold B to C, folding triangle in half.

3. Fold AD to BC, folding triangle in half again.

4. Flip folded triangle over and rotate so that folded edges fall on the left and lower sides before tracing letters on folds to cut.

3L Corp. (800) 828-3130
3M Stationery (888) 364-3577
All My Memories (888) 553-1998
All Night Media (800) 842-4197
Amy's Magic (724) 845-1748
Anna Griffin, Inc. (888) 817-8170
Art Accents (800) 937-7686
Artistic Wire Ltd. (630) 530-7567
Autumn Leaves (800) 588-6707
Bazzill Basics Paper (480) 558-8557
Beary Patch Wholesale, Inc., The
(877) 327-2111
Bo-Bunny Press (801) 771-4010
Caren's Crafts (805) 520-9635
Carl Mfg. USA, Inc. (847) 956-0730
Carolee's Creations (435) 563-1100
Colorbök, Inc. (800) 366-4660
Colors By Design (800) 832-8436
Color Wheel Company, The (541) 929-7526
Crafter's Workshop, The (914) 345-2838
Craf-T Products (507) 235-3996
Creating Keepsakes (888) 247-5282
Creative Imaginations (800) 942-6487
Creative Memories (800) 341-5275
C-Thru Ruler Company, The (800) 243-8419
Cut-It-Up (530) 389-2233
Deluxe Designs (480) 497-9005
D J. Inkers (800) 325-4890
DMC Corp. (973) 589-0606
DMD Industries, Inc. (800) 805-9890
Doodlebug Design Inc. (801) 524-0050
Dover Publications (800) 223-3130
EK Success Ltd. (800) 524-1349
Ever After Scrapbook Company (800) 646-0010
Family Treasures (949) 643-9526
Fiskars, Inc. (800) 500-4849
Frances Meyer, Inc. (800) 372-6237
Glue Dots International (888) 688-7131
Hallmark Cards, Inc. (800) 425-6275
Hero Arts (800) 822-4376
Hot Off The Press, Inc. (888) 300-3406
Impress Rubber Stamps (206) 901-9101
Inspire Graphics (801) 235-9393
K & Company (888) 244-2083
Karen Foster Design (801) 451-9779
Lake City Craft Company (417) 725-8444
Lion Brand Yarn (800) 258-9276
Magenta Rubber Stamps (450) 922-5253
Making Memories (801) 294-0430
McGill Inc. (800) 982-9884
me & my BIG ideas (949) 583-2065
Memory Muse Designs (503) 287-7952
Microsoft www.microsoft.com
Mrs. Grossman's Paper Company (800) 429-4549
My Mind's Eye, Inc. (866) 989-0320
Nature's Pressed (800) 850-2499
Northern Spy (530) 620-7430
NRN Designs (800) 421-6958
On the Surface (847) 675-2520
Paper Adventures (800) 727-0699
Paper Company, The (800) 426-8989
Paper House Productions (800) 255-7316
Pebbles in My Pocket (800) 438-8153
Plaid Enterprises, Inc. (800) 842-4197
PM designs (formerly Puzzle Mates) (888) 595-2887
Pressed Petals (800) 748-4556
PrintWorks (800) 854-6558
Provo Craft (800) 937-7686
Punch Bunch, The (254) 791-4209
Ranger Industries, Inc. (800) 244-2211
Robin's Nest Press, The (435) 789-5387
Sakura of America (800) 776-6257
Sandylion Sticker Designs (800) 387-4215
Scrapbook Wizard, The (435) 752-7555
Scrap Ease (now Creating Keepsakes) (800) 642-6762
Scrap Pagerz (435) 645-0696
Scrappin' Dreams (417) 742-2565
Sonburn, Inc. (800) 437-4919
Stamp Doctor, The (866) 782-6737
Stampa Rosa, Inc. (800) 554-5755
Stampendous! (800) 869-0474
Stamping Station Inc. (801) 695-3426
Stampin' Up! (800) 782-6787
Strathmore Papers (800) 628-8816
Westrim Crafts (800) 727-2727
Wordsworth (719) 282-3495
Wübie Prints (888) 256-0107

Artist Index

Amidei, Jodi (Lafayette, CO)
Angard, Kelly (Highlands Ranch, CO)
Anning, Cynthia (Virginia Beach, VA)
Bishop, Alex (Honolulu, HI)
Christensen, Lorna (Corvallis, OR)
Cotter, Margie (Louisville, CO) Iris folding patterns
Fishburn, Sarah (Fort Collins, CO)
Frye, Pamela (Denver, CO)
Ghumm, Erikia (Brighton, CO)
Ginn, Brandi (Lafayette, CO)
Kitayama, Ann (Broomfield, CO)
Klassen, Pam (Westminster, CO) 6
Korf, Nancy (Portland, OR)
Mason, Ruth (Columbus, OH)
McDonald, Debra (Post Falls, ID)
McMurry, Donna (Sanford, FL)
Miller, Torrey (Westminster, CO)
Moore, Sharon (Alcoa, TN)
Morgan, Lynn (Anna Griffin, Inc.)
Navone, Joanna (Springfield, MA)
Peters, Chris (Hasbrouck Heights, NJ)
Shepherd, Stacey (Highland Village, TX)
Shigaya, Stacey (Denver, CO)
Strauss, Linda (Provo, UT)
Stutzman, Pennie (Broomfield, CO)
Taylor, Shannon (Bristol, TN)
Williams, Jan (Streamwood, IL)

Photo Contributors

Aldridge, Leslie (Broomfield, CO)
Anning, Cynthia (Virginia Beach, VA)
Benedict, Jennifer (Cardiff, CA)
Campbell, Cristana (Bothell, WA)
Duncan, Lois (Southern Shores, NC)
Escobedo, Sandra (Manteca, CA)
Finger, Heidi (Brighton, CO)
Gerbrandt, Michele (Denver, CO)
Martinez, Brenda (Lakewood, CO)
Miller, Torrey (Westminster, CO)
Regier, MaryJo (Littleton, CO) 70, 114, 117
Schwartz, Helena (Los Angeles, CA)
Urban, Mary (Denville, NJ)

Professional Photographers
Kirigami heart frame
Mardel Photography
9424 S. Union Square
Sandy, Utah 84070

Bibliography
The Bargello Page
locutus.ucr.edu/~cathy/barg/barg.html

Azaleas

One of the flowers that I fell in love with when I moved to the south was the azalea. When we built our house, we made sure that lots of azaleas surrounded us. The beautiful blossoms are my favorite part of the spring season.

Getting the Most From Your

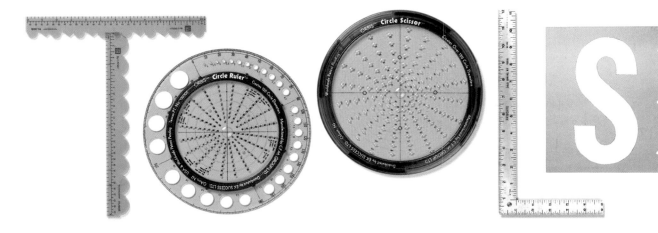

SCRAPBOOK TOOLS

MEMORY
MAKERS
BOOKS

Table

142 Cutting Tools

From craft knives to paper trimmers, cutting tools are the meat and potatoes of scrapbook tools. These indispensable supplies allow the scrapbooker to consistently make straight cuts with ease and accuracy, creating precise borders, mats and other page elements. Decorative scissors turn cuts into eye-pleasing patterns that add something special to page elements such as journaling blocks and titles or embellishments.

170 Shape Cutters, Punches, Die Cuts

There is no easier way to make perfect circles and basic shapes than by using shape and circle cutters, punches and die cuts. Most scrapbookers have an ample supply of these nifty tools on hand, or have ready access to a selection through their local scrapbook or hobby store. These specialized tools make it possible for a scrapbooker to repeatedly carve the same shape multiple times to form creative and consistent borders, embellishments, corners and other page elements.

196 Stencils, Templates, Decorative Rulers

Considered a luxury to some scrapbookers, these tools have become indispensible to others. Lettering templates allow scrapbookers to design and create beautiful titles. Shape templates and stencils can be the answer to many embellishment challenges. Decorative rulers help artists coax straight edges into pretty patterns. All of these versatile tools allow the scrapbooker to create complex designs with finesse.

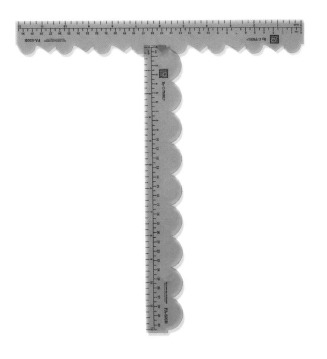

Even the rain couldn't dampen our spirits or spoil our mood on this glorious day at Discovery Cove. Daniel, Anna and Sasha Florida - 2001

Introduction

If you're like me, over time you have accumulated an extensive and sophisticated array of scrapbook tools. There is just something about purchasing the latest tool that whets the creative appetite, inspiring us simply by its "newness" and promise to perform its given function. And yet, as wonderful as they are, investing in scrapbook tools can take a substantial bite out of any budget and so it behooves us to get as much bang for our buck as possible from those that we already own. Finding innovative ways to use scrapbook tools can be a satisfying process of experimentation and discovery. After all, at the very foundation of creativity is resourcefulness.

This book was created to help jump-start your imagination and inspire you to think of new ways to use the tools that are currently part of your scrapbook arsenal. Along with an idea gallery full of great layouts, you'll find a wide range of innovative techniques that can be used for numerous page themes.

The art you'll see inside came from a number of sources. In an effort to provide you with the most comprehensive sampling of fresh ideas, we challenged tool manufacturers and professional scrapbookers to submit cutting-edge concepts. We also held a contest and encouraged readers like you to send us pages displaying new tool usage. The result? This terrific volume featuring ways to use stencils to create stamps, templates to produce polymer clay page accents, cutting tools to craft unique paper art, and much more.

We thank those artists and manufacturers who accepted the challenge and submitted concepts for this book—those whose pages are included as well as those whose work does not appear due to space limitations. Now the challenge is put to you. Get set to explore and most of all have fun!

Michele

Michele Gerbrandt
Founding Editor
Memory Makers magazine

Basic Tools Every Scrapbooker Needs

As the scrapbooking phenomenon has grown, so has the outcry for more and better tools. Manufacturers have stepped up to the plate to provide a seemingly endless parade of tools to make scrapbooking easier and more enjoyable. In this book, we've focused on the most popular and most basic tools available to scrapbookers today—those found in most scrapbookers' workboxes. These are the tools used by artists to create the spectacular scrapbook pages featured in this book.

Trimmer

Today's trimmers are updated versions of the old guillotine-type paper cutters we remember from school. These modern renditions are compact, safe and far more affordable. They are a convenient way to quickly cut straight lines.

Craft Knife

Craft knives have been in office supply and hardware stores forever. They've finally found their niche in scrapbooking. Craft knives offer the scrapbooker a means to create highly detailed cuts with ease. They have inexpensive disposable blades which ensure effortless, clean cuts every time.

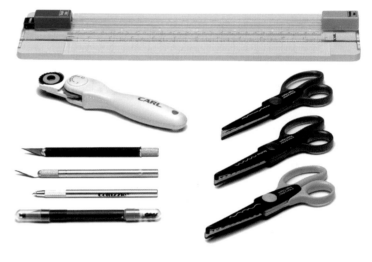

Decorative Scissors

For years Mother's pinking shears were the only decorative-edge scissors available. Not anymore. Now the patterns on the market are endless, including deckle, scallop, stamp-edge and fancy Victorian designs. These creative cutting tools are a welcome addition to the scrapbooking family.

Decorative Rulers

Gone are the days when straight-edge rulers dominated the scene. Decorative rulers have made the move from the drafting table to the scrapbooking table. We are no longer just limited to cumbersome French curves either. Decorative rulers are available in a variety of styles including wavy, scalloped Victorian and Grecian key designs. The choices are boundless.

Templates and Stencils

Templates help create perfect circles and ovals as well as other distinct shapes. Some come with cutting tools, allowing scrapbookers to skip the tedium of tracing prior to cutting, by performing the tasks consecutively. Stencils, including brass stencils, provide complex designs and patterns to add that finishing touch to scrapbook spreads.

Shape Cutters

Shape cutters such as circle, oval and nested-template cutting systems make it possible for scrapbookers to make clean and precise cuts every time. Durable and inexpensive, these tools are available from many major manufacturers and various systems provide unique results.

Punches

Who would have guessed that the humble beginnings of the punch craze started in an office supply store with a single hole punch? Punches have become a major staple in scrapbookers' tool collections. Just when we think we've seen all the designs there can be, here comes a whole new line of must-have punches in sizes from tiny to jumbo. There's a punch for just about every scrapbooking need.

Die cuts

Like paper trimmers, these paper cutters have also found life beyond the classroom. From their modest beginnings as tools used to create bulletin board decor, die cuts have evolved into multifaceted phenomena. Whatever the image you are seeking for your scrapbook page, you can bet you will find it immortalized in die-cut form. Simple die-cut shapes can be customized with colorful embellishments that add dimension and pizazz.

Beyond the Basics:

Other great tools to add to your scrapbook toolbox

- Adhesive application machine: a tool that adds an adhesive backing to flat objects
- Paper crimpers: create three dimensional wavy ridges and designs in paper
- Wire tools: round nose pliers, wire cutters, peg boards, coiling rods
- Rubber stamps: create simple and complex stamped designs
- Heat gun: makes ink and other materials dry more quickly and aids embossing
- Eyelet setting tools: punch tiny holes anywhere
- Piercing tools: create holes for stitching or creating patterns
- Styluses: used to impress a design into paper, metal or other surfaces
- Button shank removers: allow easy removal of shanks so buttons can lay flat against a page

Care and Storage of Tools

How many times have you sat down to scrapbook only to find yourself spending more time and energy locating the right tools than actually creating layouts? One of the keys to enjoyable and productive scrapbooking is having your tools both accessible and in great working condition. Follow our tips for organizing, storing and caring for your tools and your scrapbooking time and money will be well spent.

Decorative Scissors

Over time decorative scissors can become dull. Some say you can sharpen them by cutting through heavy foil. Gently file down any rough spots along the pattern teeth to ensure smooth cutting. Check with the manufacturer before adding lubrication which may damage the plastic hinges and housings of decorative scissors. Store scissors by hanging them on a pegboard or expandable wooden coat rack. Sort them by pattern and tuck them away in a plastic tub. Stand them on end in a partitioned plastic Lazy Susan or wooden box. Keep them holstered in the elastic loops of a cropping bag. Place them in the compartments of an over-the-door hanging shoe rack. Do not expose scissors to high heat or humidity.

Paper Trimmers

Blades can become dull with repeated use. Be sure to keep extra blades on hand and change them frequently. If your trimmer is creating crooked cuts, contact the manufacturer. Many offer limited lifetime warranties on the trimmer's parts and provide repair or replacement at no charge. Store trimmers flat. Do not expose them to high heat as this may cause warping.

Craft Knives

Craft knives can become sticky with adhesive. Clean them with a product intended to remove adhesives and glues. Lost lids can be replaced with small pieces of clear plastic tubing from the hardware store, or with discarded marker lids. Some artists plunge their craft knives, blade first, into an eraser for storing, although this may dull the blade. Replace the blade often and discard used blades carefully.

Templates, Stencils, Shape Cutters

Templates are delicate and can easily be damaged either with a cutting tool or by catching upon one another. To minimize damage, do not use a craft knife against the edges of the template or stencil. Instead, trace the pattern with a pen or pencil, remove the template or stencil and then cut the design out of the paper. Sort plastic lettering templates by category and store them out of direct sunlight in page protectors within three-ring notebooks. By placing a piece of dark paper between each stencil/template in the notebook, it is much easier to see patterns. Place brass stencils in the sleeves of a 4 x 6" photo album. File heavier templates in hanging folders or zippered plastic bags.

Decorative Rulers

Decorative rulers can become dirty with ink, lead and adhesive which can transfer to your next project. Clean off all pen/pencil marks and adhesive after each use. If possible, store rulers flat, as storing on edge or standing up will cause warping. You may wish to punch a hole on the end of rulers and place them on a metal ring or hang them from a pegboard. Consider storing rulers in partitioned sheet protectors made for long border stickers and place them in three-ring notebooks. Avoid high heat and direct sunlight to prevent warping. Always trace your pattern and cut by hand. Avoid using decorative edges as direct cutting guides for your craft knife, as the edge can be easily nicked and sliced.

Punches

Clean adhesive from punches with a commercial adhesive remover. Sharpen dull punches by cutting through heavy foil. Gently file down any rough spots along the pattern to ensure smooth cutting. Keep them from sticking by punching through waxed paper. Punches can be taken apart relatively easily for internal lubrication with a lubricating spray (check with manufacturer first). Store punches by category in labeled plastic tubs or in an over-the-door organizing system specifically designed for punches. Stow them in the plastic compartments of a cropping bag, in the pockets of a hanging plastic shoe organizer or in labeled drawers of a plastic multi-drawer chest. Make skinny punch shelves from 2 x 2" pieces of wood. Do not expose punches to high heat.

Die cuts

When die cuts become dull, sharpening should be done by the manufacturer or the manufacturer's agent. Contact the manufacturer about replacing damaged rubber matting as well. Before storing dies, remove all stray bits of paper from the die surface. Categorize dies and store dies flat, if possible, away from high heat or direct sunlight. Dies can be stored in much the same fashion as punches.

The Cabin

We rented this great little cabin when we went to South Dakota. It had three rooms and a great kitchenette. Just outside the door was a wonderful fishing pond. John & the boys didn't catch anything, but they had a lot of fun trying. There was also a fire pit and we had a blast making s'mores and cooking hotdogs over the open flame. I would love to own a little cabin just like this, but in the Colorado Mountains.

Des and the boys really enjoyed their first Camel Ride at the Cheyenne Mountain Zoo. Miah rode with Joey because he was a little scared to ride alone. I think Joey was a little scared to ride by himself too. Des wasn't going to ride the camel at first, then changed her mind. Everyone said it was a little bumpy but lots of fun.

Des

Camel Ride

Joey & Miah

Cutting Tools

In construction, you start building from the ground up. In cooking, you make the cake before you frost it. It's only logical. Scrapbooking is no different. That's why so many scrapbookers invest first in cutting tools such as paper trimmers, craft knives and decorative scissors. These are the foundation blocks of scrapbook equipment. While familiarity with these tools by no means breeds contempt, it can result in many scrapbookers overlooking and underestimating the value of these tools. They reach for them only to trim paper to size and cut photo mats. However these toolbox staples hold a wealth of possibilities and potential. With some imagination, you can utilize cutting tools to create unique decorative accents for your layouts. This chapter presents some interesting techniques that will help you view cutting tools from a different angle.

Valerie Barton, Flowood, Mississippi

Scootin' Along

Use a paper trimmer to create a border that meanders around the page like a complex sidewalk that just calls for a scooter ride (see adjacent page for border instructions). Place pictures on background. Enfold photos with border strips. Embellish with tiny mirrors and eyelets. Attach the vellum journaling block to the page with eyelets. Make the "Scootin'" title by embellishing a metal-rimmed tag with stickers, fibers, tiny mirrors and a ball chain. Attach a metal nameplate with decorative brads.

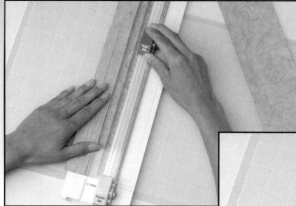

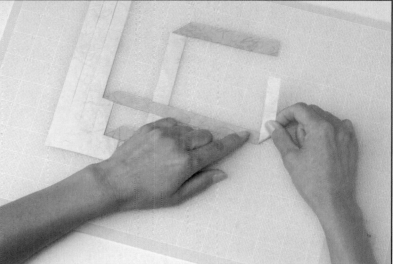

ONE To create the sidewalk border seen on the Scootin' Along page (left), cut a 3 x 12" double-sided mulberry strip. (Double-sided cardstock or patterned paper can also be used.) Use a paper trimmer to make parallel cuts along the length of the paper strip. Space the slices ½" apart. Leave 1" at the bottom of the strip uncut to hold section together.

TWO Randomly fold cut paper strips to form the desired design. Adhere the folded pattern to the page.

Valerie Barton, Flowood, Mississippi

Girls Just Wanna Have Fun

For a funky variation on the method shown above, use double-sided patterned paper strips and torn vellum to create a title. Adhere your title to a patterned paper background. Tear cardstock into a photo mat and chalk the torn edges; embellish with fibers, 3-D vellum flower stickers and buttons. Add metal-rimmed vellum tags for journaling. Place a small piece of the title paper behind each tag. Secure tags to page with decorative brads. Finish the page with a torn vellum tag accent. Chalk torn edges and tie with fiber.

Ruth Anne Oliver, Lafayette, Colorado

Wild Wild West

No need to cut perfect rectangles and squares for this rootin' tootin' layout! Choose five contrasting or coordinating colors of cardstock. Select one color for the background and four colors to be used for the embellishments. Use a paper trimmer to cut random, asymmetric four-sided shapes from those papers selected for the embellishments (see instructions on adjacent page). Mat photos using asymmetric shapes as well. Create the journaling block and title by either hand lettering or stamping. Add penwork to journaling block, title, mats and embellishments and mount to page.

Alone We Can Do So Little…

Use the paper-slicing technique seen in Wild Wild West (left), to create this unique border. Use a paper trimmer to cut a 3 x 10" strip of cardstock into asymmetric pieces. Reassemble the cut pieces on background paper, replacing just one piece of the cut border strip with a block of contrasting colored cardstock. Adhere the cut pieces to the background leaving small gaps between blocks. Mat small photos off-center on colored blocks; adhere to border strip. Double mat the focal photo. Cut a 2 x 2" piece of colored cardstock for the journaling block. Mount cut pieces along another strip of asymmetrically cut cardstock. Journal.

Ruth Anne Oliver,
Lafayette, Colorado
Photos, Tracy Trulove Young,
Meadow Sweet Studio

ONE To create the asymmetrical page elements seen on the Wild Wild West spread (left), place cardstock in trimmer at an angle and smoothly cut into four-sided shapes. Vary your angle and size of paper blocks for more visual appeal.

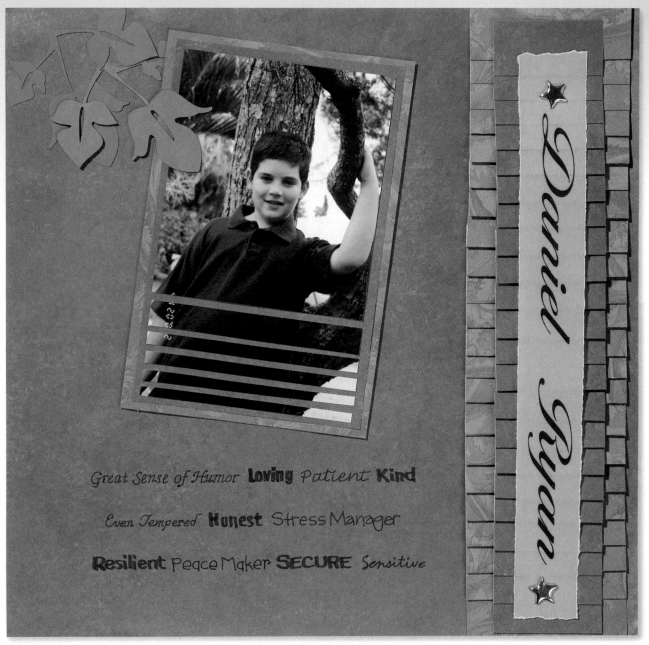

Kim Morelli, Coral Springs, Florida

Daniel Ryan

This unique all-boy page was made using parts of a Fiskar's personal trimmer that some people don't even know exist! Begin by printing the title text onto vellum. Tear the vellum to size by sliding it under the trimmer's cutting guide. Use the guide's edge to tear the vellum. Fashion the dimensional pleat accent by using the trimmer's scoring blade and cutting blade (see instructions on adjacent page). Adhere the pleat to the page and fasten the title over the pleat with decorative brads. Complete the page by hand journaling in varied fonts and add leaf laser die cut in corner for final embellishment.

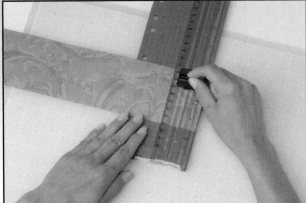

ONE To create the dimensional pleat accent seen on the Daniel Ryan page (left), cut patterned paper into three 3 x 12" strips. Use a scoring blade to score across the width of the strips. Begin the first score 1" from the end of the paper strip. The following score will be ½" from the primary score. Continue to work down the strip alternating between 1" and ½" scores. Repeat the process with three 2 x 12" strips of contrasting patterned paper.

TWO Accordion-fold the paper strips along the score lines. Lay the folded strips end-to-end, pattern-side down on a work surface. Overlap the ends slightly. Apply adhesive tape lengthwise to the strips to secure all three strips together and to hold the folds. Repeat the process in assembling three strips of 2 x 12" contrasting patterned paper to create the layered border effect.

Hula-Little Grass Shack

You can almost feel warm breezes wafting across this tropical layout which utilizes a paper trimmer to create the swaying fringe. For grass-skirt accents, make tiny parallel cuts into 1" wide strips of cardstock. Do not allow cuts to completely sever the strip (leave a ⅛" border along one edge uncut). Use a lettering template and craft knife to cut cardstock letters for the title. Sprinkle with clear embossing powder for texture. Complete by gently daubing a dark green ink pad along the edges of the letters and the mat of the focal picture; add stamps to the title. Create floral lei accents by loosely stringing punched flowers across page.

Brandi Ginn, Lafayette, Colorado
Photos, Donald Bryant Sr., Aurora, Colorado

It's hard to convince people that this is a real, live alligator, but trust me...it is! His name is Scarface and those are really my hands in his mouth. He was 10 feet 8 inches long and weighed about 500 pounds. Tom found this tacky little tourist spot outside of Alamosa, CO and had to take us there on our trip to the Sand Dunes. At first Haley and I had no intentions of sitting on one, but as more and more people stepped up and did it, I couldn't resist taking this chance. I mean, when else in my life will I be able to touch a live alligator, let alone sit on one.

Scarface

Jodi Amidei, Memory Makers

Scarface

It takes little courage, but some know-how, to create this striking page. Make the realistic-looking 3-D border from the background paper using a paper trimmer or craft knife and foam dots (see instructions on adjacent page). Double mat photos. Print journaling on vellum and tear edges. Add chalk to torn vellum edges. Tear and chalk vellum backdrop for the title and add letter stickers. Mat the entire page on cardstock.

ONE To create the alligator border seen on the Scarface page (left), fold back a 2" strip along the left side of the background paper. Right sides will be together. Draw a line lengthwise, 1" from the creased edge. Make pencil marks every 1" along the drawn line, beginning 1½" from the top of the page. Create another set of pencil marks every 1" along the folded edge of the paper. This set of marks should begin at the top of the page. Connect pencil marks on the crease with marks on the line, creating diagonal lines. Cut along the diagonal lines with a paper trimmer or craft knife.

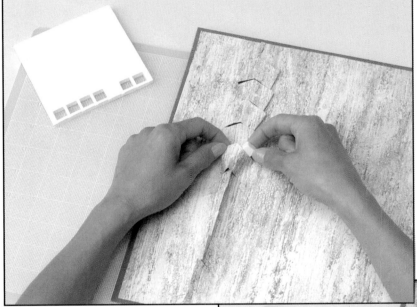

TWO Open the folded sheet of paper and turn it pattern-side up. Place hand on either side of the sheet of paper and gently push toward the paper's center. This will create a "peak" along the previously creased section. Adhere the paper to a piece of cardstock background in this "peaked" position. Place self adhesive foam spacers under each V-shaped section of the peak. Gently push down each peaked section to adhere it to the background.

THREE Lightly chalk the edges of each raised, "scale" platform with both green and brown chalk to create dimension.

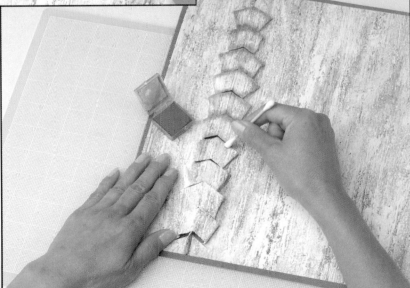

My father doesn't tell me how to live; he lives, and lets me watch him do it.
Adapted from Clarence Budington Kelland

Trying to describe my love for my father is not easy. Words that convey my admiration of him just don't come without effort. He has had such an influence and impact on my life. I know that he shaped who I was as a child, but more noticeable to me now is how he still guides me as an adult — not by telling me how to live, but by setting an example of the type of person I still strive to become. His integrity, compassion, sincerity, and virtues will always seem out of reach for me, but they will continue to give me something to aspire towards in my own life.

Jodi Amidei, Memory Makers

Father

This beautiful border, created using a technique similar to that featured on the Scarface layout (page 150), can add dimension and drama to just about any layout. Make two border sections (see illustrations below). Place the first border section on a strip of torn patterned paper. Place a second border section on the strip so that it precisely mirrors the previously positioned border section. You may need to flip one strip over to get the pattern to work. Embellish the page with metal letters. Affix journaling and quotation blocks with decorative brads. Mat photo and adhere with metal photo corners. Embellish with fiber.

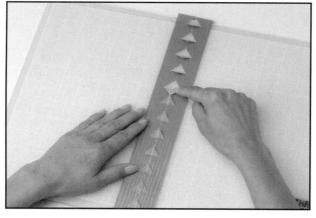

ONE Cut two 2 x 12" strips of double-sided patterned paper. Fold the first strip in half lengthwise. Mark the strip in a manner similar to that detailed in the Scarface instructions (page 151), with one major exception: The vertical line for this border should be drawn ½" (rather than 1") from the paper crease. Once all marks have been made and diagonal lines drawn, cut along diagonals. Unfold paper. Fold up the point of each V cut so that it touches the point of the next V.

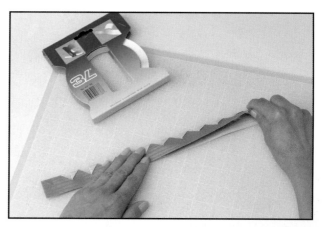

TWO When all V's have been folded, refold the strip along its crease. (Take care to assure that folded V's remain in place). Adhere the folded strip together so that the fold will stay in place. Create a second strip. Mount both strips with notched edges facing each other on torn paper strip to form the border.

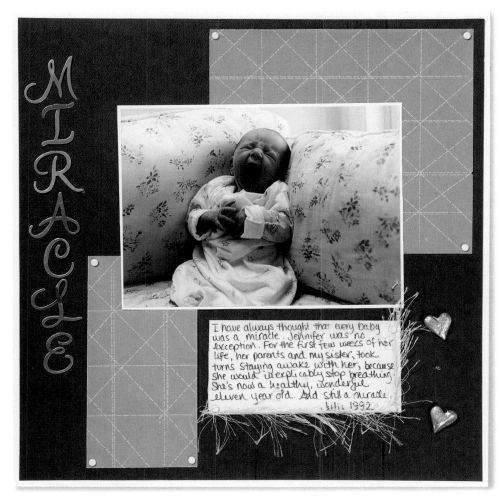

Jill Tennyson, Lafayette, Colorado

Miracle

Re-create the look of a quilt without ever picking up a needle. Mat photo on cardstock. Create the scored patterned paper by following the instructions on the right. Cut the scored paper into two pieces (one should be larger than the other). Attach these cut vellum pieces to the page with decorative brads. Place photo over vellum. Add a journaling block and adorn it with fiber. Adhere metal eyelet letters and metal hearts to the page. Mat the entire page on contrasting cardstock.

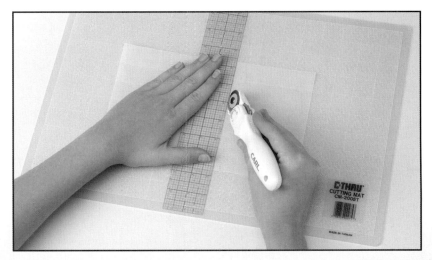

ONE Cut a 6 x 10" vellum rectangle. Using the perforating blade on a rotary trimmer, make 1" vertical passes across the piece of vellum. Turn the vellum 90 degrees and repeat the process, creating a grid. Turn the vellum on the diagonal and mark it in a similar fashion. Turn the vellum once again in the opposite direction and continue making diagonal scores.

I love these photos of John and me at two years old. We had a lot of similar experiences growing up. We both grew up in the Denver area, had blue-collar fathers, and stay-at-home moms. Our families loaded up the station wagon for vacations in Yellowstone and the Grand Canyon, had barbeques with the neighbors on summer weekends, and holiday dinners with the extended family. As children, we were allowed to run free in our suburban backyards. Life was good and we both have memories of a happy childhood.

Kelli Noto, Centennial, Colorado

View of Two

Create your own custom "metal" frames with decorative scissors (see instructions on adjacent page). Double mat photos and die cut the title. Add ribbon for decoration. Journal to complete the layout.

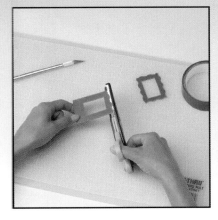

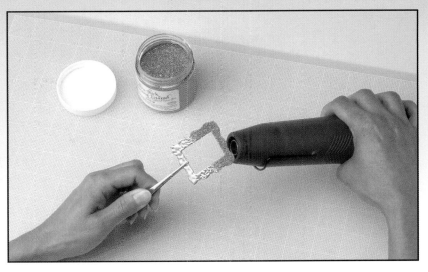

ONE To create the decorative frames seen on the page View of Two (left), cut tagboard rectangles or squares to the desired size. Cover the tagboard pieces with double-sided tacky tape. Cut out the middle of each piece to create a rough frame. Trim the edges of the frame with decorative scissors.

TWO Remove the backing from the tape. Holding the frame with tweezers, dip it into ultra thick embossing enamel (UTEE) until completely covered. Gently shake off the excess enamel. Heat from underneath with a heat gun to melt the embossing powder. For a smoother finish, apply two to four coats of embossing powder, heating between each coat

Renaissance Festival

The word "Renaissance" conjures up dreamy images of castles and kings, a theme supported by this layout of misty borders and elegant frames created by decorative scissors. Cut a 12" piece of cardstock using decorative scissors. Lay the cut strip near the edge on the background paper. Apply chalk using the decoratively cut strip as a template. Move the strip inward slightly and apply a second color of chalk. Cut mats for pictures. Cut mat edges using decorative scissors. Apply embossing ink to mats and emboss with soft metallic peach embossing powder.

Dawn Mabe, Lakewood, Colorado

The Harris Family

Robert Moe Harris 1840 – 1924

Eloise Andrews Harris 1842 –1909

50th Wedding Anniversary
Edwin Andrews Harris
&
Dora Anderton Harris

June 1960

Kim Rudd, Idledale, Colorado

The Harris Family

Use both the positive and negative pieces of chains created with decorative scissors to form an elegant border (see instructions below). Adhere the border to the background page, making sure to start and finish the process with a negative piece. Add triangle pieces of cardstock over corners to conceal ends of strips. Double mat photos. Print title and journaling blocks on vellum. Use an oval cutter to trim the edges of two journaling blocks so that they follow the curve of the photos. Attach vellum to the page with gold thread.

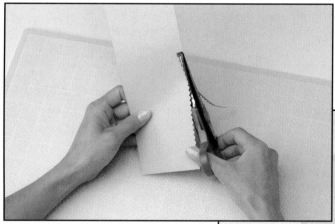

ONE To create the elegant border seen above, use decorative scissors to cut the edge of a 12" piece of cardstock. Set aside this cut piece.

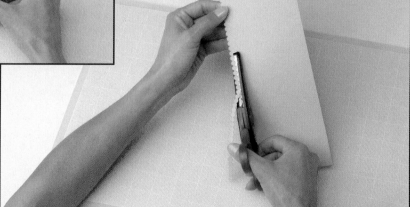

TWO Turn the 12" piece of cardstock over and make a second cut to create a beaded chain effect. Set this piece aside. Use a trimmer to cut a straight ⅛" strip along the edge of the 12" piece of paper. This final border strip should be similar to the first piece you set aside.

Rain

Create themed charms using shrink plastic. Lightly sand shrink plastic. With colored pencils, draw designs on shrink plastic. Make designs three times larger than you wish the final charm to be. Use decorative scissors to cut out the design. Before baking, punch a ⅛" hole in each charm for hanging. Bake plastic according to the manufacturer's directions. Note: Plastic curls during shrinking process but will usually flatten out when the shrinking process is complete. Place mesh down the right side of the page. Cut irregular shapes out of cardstock and adhere to the mesh. Attach the charms to the cardstock shapes with connected jump rings or pieces of chain. Die cut the title and place it on the torn cardstock. Ink the edges of the title letters. Mat photos on one piece of contrasting cardstock and mount.

Kelli Noto, Centennial, Colorado

Keychain Variations

Use shrink plastic and decorative scissors to create keychains, luggage tags, jewelry and other fun pieces. Use them on scrapbook pages, or keep them for collections.

Kelli Noto, Centennial, Colorado

One of the flowers that I fell in love with when I moved to the south was the azalea. When we built our house, we made sure that lots of azaleas surrounded us. The beautiful blossoms are my favorite part of the spring season.

Valerie Barton, Flowood, Mississippi

Azaleas

Create this fractured mat with decorative scissors and silver thread. Cut the mat out of cardstock. Wrap metallic thread randomly around the mat (see instructions on adjacent page). Adhere the mat to the background and mount the focal photo. Print the vertical title on torn vellum and adhere it to the background. Mount supporting photos. Print journaling block on torn vellum and place it over the supporting photos. Attach with decorative brads.

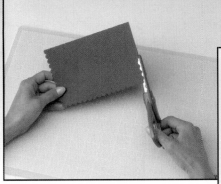

ONE To create the "shattered" mat seen on the Azaleas page (left), cut the edges of a mat with decorative scissors.

TWO Wrap metallic thread in random patterns around the cut mat using the notches created by the scissor pattern to secure the threads. Adhere the ends of the thread on the backside of the mat.

Dawn Mabe, Lakewood, Colorado

Spirograph

Childhood memories of playing with the Spirograph come sweeping back with just one look at this page. Cut cardstock circles using three decorative scissors that have three different patterns. Wrap funky fibers around the circles, using the notches created by the decorative scissors to secure the fibers. Set an even number of mini-eyelets in a circle on background page. Thread colored wire through eyelets in desired pattern. Mat photos, title and journaling block.

Kelli Noto, Centennial Colorado

Winter Walk

Add a modern twist to good old fashioned paper snowflakes by cutting them with decorative scissors (see instructions on the right and on adjacent page). Embellish snowflakes with glitter and adhere them to the page. Triple mat focal photo and add wrapped fiber. Single mat secondary photos. Mount photos. Die cut a title and journal.

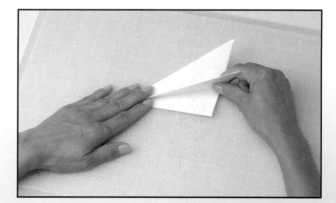

ONE Cut snowflakes from a 3 x 3" sheet of paper. Fold paper in half diagonally to form a triangle. Refold three more times, creating smaller triangles with each fold.

Bloom Where You're Planted

The illusion of pressed flowers is created with decorative scissors on this colorful page. Make the flower border by cutting different sizes of circles out of colored tissue paper using a variety of decorative scissor patterns. Gather each circle in its center to form a flower shape. Combine multiple circles of the same or varying colors to create more interesting flowers. Secure flowers by wrapping wire around the back of the gathered centers. Cut leaf shapes from mulberry paper and twist wire around their bases to secure. Journaled tags and fibers round off the embellishments.

Jennifer Mason, Longmont, Colorado

TWO Use decorative scissors to cut away small portions of paper along all three sides of the triangle. Make sure that portions of some folds are left intact. Cutting away all edges results in a snowflake that will fall apart.

THREE Unfold paper and flatten. Decorate the snowflake with glitter glue, chalks or watercolors to customize the snowflake and make it truly one of a kind.

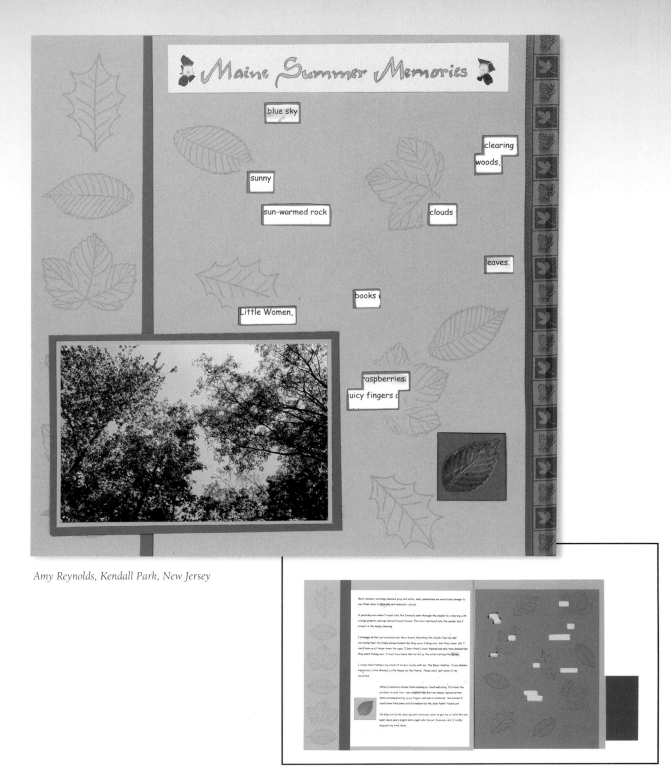

Amy Reynolds, Kendall Park, New Jersey

Maine Summer Memories

Create peek-a-boo windows in a dramatic layout. Stamp watermark leaf images on light green and darker green cardstock. Cut a 3" strip from the left side of the stamped cardstock and set the strip aside. Create windows (see instructions on adjacent page). Double mat photo and mount to the top page overlapping left side edge. Attach the printed journaling block to the bottom page along with the 3" strip which you previously set aside and a ¾" wide strip of purple cardstock. Embellish the page with dried flowers, leaves and a title.

ONE Print journaling on paper. Choose words to be highlighted in "windows." Use a ruler to measure the placement of those words in relation to the edges of the paper. Also note the height and length of the words in order to determine the size required for each window. Transfer your measurements to the previously stamped dark cardstock and draw window rectangles. Cut out windows in dark cardstock with craft knife.

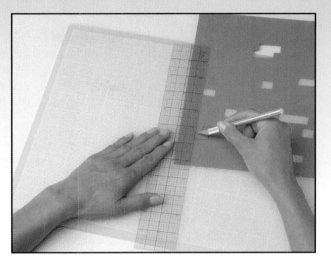

TWO Position dark cardstock on top of stamped light green cardstock. Trace along the inside edges of the windows. Lift dark cardstock and set aside. Use a craft knife to cut windows that are slightly larger than the traced lines on the light cardstock. Punch a 1½" square from the light green cardstock. Mount a dried leaf on the dark green cardstock so the leaf can be viewed through punched square. Cover the leaf with a piece of acetate. Adhere light green stamped cardstock to the front of the darker green page, aligning the windows and creating a matted effect for each window.

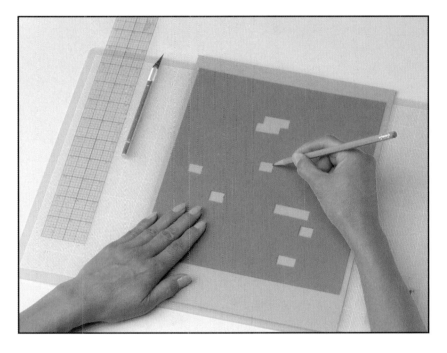

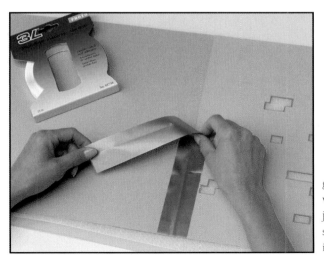

THREE Mount journaled paper along the right edge of a separate sheet of 12 x 12" light green cardstock. Turn journaled page over. Place the page in which you've cut windows face up to the right of the overturned journaled page. To create the binding which will hold these two sections together, place double-sided adhesive tape along the inside edges of both pieces of paper; apply ribbon along edges.

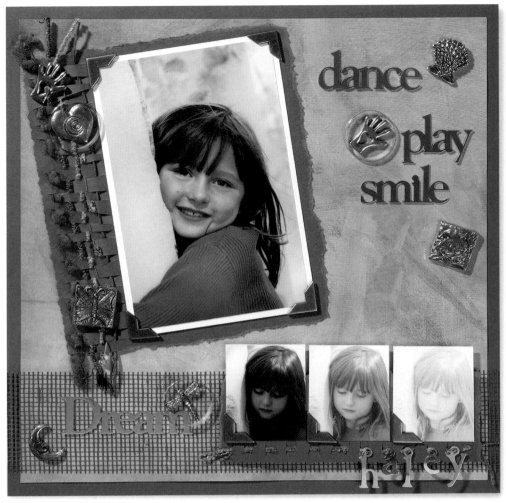

Torrey Miller, Thornton, Colorado

Dance, Play, Smile…Dream

Create a textural mat using a craft knife, fibers and embellishments of your choice (see instructions below). Mat the photo and add metal corners. Adhere metal charms and words to the page. Cover a few charms with plastic watch crystals. Adhere a mesh border across the bottom of the page. Mat a grouping of small photos on torn cardstock. Weave fiber and eyelet letters through slits cut in the bottom of the mat. Use self adhesive foam spacers to mount this photo block to the page.

ONE To create the woven mat on the Dance, Play, Smile…Dream page (above), mark two parallel lines ½" and 1½" from the mat's left edge. Use a craft knife to make random perpendicular slits between these lines. Weave fibers, threaded through a tapestry needle, through the slits. Turn the mat over and adhere it to the background.

Path to the Sea

Weave a decorative border using the same technique featured on the Dance, Play, Smile...Dream page (left). Mat the border on contrasting cardstock. To create the mat, cut cardstock, adhere photo and embellish with fibers. Print the title, mount and decorate with contrasting colors of cardstock strips.

Pat Lingwall, Kennesaw, Georgia

Customize Your Woven and Embellished Border With...

Ribbon and tiny silk flowers

Film negatives and slide frames

Measuring tape and buttons

Hemp and leaves or small pebbles

Paper strips and punches

Wire and beads

Metallic thread and rhinestones

Embroidery floss and charms

Unraveled paper yarn with flat wooden shapes

Grasses and dried flowers

Rickrack and decorative buttons

Lace with string of pearls

Chain and nuts or washers

Leather strips and conchos

Cotton packing twine, brown paper and postage stamps

Satin cording and movie tickets

Curling ribbon and mini bows

Fake fur or braided doll's hair and tiny barrettes

Kelli Noto,
Centennial, Colorado

Custer State Park, South Dakota 8/02

Where the **Buffalo** Roam

Where the Buffalo Roam

Cut-out features embellish this Wild West layout (see instructions below). Use the same technique to cut out title words. Create slits for photos in background paper. Mount the entire page on black cardstock with self adhesive foam spacers to lift it off of the background.

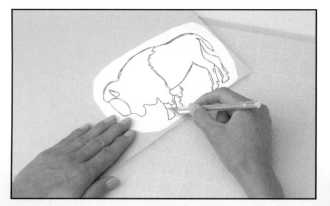

ONE To create the buffalo seen on the page above, draw or copy the desired image on a separate sheet of paper. Use temporary adhesive to stick the drawn image to the front side of cardstock background. Cut on top and bottom of the drawn pattern lines with a craft knife. Leave portions uncut for added visual impact and to secure design.

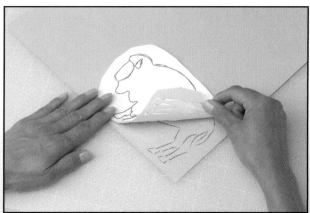

TWO Peel off the pattern and remove residual adhesive with adhesive pickup. Complete page as described above.

Nicole La Cour (Memory Makers), Lochbuie, Colorado.

Dad, Jen and Jacque
May, 2001

Dad and Jen came came out to visit us for a week in may, during labor day weekend. We had such a great visit. We spent time wandering the shops in fort collins and estes park. They taught us how to play spades, and we had a ton of fun. We had jacques family up for memorial day and had a big barbecue. Dad made ribs that were out of this world. Although the visit was short, and we live states apart, the time we spend together, I will always cherish.

Estes Park

Use a craft knife and cardstock to create powerful photo frames. Mat photo on cardstock, leaving a ½" mat border on all sides. Use a craft knife to cut parallel slices around the mat, creating a rough "fringe." Weave a thin strip of patterned paper through the slices along each side of the mat and secure the ends with glue. Create a hidden journaling block by mounting journaling on a tri-folded piece of cardstock. Use buttons and tinsel to fasten. Embellish with punched cardstock shapes wrapped in tinsel. Chalk tags and place title letter stickers on top. Adhere metal letters. Mat the entire page.

Jodi Amidei, Memory Makers
Photo, Kelli Noto, Centennial, Colorado

Daddy's Girl

Use punches to create a stunning frame (see instructions on adjacent page). Adhere framed photo to background. Print title and journaling on patterned paper and cut it into strips. Stick strips on the background and secure with brads. Wrap fiber between brads. Mount the entire page on solid cardstock.

ONE To create the frame seen on the Daddy's Girl page (left), draw the appropriately sized frame outline on a sheet of paper. Punch your preferred shape from a sheet of cardstock. Randomly place the punched shape within the frame's border, leaving a connection at the side or middle of the frame. Trace around the punched shape. Move the punched shape to a new spot, placing it at an arbitrary angle. Trace. Repeat until the frame is filled. Lightly color in the traced shapes. These will remain uncut.

TWO Adhere the marked frame to a sheet of patterned paper with temporary adhesive. Use a craft knife to cut away the portions of the image which remain uncolored around each punch shape.

THREE

Carefully peel away the frame pattern and remove excess adhesive from the patterned paper with adhesive pickup. Apply a thin strip of tacky tape to the outside and inside edges of the frame. Remove the tape backing and cover with clear microbeads.

SHAPE CUTTERS PUNCHES DIE CUTS

Imagine, for a moment, a scrapbooking world without shape cutters. Picture yourself drawing and laboriously cutting intricate shapes by hand. True, it could be done, but few of us would take the time or put forth the effort to agonize over carving complex patterns or designs. So, thank goodness for shape cutters, punches and die cuts! They open up a world of possibilities and save us oodles of time. Most scrapbookers have purchased their fair share of these tools; however, cost prohibits many from owning a true collection and that is reason enough to breathe new life into the ones you do own. This chapter offers some truly unique uses for these tools to produce some fabulous design elements. So dust off those die-cut machines, polish those punches and shine up those shape cutters. It's time to create!

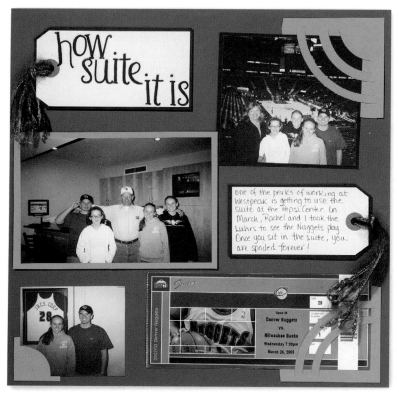

How Suite It Is

The Circle Scissor by EK Success is used to create unique corners for this special page. Use the Circle Scissor to cut a number of concentric quarter circles out of cardstock. Mat photos and weave the corner of one mat through the rings created by Circle Scissor cuts. Corners can be made in various sizes and may hold memorabilia as well as photos. Add fiber-embellished tags with letter stickers to create a title and journaling.

It Is a Happy Talent...

Simplicity is beauty, as evidenced by this page, created with the use of a nested-shape template. Print the title and journaling directly onto the background page. On the upper left side and bottom right corner of the page, cut seven concentric half circles using the template and a swivel craft knife. Use the craft knife to cut away every other ring. Bend the inner circle over to secure the photo. Mat the entire page on contrasting cardstock.

Sonja Chandler, Brentwood, Tennessee

Austin

Play peek-a-boo on your scrapbook page with hidden journaling windows created by cutting half circles in cardstock with a circle template and a craft knife. Score a straight line at the back of the half circle to aid in opening the window. Adhere a journaling page behind the windows so that words peek through the openings. Make larger windows to accommodate photos. Use a lettering template to cut out a title; add penwork for detail. Mat the photos with patterned paper. Label windows with stamped numbers for easier identification.

that you give sweet hugs and kisses

What I love about you...

that you want to sleep with your sister at night instead of in your own crib

your genuine excitement about life

FEB 2003

that you try soooo hard to talk

that you love your big sister

that you call and call and call my name in the morning until I come and get you

BRINLEY

Brandi Ginn, Lafayette, Colorado

Brinley

Circle and oval cutters were used to create the journaling tags and envelope on this layout. Print journaling on cardstock and cut into varied sizes of circles and ovals. Make a cardstock envelope using an oval cutter. Fold up bottom edge and fold sides in to create the envelope. Emboss the edges of the envelope with copper embossing powder and stamp title. Emboss tags with copper embossing powder, using smaller tags as masks. Embellish tags with eyelets, small punches and fibers. Create a textured frame using modeling paste spread upon cardstock and washed with walnut ink. Finish the frame with brads and metal tag accents. Add torn papers to the background, stitching one into place before securing page elements with adhesive.

Don't Judge Each Day...

This fun and innovative envelope, made with a circle cutter, can be used as an embellishment to hide journaling or to hold a photo or memorabilia. You can even use it as an envelope for handmade cards. Print journaling on vellum. Tear vellum into a strip and wrap it around the envelope. Decorate with stickers, die cuts, tags, fibers or brads!

Denise Johnson for EK Success Ltd.

Create the envelope by cutting a 4 x 4" square of cardstock. Cut four 4" diameter circles. Fold each circle in half to crease. Open each circle. Place a circle crease along the outer edge of the 4 x 4" cardstock square. Adhere. Turn the cardstock square 180 degrees and repeat the process with subsequent circles. Turn the envelope over. Fold the envelope's sides inward and follow with the bottom and top. Decorate the envelope as desired. Create a torn vellum journaling sleeve to hold the envelope closed.

Jodi Amidei, Memory Makers
Photos, Kelli Noto, Centennial, Colorado

*should you ever wonder if my love is true
there's one thing that I want to make clear to you*

*if I had to survive without you in my life
I know I wouldn't last a day*

*there's no way I could make it without you
there's no way that I'd even try*

Tom and Jodi

Positive and negative space work together to create a big-hearted page. Use a nested template to create the hearts (see instructions on adjacent page). Apply a thin line of glue to the edges of cut hearts and sprinkle with gold micro beads. Adhere photos to page and embellish photos with micro beads. Add vellum journaling strips to the bottom of each photo. Use gold letter stickers to create the title. Mount the entire page on a contrasting background.

ONE Place a nested heart template on patterned background paper. Use a swivel blade to carefully cut all channels. The top and bottom portions of the heart shapes must remain separated by a small portion of uncut paper. Cut along this uncut line when removing unwanted sections of the heart, as follows: Cut away every other section of the upper half of the heart and every other section of the lower portion of the heart. Upper and lower sections being removed should be offset. Repeat the process to create the second heart.

TWO Trim off a small portion of both the top and left sides of the page. Mat the page on a patterned paper background. Embellish the hearts with gold microbeads, as described.

Dawn Mabe, Lakewood, Colorado

Moonlight Dreams

Romance is in the air on this dreamy page decorated with moon shapes cut from cardstock with a circle cutter. Cut a circle. Remove the circle cutter and reposition it, slightly skewed, on top of the previously cut circle. Re-cut to form a crescent shape. Repeat until all moon shapes are cut. Embellish the crescents with glitter along one edge. Adhere coordinating lace stickers, silk flowers and crescents on the page.

May 8, 1992   Gateway Senior Prom

"Set The Night To Music" was the theme for my prom which took place at the Palace Inn in Monroeville, Pennsylvania. I took Mark Paat, a very good friend of mine, and we danced, laughed, and had a great time. The dress I picked out was a Spanish styled dress that "poofed" out on the shoulders and on the bottom. (In my defense, that was the style at the time!) Mark and I even made the local newspaper. Ah, high school memories.

Janetta Wieneke, Memory Makers
Photos, Erlinda Abucejo, Broomfield,
Colorado; Flor Paat, North Huntington,
Pennsylvania

Prom Memories

Make a quick layout embellishment using a circle scissor as a template. Start with black cardstock and draw concentric circles (see instructions on adjacent page). Adhere circles to the page. Add photos and journaling. Build the title out of two sets of letters die cut from metallic papers. Overlap letters when mounting them to the page in order to create the shadow effect. Complete the layout with decorative photo corners.

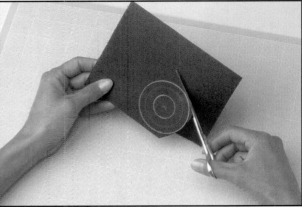

ONE To create the Prom Memories page (left), lightly mark a piece of black cardstock to indicate the center of the circle you will be creating. Place the circle scissor above that mark. Using the circle scissor as a guide, draw concentric circles with silver and red pencils, alternating colors.

TWO Use a craft knife, scissors or the circle scissor to cut along the rim of the circle you have drawn. Erase the center mark and place a brad in the middle of the circle.

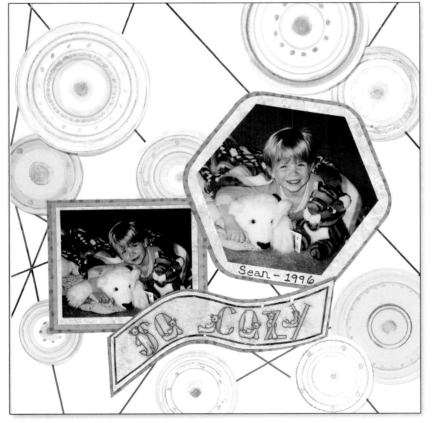

Pennie Stutzman, Broomfield, Colorado

So Cozy

Use a circle scissor to create an effect similar to that featured on the Prom Memories page (left). On a white piece of cardstock, lightly mark pencil guidelines which will help you align the scissor. With a watercolor pencil, draw a circle using the circle scissor as a template. Remove the scissor from the page and lightly brush water over watercolor pencil guidelines to bleed the color. Dry. Place the circle scissor back on the paper using the penciled guidelines to realign. Continue drawing concentric circles, one at a time; paint and dry. When the desired circle size has been achieved, cut it out. Erase penciled guidelines. Adhere thin metallic sticker strips randomly to the background page. Adhere cut circles. Double and triple mat photos. Add a vellum sticker title edged with sticker strips.

Bodie Island Lighthouse

Make a woven paper border using a shape template and decorative scissors (see instructions below). To create the background, cut a "light beam" out of yellow paper mounted on top of blue background paper. Cover background with printed vellum. Adhere the border to the background. Double mat photo and add matted journaling block.

BODIE ISLAND LIGHTHOUSE

BODIE ISLAND LIGHTHOUSE IS LOCATED HALFWAY BETWEEN THE CURRITUCK BEACH AND CAPE HATTERAS LIGHTHOUSE. IT WAS COMPLETED IN 1872 AND THE HEIGHT OF TOWER IS 165 FEET. NC LIGHTHOUSES ARE TRULY BEAUTIFUL AND OUR VISITS TO SEE THEN HAVE BEEN A HIGHLIGHT FOR OUR FAMILY SINCE WE MOVED HERE.

Diana Swensen for Fiskars

ONE Cut a 1¼ x 11" strip of white cardstock; set aside. Cut another strip of blue cardstock 2 x 11". Use a pencil to lightly mark the center of the backside of the blue strip by creating horizontal and vertical lines which cross in the middle. Place the tip of the diamond shape template on the center mark. Use a pencil to trace only the top half of the diamond. Move the template ½" down the strip and trace the entire diamond. Move template ½" farther down the strip and trace only the bottom half of the diamond. Turn the blue strip upside down and repeat the process for the second half of the strip. Make vertical pencil marks ¼" in from both sides. To make cutting easier, erase all lines that fall beyond these vertical lines toward the outside edges. With a craft knife, cut along pencil marks of diamond shapes.

TWO Use the white strip of cut cardstock to weave through the cuts made in the blue strip. Use decorative scissors to cut the right side of the blue strip. Cut another strip of white paper with the same decorative scissors and place it behind the blue strip's edge to shadow. Stamp images on the white strip. Stamp a separate image onto white cardstock and cut it out with the diamond template. Mount this element and adhere to the middle of the border strip.

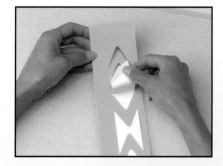

Sisters Are Forever Friends

Breezy punched pinwheel ornaments adorn this sweet layout. Double mat photo and place it on a patterned paper background. Print the title on vellum and cut it out. Tear a solid-colored cardstock strip and adhere it across the bottom of the page to build the border's base. Attach colored brads to the torn cardstock strip. Create pinwheel ornaments (see instructions below). Adhere pinwheels to the cardstock border. Add a printed journaling strip.

Emily and Kayla Swensen 1999

Sisters are forever friends

Diana Swensen for Fiskars

ONE Punch cardstock using a 1½" square punch. Along one edge of the punched square, align a border punch on the left half and punch (see photo). Rotate the cardstock square 90 degrees and punch again in the same manner. Continue rotating the cardstock square and punching until all sides are punched. Round corners, if desired.

Jordan Kennedy

Make this decorative frame using punches to create a unique stencil (see instructions below). Place a mesh strip along the right side of the background page. Tear strips of coordinating patterned paper and adhere them across the bottom of the layout. Mat photos on cream cardstock and gently ink with dauber. Print journaling and title on transparency film and attach them to the page with colored brads. Mat the entire page and focal photo on contrasting cardstock.

Jodi Amidei, Memory Makers

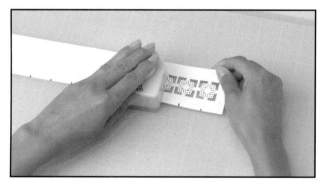

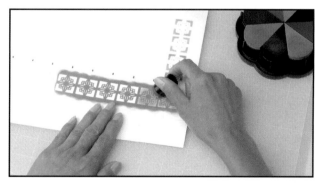

ONE Cut a 2 x 12" strip of light-colored cardstock. To make perfectly spaced punches, boldly mark 1" increments along the strip's edge. Align the left outer edge of the punch casing on a mark and press firmly. Continue punching along the strip, moving the left side of the punch to subsequent marks. When completed, this punched strip will serve as a stencil for inking.

TWO Place the punched stencil on white cardstock and daub ink through the pattern. Rotate the cardstock 90 degrees and repeat the inking process. Continue rotating the cardstock and inking until all four sides are complete. Trim outer edges as needed. Cover the stamped mat with tacky tape and adhere clear micro beads.

What a Clown

Create a cute 3-D doll from tiny circle punched shapes (see directions below). Triple mat photo and adhere it to the background paper. Hand letter or use a template to make the title and journaling blocks and mat. Add the doll embellishment to the page.

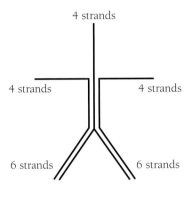

4 strands

4 strands   4 strands

6 strands   6 strands

Alison Lindsay, Edinburgh, England

ONE To make paper "sequins" for the clown (above) use a ¹⁄₁₆" hole punch to make several holes along the edge of a piece of cardstock, leaving ¼" between holes. Take a standard hole punch; center it over each tiny hole and repunch. To create the doll's legs, thread a needle with six-strand embroidery floss. Knot one end. String on sequins. Alternate colors as desired. Set aside, and repeat for the second leg. When the second leg is complete, gather all twelve-strands of floss through the needle and string on sequins to create the doll's body.

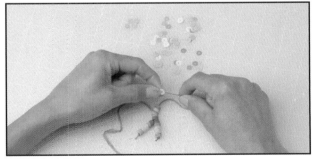

TWO When the body is complete, remove the needle and separate the floss into three sections. Each section will now have four strands (see diagram). Rethread the needle with one section of the floss. String on sequins for the arm and finish with a knot. Repeat for the second arm. To form the head, string a few sequins onto the remaining floss section. Add a pearl bead, followed by a few more sequins for the 'hat.' When complete, knot the floss above the hat, leaving extra floss from which to hang the embellishment on the page. Trim away excess floss.

Traci Armbrust for Accu-Cut

The Giant Snowman

Use a die cut to create a fun shaker box (see instructions on adjacent page). Mat photos on white cardstock and outline both photos and mat with chalk, using a blender pen to intensify the color. Adhere photos to the patterned paper background. Die cut a snowflake and place it under a vellum journaling block; attach with colored brads. Adorn photo mats with torn strips of coordinating patterned paper, wire and beads. Secure wire to brads. Embellish the layout and shaker box with decorative snowflake buttons. Attach the shaker box to the page and decorate with chalked paper elements and tiny buttons.

ONE Cut 5 x 5" pieces of foam core and solid color cardstock. Place the foam core and cardstock together on top of the rubber cutting surface of a snowman-shaped die. Run the die through a die-cut machine. Remove the snowman shapes and set aside. Mount on patterned paper the piece of foam core from which the snowman has been cut. Seal carefully along all edges. Adhere a sheet of acetate (slightly smaller than 5 x 5") to the backside of the piece of cardstock from which the snowman has been cut. Cut snowman arms, hat and scarf from cardstock using the die-cut machine. Insert the arms in the cardstock snowman shape and adhere to acetate. Chalk the hat and scarf, and adhere to the snowman.

TWO Fill the foam core snowman shape with beads and shaved ice. Adhere the blue cardstock snowman cover, acetate side down, to the foam core snowman. Make certain all edges are sealed so the shaker box contents don't leak out.

Sun Kissed

Shake up your page with a sunny shaker box. Punch three large squares out of a decorative border strip. Save punched squares to use as embellishments. Mount the border strip on torn cardstock. Create the shaker box by adhering a piece of acetate behind the punched windows. Lay strips of foam tape around the outer edges of the punched window piece, taking care to avoid gaps (it is unnecessary to lay foam around each individual window). Sprinkle small punches, beads, and other trinkets into windows. Peel the backing away from foam tape and adhere to torn cardstock strip. Mat photo and page. Add a sticker title.

Denise Johnson for EK Success Ltd.

Heidi Schueller,
Waukesha, Wisconsin

Watcing a little boy watching frogs is an unforgettable experience! Exploring one afternoon while camping at Upper Gresham Lake, we came across some children playing with two huge bullfrogs. After they let them go, Evan, Karen and I grabbed a camera and took some pictures. Evan was amazed and entranced watching it hop around.

Camp Hop

Make movable embellishments that "spring" to life using your die-cut machine (see instructions on this and adjacent page). Cut "camp" title letters out of cardstock, mat and mount on background. Cut out "hop" from colored vellum, embossing the letter edges. Mat and mount on background. Mat photos using fibers on the edge of the focal picture. Suspend fibers and beads from brads. Print the journaling on vellum and emboss the edges.

Make the frogs "hop" by gently pulling back and forth on the end of the base strip.

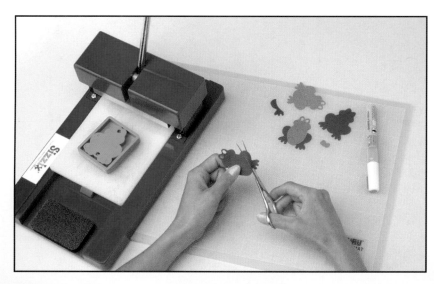

ONE Die cut five frogs from two shades of cardstock (three light/two dark). Cut apart the legs of the darker frogs. Glue dark sets of legs on two of the lighter colored bodies. On the remaining light colored frog, adhere a dark body. Glue a small piece of colored cardstock behind each frog's eyes to add stability when securing the brads.

These Boots Are Made For Walking

Make a border that literally dances (see instructions for Camp Hop below and on adjacent page). Die cut small cardstock dolls. Add embellishments such as hair and shiny black embossed cardstock boots. Make a doll border strip. Create shiny cardstock photo mats with black embossing powder. Add decorative metal brads and flowers. Mat a vellum journaling block on cardstock. Add strips of foil as accents. Attach flower accents with bits of chain.

Heidi Schueller, Waukesha, Wisconsin

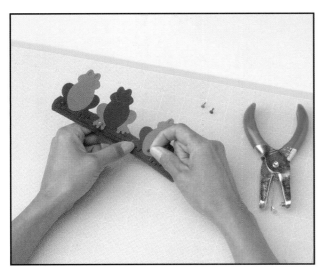

TWO Punch a ¹⁄₁₆" hole in the right foot of each frog. Cut two ¼ x 8" strips of brown cardstock, and adhere them to each other to create the "log" pull strip on which frogs are attached. Align the frogs evenly along the log, leaving 1" on the right end. Make pencil marks through the holes in the frogs' feet onto the log. Punch ¹⁄₁₆" holes into the log on the marks. Attach the frogs' right feet to the log with brads.

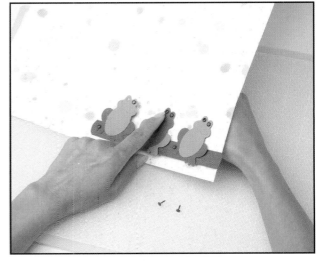

THREE Punch ¹⁄₁₆" holes for the frogs' eyes. Line up the frogs on background paper and mark through each right eye-hole to the background paper underneath. Punch holes in the background paper. Use a brad to fasten each frog's right eye to the background paper. Place a brad in the left eye openings for decoration. Add penwork details to the log. Add a decorative eyelet or brad to the end of the handle.

*Jodi Amidei, Memory Makers
Photos, Chrissie Tepe, Lancaster,
California*

Children Are God's Way…

You'll love the effect you'll get by softly tearing heart edges with a die (see instructions on adjacent page). With watermark ink, randomly stamp a design onto solid cardstock background. Tear patterned paper and cardstock to create the border; adhere it to the background and gently roll the torn edges. Create the frame by adhering printed and solid paper together. Mark guidelines to indicate the size you wish the frame's opening to be. Note: Make the opening slightly smaller than you envision the finished frame. Cut a small hole in the center of the frame and begin to gently tear away paper until you reach the guideline. Gently roll back the remaining torn edge. Tear the outside edges of the solid paper to desired size. Place photo under the frame opening and mat the entire frame on patterned paper with foam tape. Print journaling on patterned paper and tear to size. Embellish journaling block and frame with wire and beads. Mount frame and journaling to stamped background.

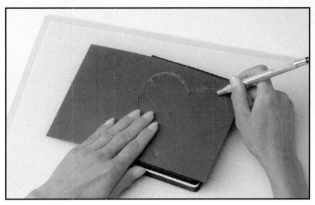

ONE Place cardstock on the rubber side of a die and rub finger gently over the design until a faint outline of the pattern emerges.

TWO While holding cardstock in place on the die, run an impressing tool along the outline until the paper tears. Note: Cutting blades are hidden within the rubber surface so you may need to exert a fair amount of pressure to expose the blades. Do not use your fingers! Adorn the top hearts with clear embossed image and beaded wire.

Flowers

Torrey Miller, Thornton, Colorado

Combine two different die cuts to create these funky flower accents and border. Cut four to five 4 x 4" pieces of contrasting cardstock. Run each piece through a die-cut machine, using a weaving die (Dayco). Set aside one of these pieces. Tear cut strips free from the remaining die cuts. Use these strips to weave alternating colors through the intact die cut. When complete, run the woven piece through an adhesive application machine. Mount the adhered woven piece on a solid piece of cardstock. Die cut flower shapes from the assembled piece. Glue loose ends of weaving to its cardstock backing. Punch holes in flowers and coil wire accent through hole. Use leftover strips of weaving assemblies for page embellishments. Mat photos and the entire page. Add metal title letters.

A day at the park makes for a great photo opportunity! Megan and her friends won a photo contest with a photo from this shoot! The photo was later displayed on the big screen in Times Square in New York City during the annual Buddy Walk.

Gotta love all those cheesy smiles!

Friendship

Discover

photo shoot
JUN 0 0

Imagination

Jennifer Mason, Longmont, Colorado
Photos by: Lucy Talbot, Sterling Heights, Michigan

Photo Shoot

Create shimmery charms and glistening background shapes using a die-cut machine (see instructions on adjacent page). Mat one photo on metal mesh and another on cardstock. Mat the third photo on both mesh and cardstock. Print journaling and adhere to the page. Arrange and adhere photos to the page. Add charms. Create the vellum metal-rimmed tag by stamping a design (in same fashion as the background paper), and adding die-cut dragonflies and fiber. Stamp words around the page. Mat the entire page on coordinating cardstock.

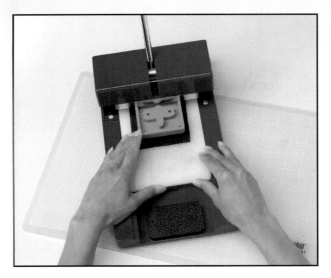

ONE Using a die-cut machine. cut a dragonfly shape out of craft foam.

TWO Adhere the die-cut-dragonfly to anything that can be used as a handle for stamping (we used the bottom of an empty film canister). Stamp images onto patterned paper background with watermark ink. With a small brush, dust images with iridescent pigment powder. Gently wipe away excess with a tissue.

Coming Home to Tennessee

Die cut cork for a unique title, aluminum foil for tree accents and hearts and burlap for leaf embellishments. Tear a background of rust-colored patterned paper. Dab dark brown stamping ink along the torn edges. Mat on green patterned paper. Mat photos with tan patterned paper. Create the title using chalked polymer letter tiles adorned with hemp and letter stickers. Cut the word "home" from thin cork and adhere to corrugated paper. Finish the title using eyelet letters and printed mulberry paper mounted on a fiber-embellished tag. Punch leaf shapes from burlap. Use the negative pieces as page embellishments. Complete the layout with die-cut-foil hearts and die-cut trees made of copper sheeting. Mount a vellum journaling block over the trees.

Holle Wiktorek, Clarksville, Tennessee

Joseph and Jan Perilli
November 3, 2001
St. Joseph's Roman Catholic Church
Summit Hill, Pennsylvania

Our Fall Wedding

Create a stained-glass border using a die-cut machine (Sizzix) and scissors (see instructions on this and adjacent page). Mat and mount photo. Add a journaled block. Create the title by cutting windows in the background paper. Print title on colored vellum and place sections behind each window.

ONE Cut four 3 x 3" squares of different colored cardstock, making certain they are all exactly the same size. Stack the squares on top of each other and cut them all together using a die-cut machine and leaf die. This will ensure they are all identical.

Michigan Lakes

Only half a die cut is needed to create this interesting effect. Mask off half the die with a piece of cutting plastic and run a sheet of two-tone grey cardstock background paper through the die cut machine. (A #3 Spiral die from Accu-Cut was used for this page.) The plastic prevents half of the die from being cut. Score the spiral die cut where the cut ends.

Fold the cut parts up, and adhere them to the background. Place black cardstock behind the cut-out portion. Cut ½" wide strips of patterned cardstock and adhere to the top and left sides of the page. Double mat photos and journaling blocks on grey and black cardstock. Print journaling on vellum and adhere. Add a ½" wide strip of patterned cardstock under the die cut feature. Finish the strip embellishment with silver brads.

Chris, Dan, and I had an awesome time on our backpacking trip to Michigan Lakes in Colorado. The air was crisp and cool and scenery amid the peaks and lakes was nothing short of spectacular!

Martha Moseman for Accu-Cut

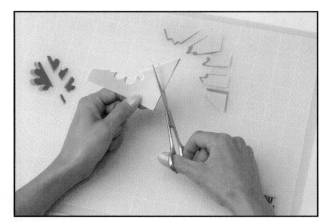

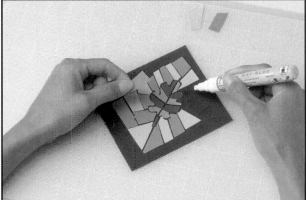

TWO Select two colors of cardstock for the leaves, and two different colors for the borders. Hold identically cut pieces together and cut into pieces as shown. Loosely arrange the pieces on cardstock, alternating colors.

THREE Glue pieces to black cardstock in appropriate position. Make certain to leave a small gap between each piece to create the look of stained glass. Repeat the process to create additional panels.

Easter 2002

We spent Easter Sunday at my mom's house in Newport Beach. The girls were looking super cute in there matching dresses that Shaya picked out. The Easter bunny was exceptionally good to Jessie and Shaya with all the wonderful goodies they got in their Easter baskets, complete with a pair of bunny ears. My mom had an Easter egg hunt in the backyard for everyone including the adults. It brought back lots of great memories of my childhood, which made it special to share with my own children. It was a beautiful sunny day and a great Easter.

Cara Mariano for Ellison

Hoppy Easter

Make bunnies that march across your page. Accordion-fold paper and use a die-cut machine to create a "paper doll" strip of bunnies (see instructions on adjacent page). To create the background, cut patterned paper on the diagonal and adhere it to a solid cardstock background. Print journaling on patterned paper and adhere it to the background with self-adhesive foam spacers. Mat photos and adhere to the background. Embellish with an extra die-cut bunny.

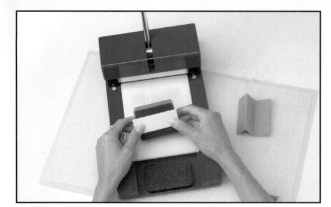

ONE Create the Hoppy Easter page by cutting six 3½ x 3½" squares of colored cardstock (three light/three dark) and folding each into thirds accordion-style. To make bunny chains, make certain the die's cutting surface is slightly wider than the folded paper. Place one piece of accordion-folded paper on the die so the blade is visible on both sides of the bunny. Run the paper through the die-cut machine. This will create a chain of three bunnies. Repeat for remaining five pieces of accordion-folded paper.

TWO Cut apart various portions of the dark bunnies and glue pieces, as desired, to light bunnies. Adhere a small piece of pink cardstock behind the opening in the bunnies' ears and noses. Place black cardstock behind the bunnies' eyes. Add penwork detail and mount the bunnies on the background. Add letter stickers for the title.

Brenee Williams for Provo Craft

Pumpkin Princess

Create this pumpkin chain by folding dark maroon cardstock, accordion-style, into thirds. While folded, use a template to cut a pumpkin shape, leaving 1" along the folded bottom left edge uncut. Print journaling on coordinating orange patterned paper. Use a template to cut journaling blocks into pumpkin shapes slightly smaller than the maroon accordion. Decorate the front of the pumpkin journaling book with patterned paper. Cut stars and place on the background. Attach gold brads to journaling book and star; connect with gold thread. Double mat photo on patterned paper; add tulle corners. Cut a tulle pocket approximately one-third the size of the page and stitch onto the bottom of the layout and around the background with gold thread. Slide the pumpkin journaling book into the tulle pocket.

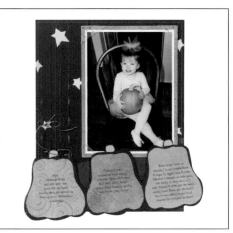

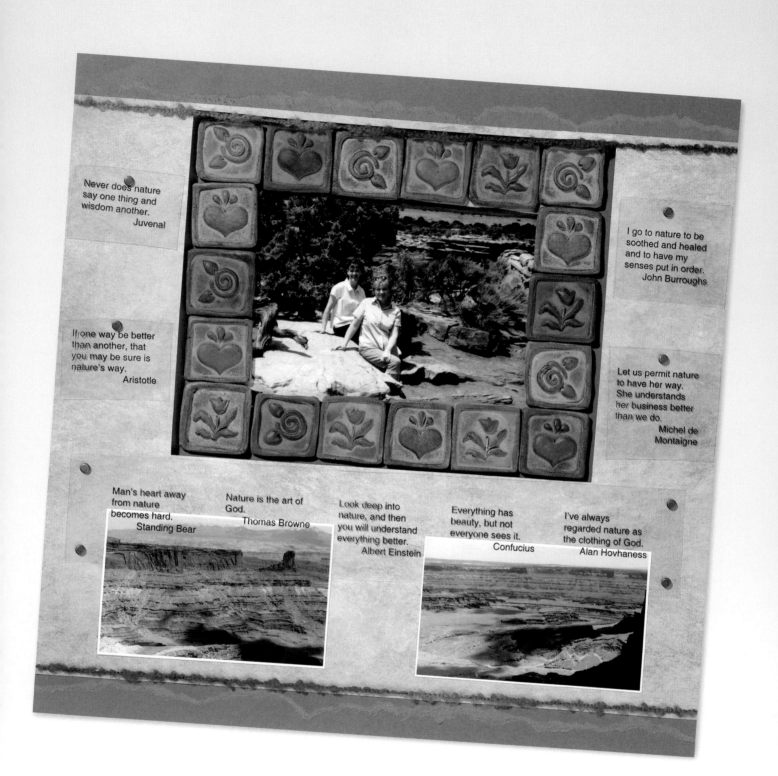

Never does nature
say one thing and
wisdom another.
Juvenal

If one way be better
than another, that
you may be sure is
nature's way.
Aristotle

I go to nature to be
soothed and healed
and to have my
senses put in order.
John Burroughs

Let us permit nature
to have her way.
She understands
her business better
than we do.

Michel de
Montaigne

Man's heart away
from nature
becomes hard.
Standing Bear

Nature is the art of
God.
Thomas Browne

Look deep into
nature, and then
you will understand
everything better.
Albert Einstein

Everything has
beauty, but not
everyone sees it.
Confucius

I've always
regarded nature as
the clothing of God.
Alan Hovhaness

Stencils, Templates, Decorative Rulers

Most of us have a penchant for perfection when it comes to making letters for titles. We want exquisite curves, impeccable lines and flawless angles…all without those tell tale pencil lines. This can be effortlessly achieved with the use of templates and stencils. But there is so much more you can do with a stencil, template or decorative ruler than use them as simple lettering guides. It's time to look at your stencils, templates and decorative rulers in a whole new way and to explore their possibilities. Learn how to use these 2-dimensional tools to create intriguing 3-dimensional embellishments and accents for your scrapbook layouts. Keep scrapbooking exciting and fresh by trying new things and your pages will evolve and grow right along with your self-confidence.

*Jodi Amidei, Memory Makers
Photos, Torrey Miller, Thornton,
Colorado*

Garden Party

Use a brass stencil and polymer clay to create these decorative floral embellishments (see instructions on adjacent page). Double mat photos and place them on the background. Mat a colored torn cardstock strip on a piece of black cardstock for the border; wrap it with fibers and attach on back side. Add polymer tiles. For the title, tear a piece of cardstock and adhere it diagonally across the upper left page corner. Add fiber and adhere the title tile.

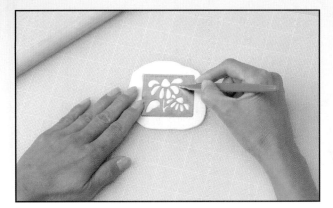

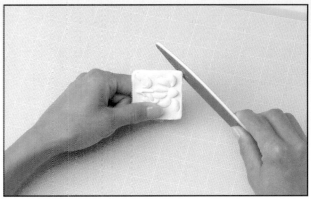

ONE Roll out polymer clay to ⅛" thickness. Use a stylus to press a brass stencil into the clay to make an image. Gently lift the stencil from the clay. Use a craft knife to trim away excess clay. Carefully transfer the "tile" to a glass baking pan and bake according to manufacturer's directions.

TWO When cooled, use an emery board or fine sandpaper to gently sand the edges of the clay tile until smooth and rounded.

THREE Apply chalk lightly to colorize the image. Add more chalk until the desired effect is achieved. When satisfied with colorized effect, spray with acrylic sealant to fix the color.

Torrey Miller, Thornton, Colorado

Celebrate

Create a unique title with black polymer clay and a word template (see instructions for Garden Party page above). Cut clay to desired shape and bake as directed. Using a metallic leafing pen, color in the raised negative spaces of the word. Mat the clay tile on silver paper with glue dots. For the background, mount patterned paper over silver paper. Place mesh over patterned paper, securing it with decorative brads. Mount the clay title to mesh with glue dots. Attach circular paper clips on torn black cardstock and add metallic fibers.

Valerie Barton, Flowood, Mississippi

Winter White

Create frosty embellishments for a winter page (see instructions on adjacent page). Tear the edges of patterned paper to create a background. Print journaling on the left side of a strip of vellum and attach the strip to the page with eyelets. Mat photos. Place focal photo over the portion of the vellum which does not display journaling. Add a strip of journaled vellum diagonally across the bottom corners of the photo. Make a title with a metal-rimmed vellum tag, letter stickers, letter beads and a ribbon. Add organza ribbon and fiber across the bottom of the page. Embellish with frosty ornaments and mat the entire page.

Lessons Learned From a Lime Green Cast

Use texture paste and stencils to create a well-"cast" title (see instructions for Winter White below). Tear out letters. Add a torn patterned paper strip at the bottom of the layout. Print the remainder of the title and the journaling block on vellum and adhere to the page with decorative brads. Cover a portion of the layout with gauze fabric. Mat the focal photo and embellish its corner with a knotted piece of gauze. Add the smaller photo and a stamped, patterned vellum metal-rimmed tag.

Valerie Barton, Flowood, Mississippi

ONE Place a brass stencil on cardstock. While holding down the stencil, use a finger to apply texturizing paste to fill in all areas of the stencil pattern.

TWO Carefully lift off the stencil. The paste will crackle as it dries. Wash paste off your hands and the stencil immediately. Allow the paste to dry completely before tearing edges and adhering it to the layout.

Surely a Star danced in heaven on the day you were born.

Faye Morrow Bell,
Charlotte, North Carolina

Surely a Star Danced

Use square and rectangular templates with paint to create a beautiful background. Print journaling on background paper. Lightly pencil outlines of square and rectangular template shapes. Thin acrylic paint with water. Place a template over penciled guide marks and use a sponge to apply paint through the template. Let the paint dry before sponging on a second color. Add photo and Chinese coins to page.

Debi Boring, Scotts Valley, California

Ya Ya Sisterhood

Use texturizing paste applied through a lettering template to create a title that says it all. While the paste is still wet, sprinkle on colored embossing powder and allow it to dry. Cut out letters and set them aside. (Use a brass stencil for a slightly different look.) With a craft knife, cut out portions of the design running through the background paper. Double mat photo and slip it underneath these cut-free portions. Mount individual title letters on torn blue cardstock. Create flower embellishments by cutting unraveled paper yarn into leaf shapes and rolling it to form flower centers. Make hat embellishments by stamping image, embossing and adding decorative flower. Print journaling onto vellum and attach it to the cardstock mat with eyelets.

Cousins

Combine a rectangle template with rubber stamping to embellish a page that is simply elegant. Print title sideways on the left side of background. Position the template on the background paper and draw the rectangular outline with a fine-tip marker. Holding the template firmly in place, stamp through the opening to create an image that has a perfectly squared border. Print journaling on colored cardstock, and embellish with a template/stamped image. Add photo and fibers.

Faye Morrow Bell, Charlotte, North Carolina

STENCILS, TEMPLATES, DECORATIVE RULERS   203

Torrey Miller, Thornton, Colorado

Sun Goddess

Make your own rubber stamp using a brass stencil and moldable foam (see instructions below). To texturize the top layer of background paper, wet and crumple cardstock. Smooth and iron it dry. Tear a second sheet of cardstock along the right side and curl its edges back. Stitch the texturized background to a second sheet of cardstock at arbitrary points. Add chalk to the cardstock edges and along stitched lines. Mat stitched background pieces to a third layer of cardstock background. Place natural fiber "ribbon" down the left side of the page and attach on the back side. Frame photo using a similar technique as described in Children Are God's Way… (page 188). Print journaling and title on cardstock and cut it into tag shapes. Embellish with fiber and charms. Add chalk to "age" frame, border, title and journal. Attach stamped paper tiles.

ONE Heat foam with a heat gun and immediately press a brass stencil into the hot foam. You may need to press a finger along the finer details to impress the image. Hold the stencil in place for a few seconds to set the image. Remove the stencil. You now have a reusable rubber stamp.

TWO Ink the impressed foam and stamp onto cardstock. Tear out the stamped designs and chalk the edges for detail. Adhere to the layout.

Love Letter

Create beautiful backgrounds with lettering templates. On an 8½ x 11" piece of white cardstock, rub chalk through the template's larger letter openings. Use a fine-tip marker to outline each letter, including any finely detailed parts that might not have been well-chalked. Mount the lettered background to 12 x 12" cardstock. Cut out a title using another lettering template, and apply it to the left side of the page. Add penwork details, hang a metal-rimmed tag and add a metal charm to the title. To create the photo mat, make a cardstock card which opens on one side and mount it to the background. Inside the card put printed journaling and another matted photo; decorate with a sticker. Place mounted focal photo on the outside of the card.

Mary Anne Walters, Monk Sherborne, Tadley, England

Mary Anne Walters,
Monk Sherborne,
Tadley, England

Reading Is Pure Dead Brilliant

Produce unique borders and mats with a lettering template. Cut cardstock mats with ½" borders. Use a lettering template and silver gel pen to decorate the mats. Create the border by drawing vertical lines 2" apart down the outer edges of the layout. Decorate with a lettering template and pen as with the mats. Scan the child's book cover and print the title onto photo paper. While the ink is still wet, sprinkle on embossing powder and heat the embossed title. Cut out the letters with a craft knife and mount them on the background. Embellish with metal letters and brads. Journal on vellum and adhere to cardstock mats.

United in Love

Tear intricate paper-pieced shapes easily and accurately using nothing but a shape template and a stylus (see instructions on adjacent page). Cut large oval windows out of background cardstock. Place photos behind the windows to create frames. Make hand-lettered title banners by tearing strips of vellum and pleating the ends. Add journaling and rose embellishments.

Roxane Kryvenchuk, Edmonton, Alberta, Canada

ONE To create the flowers on the United in Love page (left) firmly hold a piece of vellum on top of a template. Using a stylus, outline the template shape until the vellum piece breaks free. Repeat for all desired shape pieces.

TWO Assemble the floral embellishments and adhere the torn vellum pieces directly to the background to form roses. Construct flowers beginning with outer pieces and working inward.

Lazy Days of Summer

Tear perfect letters and shapes out of vellum using a template. Run vellum through an adhesive application machine and peel off the top plastic covering. To make bubble shapes, roughly cut the prepared vellum slightly larger than the bubble shape. Place wax paper on a work surface and lay the template on top. Peel the backing off of the vellum and place the adhered vellum on the template, completely covering the template opening. Using a stylus, trace around the template shape several times until the vellum is cut through and falls onto the wax paper underneath. Remove the vellum shape from the wax paper and adhere it to the page. Create letters the same way using a lettering template. Cut photos with a circle cutter. Mount photos and the title on bubbles. Journal.

Roxane Kryvenchuk, Edmonton, Alberta, Canada

Linda Strauss, Provo, Utah

Help I'm Being Eaten

The scales on the snake's back are made by mirror imaging the boy's name (Mario) with letters cut from a template (see instructions below and on adjacent page). Make the background by crumpling cardstock, flattening it and then securing it to the mat with eyelets. Create a title by hand-lettering on random shapes of torn cardstock and add details with a black pen. Mat photo on torn cardstock. Embellish with gold jewelry findings. Include a real snake skin, enclosed in a memorabilia pocket.

ONE Sketch a snake shape on cardstock and free-hand tear along pattern lines. Attach a cut or torn tongue and tail pieces to the body with glue.

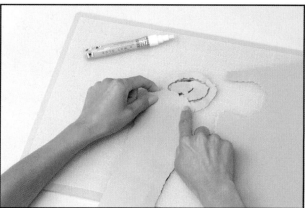

Summertime and the Living Is Easy

The letters that make up your page title can also be part of the page embellishment. Use a computer to write the title. Print the word on plain copy paper in the size desired. Adhere the title to patterned paper with temporary adhesive. Using a craft knife, cut out the individual letters. Peel off the copy paper and remove excess adhesive. Adhere the letters to patterned background in a circular pattern of sun rays. Embellish the page with unraveled paper yarn, eyelets and die cuts. Make journaling tags out of the same patterned paper as used for the title.

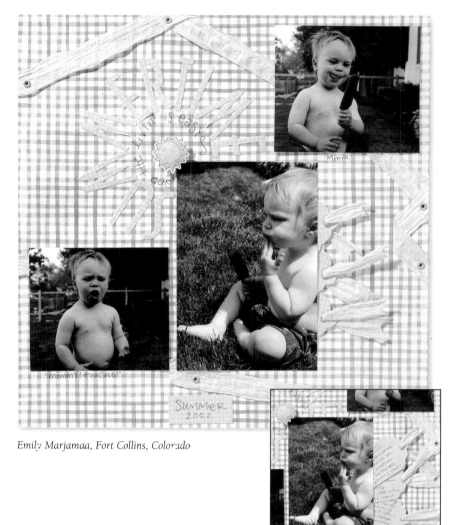

Emily Marjamaa, Fort Collins, Colorado

TWO From cardstock, die cut two of each letter needed to spell out the boy's name. One set of letters should be reversed. Mat letters on black cardstock, and decorate the letters with torn pieces of contrasting-colored cardstock. Place the letters mirroring each other onto the snake.

THREE Add torn bits of paper and metallic embellishments to complete the snake.

Brenee Williams for Provo Craft

Grandma Karen's First Grade Class

Make 3-D metal embellishments using a shape template. Place a medium-weight metal sheet over a template. Using a stylus, trace and "color in" the shape to create a gentle concave-shaped image. Cut out the shape and turn it over. Adhere it to cardstock circles with self-adhesive foam spacers. Cut several circles out of patterned paper for the journaling book. Print journaling onto vellum. Cut the vellum in circles that are slightly smaller than those on the primary page. Adhere them to the pages of the journaling book. Double mat photo and mat the entire page. Use eyelets to secure the fiber holding the embellishments.

JD

Create your own metal letter hanging tags easily. Place a metal sheet over a letter template and place on a neoprene-style mouse pad. Trace around the letter with a stylus. Add your own decorative designs such as swirls, polka dots, stripes, checkerboards, or flowers. Cut out the letter and mat it on cardstock. Hang the letter with wire, eyelets, brads or fibers. Use a precut cardstock background, or make your own by dry embossing the cardstock and cutting out windows with a craft knife. Journal.

Lori Pieper for C-Thru Ruler

Paula Hallinan for Heritage Handcrafts

Nativity Card

Create an ornate nativity card with metal embossing (see instructions). Trim edges with decorative scissors and adhere to cardstock. Mat cardstock with silver paper.

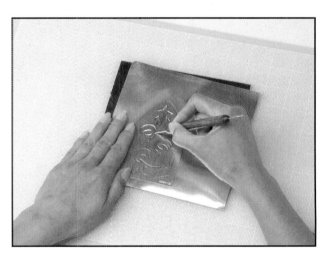

ONE To create an embossed card, place a metal sheet on a neoprene-style mousepad. Cover with a brass stencil and trace the image into metal using a stylus. When complete, remove the stencil and turn the metal sheet over.

This picture of Elizabeth and Zachary is one of Mom's all time favorite shots. It was taken in August of 1999 at the Au Sable Valley Railroad in Fairview. Zach was 10 and Elizabeth was 2. There are so many reasons why this photograph is special to Mom. She loves all of Zach's freckles. She loves all the whispy curls in Elizabeth's hair. She loves Zach's sweet smile. And, she loves Elizabeth's hands with one holding onto Zach and the other with her thumb in her mouth. Mom never gets tired of looking at this picture and every time she does, it pulls at her heart strings.

Beth Wakulsky for Provo Craft

Heart Strings

Specialty papers such as mulberry or thin handmade papers don't stand up well when cut with a craft knife. Make the job easier by applying temporary adhesive to the paper's backside and sticking the fragile paper to a sheet of wax paper. The wax paper backing allows easier cutting with less wear and tear on the paper. When finished cutting out letters and shapes, peel off wax paper backing and adhere cut elements directly to page. Embellish the layout with fabric mesh, buttons and fibers. Secure a vellum journaling block with colored brads.

Sorting Hearts

Make a border using a shape template. Use a pencil to outline the template shape on one side of a piece of white-core cardstock. Move the template over so that the second shape slightly overlaps the first and trace the shape once more. Continue moving the template and tracing until the border is the desired length. Use scissors or a craft knife to cut out the border. Erase pencil marks. To "distress" the border, use fine grit sandpaper to lightly sand the border's edges. Create additional embellishments by chalking through a template onto a piece of cardstock, cut to size. Or trace template shapes, cut out the design, and place mesh or fabric behind the opening left behind. Create a stitched title with embroidery floss and chalk. Adhere mesh and torn strips of patterned paper to a cardstock background. Finish the layout by stamping with a small letter and date stamp.

Marilyn Healey for Provo Craft

Marilyn Healey for Provo Craft

Wind Cave

Use whimsical patterned paper and a lettering stencil to create a unique title. Trace title letters onto white cardstock. Randomly stamp letters over the traced title letters using brown ink. Chalk the letter edges and lightly dab red ink across the letter. Cut out the letter and dab the edges in black ink or hand color the edges with a felt pen. Mount title letters on vellum and weave through them with handcut chalked "wind" swirls. Make background paper by placing large sections of torn patterned paper on a brown cardstock background. Embellish the layout with bits of torn cardstock fiber and chalking. Use both letter stickers and hand lettering to create the remainder of the title and journaling

Diana Swensen for Fiskars

Fall

Create a woven border using the decorative edge of a shape template (as seen below). Double mat photos and decorate mats with tiny punched leaves. Watermark stamp leaf images onto the background. Mount photos on the background. Cut out letters for titles using a shape-cutting system. Print journaling words on cardstock and cut them into small rectangles. Mat the title and journaling words and adhere them to the background.

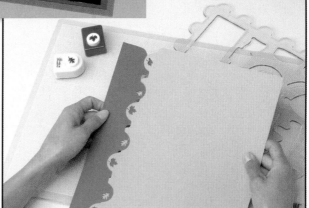

ONE Use a Fiskars shapecutter and Celebration template to cut borders along the paper's edge. Punch every other "scallop" with a small leaf punch. On the side strip, punch opposite "scallops" with a different leaf punch. Intertwine the borders so that punched scallops are showing.

Sonja Chandler, Brentwood, Tennessee

Never Lose Your Joy

Create a positive/negative effect across your layout with a wavy ruler (see instructions below). Once wavy pieces have been cut, adhere them to a white cardstock background. Print a title and journaling blocks on vellum and cut using the same wavy ruler used to create the decorative page elements. Mat photos and slide them under the edges of the wavy accents.

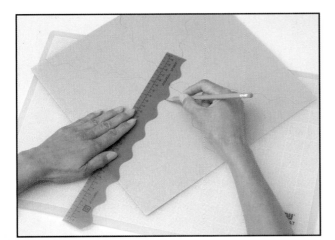

ONE In the center of a 12 x 12" piece of grey cardstock, adhere a 6 x 8" piece of aqua cardstock. Slightly overlapping the aqua, adhere a 5 x 7" piece of blue cardstock to create a layered effect (not shown). Turn the assembly over, and mark the center of the back side of the grey cardstock. Use a decorative ruler to draw "sunburst" rays from the center mark to the edges of the paper. Cut on the lines.

TWO Arrange and adhere the pieces on two separate sheets of white 12 x 12" cardstock to create a two-page layout in a chosen design.

Jill Tennyson,
Lafayette, Colorado
Photos, Torrey Miller, Thornton,
Colorado

Colorado

Create a pattern for a stitched border using a decorative ruler (see instructions below). For the beaded section of the border, lay tacky tape on a separate strip of cardstock and trace the ruler's edge along both long edges of the strip. Cut out the design. Remove the protective backing and adhere gold micro beads along the strip. Adhere the beaded strip onto the background page. Stitch remaining sections of the border. Mat photos and adhere to the background. Stamp a title on vellum and apply journaling sticker. Secure vellum elements to the background with decorative studs. Mat the entire page on colored cardstock.

ONE Lay a decorative ruler on cardstock background to use as a pattern. Following the ruler design, pierce holes along the edge of the ruler. Stitch with silk ribbon or embroidery floss.

Janetta Wieneke, Memory Makers

First Time Grandma

Use the edge of a decorative ruler as a template for gluing down a fiber border. Transfer the ruler pattern to cardstock using one of the following methods: Trace the pattern on the backside of paper. Turn the paper over and place it on a light box, (or) use a vanishing pen on light colored cardstock to trace the ruler directly onto the background, (or) lightly outline the ruler pattern on dark cardstock. Adhere fiber along the ruled line. Create background paper by mounting a 9½ x 9½" piece of patterned paper in the center of solid-colored cardstock. Attach the thin ribbon border to the edges of the cardstock background with eyelets. Mount photos with photo corners. Print a title and journaling on vellum mounted on contrasting vellum. String letter beads on embroidery floss and attach them to photos. Add punched shapes decorated with rhinestones.

Friends

Lettering and shape templates act as guides for easily stitched page embellishments. Place a lettering shape template on background paper and pierce holes approximately ⅜" apart. Stitch through the holes with embroidery floss. Use a different template to add the decorative flower, working in the same manner as previously described. Mat photo and page and add a journaling block.

Tracey Mason, Gahanna, Ohio

Roxane Kryvenchuk, Edmonton, Alberta, Canada

Four Wheelin'

A decorative template can help create woven borders and mats (see instructions on adjacent page for border). Cut an oval window from black cardstock and frame the photo. Mat the framed photo on red cardstock and then again on another piece of black cardstock measuring ¼" larger than the red mat. Using a square design decorative template, cut slits in the mat along the sides of the template's "teeth." Work from the center of each side and move toward the corners. Cut a rectangular hole in a separate sheet of red background paper. Make the hole ⅛" larger than the red photo mat. Place matted photo over the cut hole. Weave the "teeth" of the template-cut black mat over and under the edge of the rectangular hole to create a striped effect. Cut off the corner "teeth." To create the title, lightly pencil a diagonal baseline. Sketch blocky letters along the line and cut slits through the background paper along the vertical lines. Do NOT cut the horizontal top and bottom lines. Weave ¼" strips of contrasting cardstock through the slits. For letters with diagonal lines, add a small diagonal strip of cardstock to fill in necessary space. Adhere strips to backside of layout and erase all pencil lines. Make additional slits in the background for journaling. Write journaling on ½" wide strips and weave through slits to anchor. Finish the title with letters cut from cardstock. Add pen details. Mat auxiliary photos on second page in similar manner. Mount diagonally. Add a journaling block.

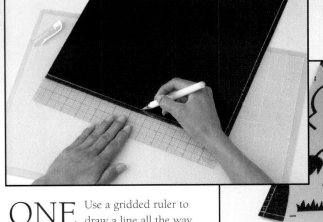

ONE Use a gridded ruler to draw a line all the way around a 12 x 12" piece of cardstock. The line should be ¼" from the outer edge of the page.

TWO To create a slanted black-and-white border, hold a template at a 35 degree angle to line and mark slanted parallel lines around all sides of the paper. Place a pencil dot on every other square in the pattern to aid in weaving.

THREE Cut along the slanted lines, stopping short of the main guideline on the page.

FOUR Cut four ¼ x 12" strips of white cardstock. Using the dotted squares along the edge as a guide, weave a strip along each side in an over-under pattern. Secure strips in each corner with adhesive. Turn over the assembly. The marked side is the back of the layout.

Jodi Amidei, Memory Makers

Hat-titudes

Make this mat and page decoration using a decorative ruler and a craft knife (see directions on adjacent page). Use those pieces you cut free for page decoration on a different page. Mat patterned paper over contrasting paper. Decorate with glitter glue. Mount the mat you have created on dark colored cardstock and add glitter glue. Tear a strip of patterned paper and place it across the top of the page. Embellish the torn edge with glitter glue. Double mat photos. Use letter stickers for a title and add a chalked vellum journaling block.

ONE
On the back side of a 12 x 12" piece of patterned paper, trace along the edge of a decorative ruler.

TWO
Flip the ruler over and trace the edge again to create a mirror image of the first line. Cut out the shape with a craft knife. Remove the cut-out shape.

Bessie Logan Sparks
1884-1958
Mother of Alberta Sparks Danley

Valerie Barton, Flowood, Mississippi

Bessie Logan Sparks

Use a decorative template with double-sided patterned paper to make this lovely heritage page. Cut two 1 x 12" strips for the border using the decorative edge of a template. Adhere patterned strips facing each other on a 2½ x 12" piece of cardstock. Mat photo and place it on a large rectangular piece of paper. Add patterned paper strips to the top and bottom of the rectangular sheet. Add punched embellishments. Adhere a journaling block, fiber and small ribbon flowers. "Age" the fabric and journaling block by chalking edges.

Additional Page Instructions

Bookplate

Torrey Miller, Thornton, Colorado

Although we used this artwork as a bookplate, it can be adapted very easily as a background for scrapbooking. Use the same technique with polymer clay and brass stencils as outlined on page 198 in Garden Party. Before baking clay, cut shape apart into five pieces. The interesting color was obtained by slightly overcooking clay on an aluminum baking sheet in a toaster oven. It was a happy "accident." Place mesh along the left side of page. Tie several different coordinating fibers together and adhere them across bottom of layout. Place clay pieces on foam dots and adhere over fibers to background. Title block is chalked torn cardstock mounted on foam squares to background. Entire page is then matted.

Rain

Michele Gerbrandt, Memory Makers

Use the same technique as "Daddy's Girl" on page 168 to create the fun frames for this layout. Add glitter details to raindrops on frames and mat frame on white cardstock. String beads on wire and twist two strands together to make each of the bead accents. Adhere to background with glue dots. Cut out die cut title. Apply clear micro beads over letters in title and add glitter to highlight. Stick to background using foam dots. Mat background paper on contrasting color, and add torn strips of patterned paper top and bottom.

Camel Ride

Jennifer Cain, Highlands Ranch, Colorado

Create a woven/layered border very easily with decorative scissors. Cut eight 8½ x 12" strips of cardstock using paper trimmer. Cut eight shorter strips of cardstock only this time cut one long edge on each strip with decorative scissors to add texture. Partially weave long vertical strips with short horizontal strips along right edge of layout. Double mat photos and add handmade photo corners using same decorative scissors. Embellish page with interesting metal accents. Attach journaling tags to photos with fiber. Stamp vellum tags for journaling and frame small photo with one of the tags. Add main printed journaling block to complete.

The Cabin

Kelli Noto, Centennial, Colorado

The rustic pattern seen on this page was inspired by a Native American blanket and was created using two sizes of decorative pinking-edged scissors. To create this effect, cut along both sides of the long edges of cardstock strips. Alternate between mirror cuts (lining up the scissors to oppose the first cut exactly) and shadow cuts (lining up the scissors so they bite into the design of the first cut, repeating the first cut's design to create a rickrack effect). When the strips are adhered to the page, the negative spaces become part of the overall design. Mat photos and add punched title and trees. Mount diamond shapes cut from cardstock on self-adhesive foam spacers to complete the effect.

Scatter Joy

Torrey Miller, Thornton, Colorado

A heart becomes a butterfly with the help of a Fiskar's shapecutter. To create the butterfly-shaped journaling windows, use the shapecutter on blue background to cut out mirrored hearts (overlapped in the middle with their points facing toward center). Leave a small section in the middle uncut on which to adhere the top wings. Use the same technique to cut the top wings out of vellum. Hand cut a cardstock frame and adhere over the vellum wings. Adhere center section of top wings to background with tacky tape for added strength. Cut butterfly bodies out of cardstock, cover in tacky tape, and coat with microbeads. Form wire antennae by hand and wrap bodies in wire. Adorn vellum wings with stickers, rhinestones and glitter. Print journaling on colored cardstock in various fonts and strategically place behind the butterfly-shaped windows on the background so that the journaling shows through the window. Adhere journaling to back of page. The top wings lift to reveal the journaling underneath. Embellish page with stickers and rhinestones. Die cut the title from cardstock and adhere. Mat page on cardstock.

Nature's Canyon

Jodi Amidei, Memory Makers
Photos, Cheryl Banner, Arvada, Colorado

The stunning tile frame was created with polymer clay using the same technique as described in "Garden Party" on page 198. To "age" tiles, rub with brown dye-based ink after they're baked. Place photo on background and surround with tiles. Make the foreground of page by adhering a 12 x 10" piece of patterned paper to foam core board. Cut window in paper/foam core to a size that will reveal photo underneath. Add torn cardstock and fiber borders top and bottom. Attach secondary photos. Print out nature-related sayings onto transparency film. Cut apart and secure to page with brads.

Supply List

Bookplate
Polymer clay (Sculpey), brass stencil (Heritage Handcrafts), patterned paper (Karen Foster Design), fibers (EK Success, On The Surface), mesh (Magic Mesh by Avant Card), cardstock (grey, mint), self-adhesive foam spacers, adhesive, glue dots, chalk.

Rain
Teardrop punch (EK Success), letter die cuts (Sizzix), patterned paper (Paper Adventures), micro beads and colored beads (Halcraft), Sparkle diamond glitter glue (PSX Design), cardstock (aqua, white), wire, glue dots, self-adhesive foam spacers, craft knife, adhesive.

The Cabin
Decorative scissors (Maxi Cuts, Family Treasures), tree punch (Carl), letter punches (Family Treasures), cardstock (oatmeal, forest green, burgundy, brown, taupe), adhesive.

Camel Ride
Deckle scissors (Fiskars), letter stamp (Hero Arts), sun paper clip and camel bookmark (Pier One Imports), fibers (On The Surface), metal-rimmed vellum tags (Making Memories), cardstock (dark brown, red, evergreen, caramel), eyelets, adhesive.

Scootin' Along
Personal Paper Trimmer (Fiskars), 2-sided mulberry paper (Pulsar Paper Products), letter stickers (Mrs. Grossman's Paper Co.), fibers (Cardladies.com), metal nameplate (Magic Scraps), mirrors (JewelCraft), metal-rimmed tag (Impress Rubber Stamps), eyelets, brads, chalk, vellum, cardstock (aqua, white), adhesive.

Girls Just Wanna Have FUN
Personal Paper Trimmer (Fiskars), Flavia patterned paper (Colorbök), double-sided patterned paper (Daisy D's), metal-rimmed vellum tags (Making Memories), fiber (Fibers By The Yard), Jolees By You flower button stickers (EK Success), flower-shaped brads, vellum, chalk, cardstock (aqua), felt pen, adhesive.

Wild Wild West
Personal Paper Trimmer (Fiskars), letter stamps (Stampin' Up!), cardstock (brown, maroon, navy, gray, yellow, tan), felt pen, adhesive.

Alone We Can Do So Little...
Personal Paper Trimmer (Fiskars), letter stamps (Stampin' Up!), cardstock (black, lavender, sage green, white), felt pen, adhesive.

Daniel Ryan
Personal Paper Trimmer with scoring blade (Fiskars), patterned paper (Frances Meyer), leaf laser die cut (Deluxe Designs), star brads (Magic Scraps), vellum, photo tape, felt pen, ruler, adhesive.

Hula-Little Grass Shack
Personal Paper Trimmer (Fiskars), Patterned paper (Karen Foster Design), flower punches (Family Treasures), letter stamps (All Night Media), cardstock (orange, forest green, white, yellow, red), lettering template (Pebbles In My Pocket), clear UTEE (Suze Weinberg), fiber (Rubba Dub Dub), dark green stamping ink, adhesive

Scarface
Personal Paper Trimmer (Fiskars), patterned paper (Rocky Mountain Scrapbook Co.), letter stickers (Making Memories), cardstock (beige, olive green), self-adhesive foam spacers, vellum, chalk, adhesive.

Father
Red plaid patterned paper, metal letters, square brads, and metal photo corners (Making Memories), fibers (Rub A Dub Dub), blue patterned paper (EK Success), cardstock (burgundy, federal blue, white), adhesive.

Miracle
Personal Paper Trimmer with perforating blade (Fiskars), fiber (EK Success), metal eyelet letters (Making Memories), vellum, brads, cardstock (eggplant, cream), 3-D metal heart charms (source unknown), adhesive.

View of Two
Decorative scissors (Fiskars), Sonja die cut letters (QuickKutz), gold UTEE (Suze Weinberg), heat gun, tweezers, ribbon, cardstock (cranberry, evergreen, caramel), gold paint pen, felt pen, adhesive.

Renaissance Festival
Decorative scissors (Fiskars), cardstock (oatmeal, powder blue), chalk, gold embossing powder, heat gun, adhesive.

The Harris Family
Decorative scallop scissors (Creative Memories), oval cutting system (Creative Memories), vellum, cardstock (wisteria royal purple), gold thread, adhesive.

Rain
Decorative scissors (Fiskars), clear shrink film (K & B Innovations, Inc), die-cut letters (Sizzix), mesh (Magic Mesh by Avant Card), colored pencils, wire, silver jump rings, cardstock (granite, navy, Christmas red), navy stamping ink, self-adhesive foam spacers, adhesive.

Keychains
Decorative scissors (Fiskars), clear shrink film (K & B Innovations, Inc.), colored pencils, ball chain.

Azaleas
Decorative scissors (Fiskars), metallic thread (DMC), vellum, cardstock (hot pink, black), brads, adhesive.

Spirograph
Decorative scissors (Fiskars, Provo Craft), wire, tiny eyelets, fibers (Rubba Dub Dub), cardstock (federal blue, turquoise, white, royal purple), self-adhesive foam spacers, adhesive.

Winter Walk
Decorative scissors (Fiskars), fiber (On The Surface), die-cut letters (QuickKutz) cardstock (navy, blue-gray, white), Sparkles diamond glitter (PSX Design), opaque white paint pen, adhesive.

Bloom Where You're Planted
Decorative scissors (Fiskars), yellow patterned paper (Bo Bunny Press), blue patterned paper (Creative Imaginations), tag punch (EK Success), fiber (Gotyarn.com), wire, felt pen, self-adhesive foam spacers, mulberry paper, adhesive.

Maine Summer Memories
Rubber stamps (Martha By Mail), ribbon, Versamark ink (Tsukineko), cardstock (light and dark green, lavender, deep purple, white faux botanical), chalk, pressed leaves/flowers (Pressed Petals, Inc.), acetate sheet, adhesive, felt pens, craft knife.

Dance, Play, Smile...Dream
Fibers (EK Success, Making Memories, On The Surface), metal corners, eyelet letters and words (Making Memories), metal charms (Global Solutions), patterned paper (Karen Foster Design), plastic watch crystals (Deluxe), mesh (Magic Mesh by Avant Card), cardstock (dark green, white), self-adhesive foam spacers, adhesive, glue dots, craft knife, tapestry needle.

Path To The Sea
Fibers (EK Success, On The Surface), ruler, craft knife, cardstock (royal purple, teal, celery), found objects, eyelets, adhesive.

Where The Buffalo Roam
Cardstock (black, oatmeal), self-adhesive foam spacers, felt pen, adhesive, craft knife.

Estes Park
Metal letters (Making Memories), stickers (Colorbök), fiber (EK Success), metal butterfly and dragonfly (Darice), metallic thread, cardstock (buckeye, buttercup, cream), chalk, fine detail pen, adhesive, decorative brads.

Daddy's Girl
Leaf punch (Nankong), patterned paper and Sonnets letter stickers (Creative Imaginations), fiber (On The Surface), clear micro beads (Halcraft), cardstock (eggplant), brads, tacky tape, adhesive, craft knife, ruler.

Scatter Joy
Heart template (Fiskars), vellum stickers (Stickopotamus), die-cut letters (QuickKutz), rhinestones (JewelCraft), Sparkle diamond glitter glue (PSX Design), clear micro beads (Magic Scraps), tape (Art Accents), wire, self-adhesive foam spacers, colored vellum (pink, buff, spring green), cardstock (navy, bright blue, buttercup, pastel green, dusty pink, canary yellow, bubble gum pink, dark pink, celery, peach, white), craft knife, adhesive.

How Suite It Is
Circle Scissor (EK Success), fibers (Fibers By The Yard), letter stickers (Doodlebug Design), tagboard tags (DMD), cardstock (burgundy, black, light brown), craft knife, adhesive, felt pen.

Supply List (continued)

It Is a Happy Talent…
Circle template (Provo Craft), cardstock (pumpkin, cream), craft knife, adhesive.

Austin
Circle cropper (Making Memories), lettering template (EK Success), patterned paper (Colorbok), number stamps (Hero Arts), opaque lavender stamping ink, colored pencils, cardstock (purple, white), felt pen, adhesive.

Brinley
Circle and Oval cutting system (Creative Memories), patterned paper (Design Originals), punches (EK Success), fibers (Rubba Dub Dub), metal tag (FoofaLa), paper yarn (Making Memories), Suede (Crafter's Workshop), metal impact stamps (FoofaLa), clear and copper UTEE (Suze Weinberg), stamps (All Night Media, Hampton Art, Raindrops on Roses), patterned cardstock (Family Treasures), cardstock (green, white, caramel), brads, texturizing paste, walnut ink (Anima Designs), eyelets, sewing machine, adhesive, self-adhesive foam spacers.

Don't Judge Each Day… (envelope)
Circle Scissor (EK Success), flower die cut (EK Success), vellum, cardstock (chili, rusty brown, caramel), fiber (EK Success), eyelets, self-adhesive foam spacers, seeds, heart punch (EK Success), adhesive.

Tom and Jodi
Heart template (Provo Craft), patterned paper (Daisy D's), letter stickers (Stickopotamus), gold micro beads (Art Accents), vellum, adhesive, craft knife.

Moonlight Dreams
Circle cutting system (Creative Memories), sparkle diamond glitter glue (PSX Design), border stickers (Mrs. Grossman's Paper Co.), silk bridal floral spray (Michael's), cardstock (cream parchment, pink parchment), adhesive.

Prom Memories
Circle Scissor (EK Success), Marisa die-cut letters (QuicKutz), square metal brads (Creative Impressions), rose photo corners (EK Success), colored pencils (red, silver), metallic paper (red, silver), cardstock (black, white), self-adhesive foam spacers, adhesive, ribbon roses.

So Cozy
Circle scissor (EK Success), patterned paper (Bo Bunny Press, Colors By Design), letter stickers (Bo Bunny Press), stickers (Mrs. Grossman's Paper Co.), watercolor pencils (Staedtler), white cardstock, adhesive, felt pen.

Bodie Island Lighthouse
Shapecutter template (Fiskars), decorative scissors (Fiskars), stamp (PSX Design), printed vellum (Fiskars), cardstock (yellow, turquoise, white, black), blue stamping ink, adhesive.

Sisters Are Forever Friends
Heart border punch and shape cutter (Fiskars), patterned paper and patterned vellum (Fiskars), cardstock (white, strawberry, Christmas red), brads, vellum, adhesive.

Jordan Kennedy
Punch (Punch Bunch), patterned paper (Karen Foster Design), mesh (Magic Mesh by Avant Card), tape (Art Accents), clear micro beads (Halcraft), brads, printable transparency film, stamping ink, white cardstock, dauber for applying ink, adhesive.

What a Clown
Embroidery floss (DMC), standard hole punch (Office Max), 1/16" hole punch (Family Treasures), cardstock (pink, turquoise, yellow, cream), large-eyed needle, pearl bead, adhesive, felt pens.

The Giant Snowman
Snowman, snowflake, and doll-clothes die cuts (Accu-Cut), buttons (Jesse James, Magic Scraps), patterned paper (Bo Bunny Press, Creative Imaginations), shaved ice glitter (Magic Scraps), foam core paper, brads, beads, wire, vellum, acetate sheet, cardstock (royal blue, brown, white), adhesive.

Sun Kissed
Punches (EK Success), Ek-streme Edges border strip (EK Success), stickers (EK Success), cardstock (pumpkin, bright blue, oatmeal), foam tape, beads, adhesive.

Camp Hop
Frog die cut (Sizzix), letter template (C-Thru Ruler Co.), patterned paper (EK Success), anywhere hole punch, brads, vellum, cardstock (dark green, yellow), fibers, beads, adhesive, craft knife, embossing powder, heat gun, embossing ink, felt pen.

These Boots Were Made for Walking
Paper doll die cut (Sizzix), metal flowers and brads (Making Memories), punch (Family Treasures), adhesed foil, black pen, chain, vellum, patterned paper (Doodlebug Design), black embossing powder, cardstock, heat gun, adhesive, anywhere hole punch.

Children Are God's Way…
Heart die cut die (Ellison), patterned paper and rubber stamp (Magenta), Versamark ink (Tsukineko), beads (Magic Scraps), cardstock (spearmint, cranberry, burgundy), beads, wire, self-adhesive foam tape, adhesive.

Flowers
Straight and wavy weaving die cuts (Dayco), flower die cut (Create-A-Cut), copper letters (Global Solutions), wire, self-adhesive foam spacers, cardstock (hemlock, evergreen, pumpkin, orange, red-orange, buttercup, white), patterned paper (Provo Craft), adhesive. Xyron machine.

Photo Shoot
Dragonfly die cuts (Sizzix), patterned paper (Creative Imaginations), wire mesh (Paragona), fun foam, clear shrink plastic (Lucky Squirrel), Pearl-Ex pigment powder (Jacquard Products), Versamark ink (Tsukineko), metal-rimmed vellum tag (Creative Imaginations), fiber (Gotyarn.com), rubber stamps (Limited Edition, 200 Plus), vellum, cardstock (cactus, pale mint), self-adhesive foam spacers, adhesive, glue dots.

Coming Home To Tennessee
Die-cut letters and shapes (Sizzix), patterned paper, polymer letter tiles, and letter stickers (Sweetwater), Fibers (EK Success), metal eyelet letters (Making Memories), copper metal sheet (Paragona), cork, burlap, stamping ink, mulberry paper, aluminum foil, heart brads (Creative Impressions), hemp, eyelets, vellum, adhesive, corrugated paper, gold metallic paper, chalk.

Our Fall Wedding
Leaf die cuts (Sizzix), colored vellum (red, orange, maroon, white), brads, cardstock (maroon, orange, golden yellow, purple, craft paper, black), adhesive.

Michigan Lakes
#3 Spiral die (Accu-Cut), Grande Mark Roller Die Cutting Machine (Accu-Cut), patterned cardstock (Crafter's Workshop), cardstock (black, two-tone gray), vellum, brads, adhesive.

Hoppy Easter
Bunny die cut (Sizzix), patterned paper (Keeping Memories Alive), cardstock (periwinkle, caramel, beige, pink, black), letter stickers (Making Memories), adhesive, felt pen, self-adhesive foam spacers.

Pumpkin Princess
Patterned paper (Provo Craft), Fall & Halloween templates (Provo Craft), sparkly tulle, gold twine, brads, cardstock (ivory, buckeye), gold metallic thread, sewing machine, adhesive.

Nature's Canyon
Polymer clay (Sculpey), brass stencils (Lasting Impressions), fibers (Rub A Dub Dub), patterned paper (Fiskars), printable transparency film, brads, cardstock (evergreen, rust, white), brown stamping ink, foam core paper, adhesive, craft knife.

Garden Party
Polymer clay (Sculpey), brass stencils (Lasting Impressions), fibers (Club Scrap, Funky Fringes Lions Brand, On The Surface), Preserve-It matte acrylic sealant (Krylon), cardstock (holly, rust, pumpkin, white), adhesive, craft knife, sandpaper or emery board, chalk.

Celebrate
Polymer clay (Sculpey), "Celebrate" brass stencil (Plane Class), metallic mesh (Robin's Nest), patterned paper (Paper Adventures), silver leafing pen (Krylon), star brads (Creative Impressions), spiral clips (Target Stores, Inc.), glue dots, silver metallic paper, adhesive, craft knife, silver floss.

Winter White
101 Crackle paste (US Art Quest), brass stencil (Heritage Handcrafts), patterned paper (Scrappin' Dreams), metal-rimmed vellum tag (Making Memories), letter stickers (Making Memories), alphabet beads (Darice), fibers (Cut-It-Up), organza ribbon (Jo-Ann Fabrics), vellum, adhesive, ribbon, cardstock (white, blue).

Lessons Learned From a Lime Green Cast
Lettering template (Frances Meyer), crackle paste (US Art Quest), rubber stamps (Hero Arts), patterned paper (Provo Craft), metal-rimmed vellum tag (Making Memories), stamping ink, gauze mesh, vellum, cardstock (celery, lime green), flower shaped brads, adhesive.

Surely a Star Danced…
Rectangle template (Provo Craft), acrylic paint (Synta, Inc), Chinese coins, cream cardstock, paint brush, adhesive.

Cousins
Rectangle template (Provo Craft), rubber stamp and ink (Stampin' Up), fibers (On The Surface), cardstock (celery, cactus), adhesive.

Ya Ya Sisterhood
"Whimsy" Lettering template (Scrap Pagerz), hat brass stencil (Lasting Impressions), printed paper (Club Scrap), paper yarn (Making Memories), texturizing paste (Dreamweaver), pave pearl accents, scalloped scissors, cardstock (peacock blue, olive green, plum, black), purple and blue embossing powders, eyelets, adhesive, felt pen.

Sun Goddess
Brass stencil (T.S.C. Designs), fibers (EK Success), raffia ribbon (Gallery), brass sun charm (source unknown), cardstock (dark brown, craft paper, cream, ivory), chalk, stamping ink, sewing machine, adhesive, self-adhesive foam spacers.

Love Letter
Fancy Caps lettering template (Wordsworth), border sticker (K & Company), metal-rimmed tag (Avery), butterfly charm (source unknown), white gel pen, chalk, cardstock (purple, white), adhesive, felt pen.

Reading Is Pure Dead Brilliant
"Mini Charmed Letters" lettering template (Crafter's Workshop), metal eyelet letters (Making Memories), silver gel pen, cardstock (black, Christmas red, violet, teal), vellum, brads, silver embossing powder, embossing ink, heat gun, adhesive.

United in Love
Shape template (EK Success), oval cutting system (Creative Memories), circle punch (Carl), colored vellum (hunter, cranberry, pink, white), black cardstock, stylus, gold gel pen, felt pen, adhesive.

Lazy Days of Summer
Lettering template (Provo Craft), Alphabet template (Accu-Cut), circle cutting system template (Creative Memories), Xyron machine, cardstock (sparkly blue-gray), stylus, felt pens, white gel pen, adhesive.

Help! I'm Being Eaten
Lettering template (Scrap Pagerz), jewelry findings (Darice), memorabilia pocket (3L), cardstock (black, celery, army green, brown, ginger), felt pen, eyelets, adhesive.

Summertime and the Living Is Easy
Patterned paper (PrintWorks, Pebbles In My Pocket), paper yarn (Making Memories), decorative eyelets, sun sticker (source unknown), self-adhesive foam spacers, adhesive, felt pen.

Grandma Karen's First Grade Class
Shape and circle templates (Provo Craft), patterned paper (Provo Craft), Art Emboss medium-weight metal sheets (Paragona), embroidery floss (DMC), black cardstock, vellum, eyelets, adhesive, stylus.

"JD"
Letter template (C-Thru Ruler), pre-cut blue offset window cardstock (C-Thru Ruler), metal sheet (Paragona), patterned paper (Keeping Memories Alive), stylus, deckle scissors (Fiskars), silver paper, cardstock (black, ivory), adhesive, felt pen, self-adhesive foam spacers.

Nativity Card
Brass stencil (Heritage Handcrafts), Art Emboss medium-weight metal sheet (Paragona), deckle scissors (Fiskars), black cardstock, self-adhesive foam spacers.

Heart Strings
Letter and primitive heart templates (Provo Craft), fiber (Magic Scraps), patterned paper (Provo Craft), mulberry paper (Magenta), vellum, brads, buttons, mesh fabric (source unknown), white cardstock, adhesive.

Sorting Hearts
Primitive heart template (Provo Craft), patterned paper (Provo Craft), decorative eyelets, brads, red mesh (Magic Mesh by Avant Card), chalk, letter stamps (Hero Arts), stamping ink, date stamp (source unknown), cardstock (white, oatmeal), self-adhesive foam spacers, adhesive, embroidery floss (DMC), felt pen.

Wind Cave
Lettering stencil, Alphabitties letter stickers, and patterned paper (Provo Craft), letter stamps (Hero Arts, PSX Design), chalk, fibers (On The Surface), cardstock (brown, red, black), vellum, stamping ink, eyelets, felt pen, adhesive.

Fall
Celebrations template (Fiskars), punches (Fiskars, Punch Bunch), leaf stamp (PSX Design), Versamark ink (Tsukineko), cardstock (pumpkin, burnt orange, evergreen, ivory), adhesives, lettering template (source unknown).

Never Lose Your Joy
Decorative ruler (C-Thru Ruler), cardstock (aqua, periwinkle, white, blue-gray), vellum, felt pen, adhesive.

Colorado
Decorative ruler (Cut-It-Up), gold micro beads (Art Accents), leaf studs (JewelCraft), journaling sticker and letter rubber stamps (Wordsworth), fiber (Rubba Dub Dub), silk ribbon, pale yellow embroidery floss, vellum, cardstock (white, black, buttercup), tacky tape, piercing tool, adhesive.

First Time Grandma
Decorative ruler (Creative Memories), patterned paper (Patchwork Design, Inc.), alphabet beads (Westrim), foil photo corners (3L), flower punch (EK Success), variegated fiber (On The Surface), vellum (white, pink), ribbon (Offray), decorative eyelets, adhesive, rhinestones (Stampa Rosa).

Friends
Letter template (EK Success), brass flower template (Lasting Impressions), embroidery floss (DMC), cardstock (ivory, sage, blush), felt pen, adhesive.

Four Wheelin'
Border template (EK Success), craft knife, cardstock (deep red, black, white), white gel pen, adhesive, black felt pen.

Hat-titudes
Decorative ruler (C-Thru Ruler), patterned paper (NRN Designs, Two Busy Moms), sticker letters (Creative Imaginations), Sparkles diamond glitter glue (PSX Design), cardstock (white, dark purple), chalk, vellum, felt pen, adhesive, craft knife.

Bessie Logan Sparks
Border Buddy (EK Success), fibers (Fibers By The Yard), double-sided patterned paper (Daisy D's), ribbon flowers (Offray), punch (EK Success), cardstock (caramel, beige), chalk, adhesive.

The following companies contributed artwork towards this book:

AccuCut
(800) 288-1670
www.accucut.com

C-Thru Ruler Company, The
(800) 243-8419
www.cthruruler.com

EK Success Ltd.
(800) 524-1359
www.eksuccess.com

Ellison Craft and Design
(800) 253-2238
www.ellison.com

Fiskars, Inc.
(800) 500-4849
www.fiskars.com

Heritage Handcrafts
(303) 683-0963
www.heritage-handcrafts.com

Provo Craft
(800) 937-7686
www.provocraft.com

POST CARD

Safari

MEMORIES

The dioramas and scenery at Animal Kingdom's "Safari Ride" in Walt Disney World seemed so realistic! From the alligator swamps to the savannah-like and root-exposed trees, we felt like we were on a genuine, exotic African Safari! David, the kids and I had so much fun!

Scrapbook
Borders, Corners
& Titles

Fresh techniques and innovative ideas for designer pages

**MEMORY
MAKERS
BOOKS**

Table of Contents

Winter

Spring

Summer

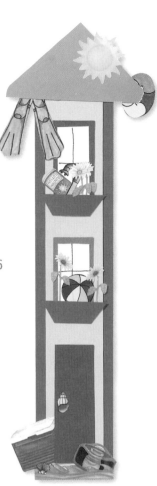

Fall

Introduction

Over the past decade I have seen my share of scrapbook pages, and generally they consist of three elements: a title, photos and journaling. Beyond these components are the embellishments that accessorize the page. Although it is true that over-accessorizing a page can take the focus away from the photos and journaling, when in balance embellishments can enhance the story behind the photos and allow for personal creativity.

In this book, we inspire scrapbookers with fresh and fun ensembles of page borders, corners and title designs for seasonal and holiday themes—including a peeking snowman, pierced egg die cuts, fiber-hung seed packets, and stamped and lacquered pumpkins, just to name a few.

Each and every scrapbook page featured also represents a different scrapbook technique, such as embossing with buttons or intaglio shrink art. Once you learn a technique, it can be applied to your own pages using relevant colors and themes to match your photos. Best of all, these custom-coordinated page accents will help you get more use out of your existing tools and supplies in ways that you may have never imagined.

This book also includes a basic list of tools and supplies, followed by helpful hints for working with color and adding texture and dimension. Each chapter represents a season and begins with an inspirational gallery of page ideas featured within the chapter. In addition, useful tips are sprinkled throughout and original patterns are provided.

All of these techniques are simple and easily mastered. So get out your scrapbook supplies and begin! Above all else, enjoy creating and personalizing your pages.

Michele

Michele Gerbrandt

Founding Editor

Memory Makers magazine

Basic tools & supplies

The following tools and supplies are used to create many of the scrapbook page projects featured in this book, although not every tool listed is used in every project. Before you begin any project, start with a clean work space that is covered with a self-healing cutting mat. Then assemble the following tools, depending on the project you've selected:

¹⁄₁₆", ⅛" and ¼" round circle or hand punches

Beading needle

Black journaling pen

Bone folder

Button shank remover

Craft knife

Decorative scissors

Embossing heat gun

Embossing stylus

Eyelet setter and hammer

Metal straightedge ruler

Mouse pad or sheet of craft foam

Personal paper trimmer

Piercing awl or sewing needle

Round needle-nose pliers

Scissors

Small paintbrush

Small, stiff brush

Stabilo pencil

Tweezers

Adhesives

Your choice of adhesive is a personal preference, but the following wet and dry adhesives are used in this book—depending on the project featured—because each is best suited for different types of tasks. Photo-safe, acid-free adhesive products are recommended.

Adhesive application machine

Bottled glue

Double-sided foam tape

Double-sided photo tape

Double-sided sheet adhesive

Glue Dots®

Glue pen

Photo splits

Powder adhesive

Self-adhesive foam spacers

Tape roller

Other tools

The following tools are unique to a number of the projects in this book. If you don't have the specific tool we used, simply substitute your own tools as your page theme dictates.

Inkworkx® bulb sprayer

Lettering templates

Punches

QuicKutz™ letter press

Reproducible patterns
(see pages 312–316)

Rubber stamps

Sizzix® die-cut machine

Paper

All projects featured use colored cardstock and/or patterned paper, as the foundation of the scrapbook page. When selecting paper colors, take the lead from your photos. Select 2-4 colors in the photos that best highlight the important aspects of the pictures, plus a neutral color—such as black, white or cream.

To help your photos "pop" off of the page, select lighter colored papers for photos with dark backgrounds and darker papers for photos with light backgrounds.

Colorants

Projects may also use one or more of the following colorants to add sizzle to the pages:

Black and colored
pigment pens

Chalk

Clear and colored
3-D crystal lacquer

Clear embossing ink

Embossing pen

Embossing powders

Glitter

Glitter glue

Metal flake

Stamping inks

Watercolor paints

White opaque pen

Other craft supplies

For texture and dimension, these craft supplies are used in one or more of the projects showcased:

Metallics

Eyelets

Fasteners

Wire

Wire mesh

Baubles

Flat and shank buttons

Seed and bugle beads

Sequins

Shaved ice®

Tiny glass marbles

Design additions

Die cuts

Paperclay®

Pre-made tags

Shimmer Sheetz®

Shrink plastic

Stickers

Organics

Pressed flowers

Tiny shells and starfish

Textiles

Embroidery floss

Fibers

Jute

Paper cord

Paper yarn

Raffia

String

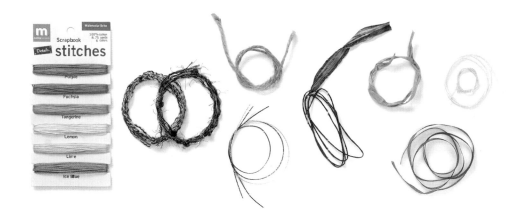

Winter

The warm memories, chilly fun and holiday happenings of wintertime are brimming with photo opportunities for scrapbookers! Make the perfect designer-look accents for those photos with:

- Progressive punch scenes • A window shaker box • Sticker reflections
- A peek-a-boo window • Embossed ornaments • Vellum stained glass
- Frosted letters • Threaded accents

These easy-to-learn techniques will give you plenty of ideas for year-round scrapbooking pleasure!

Progressive Punches
LAYER CHANGING SCENES

Joan Gosling, Keizer, Oregon

This technique, which resembles subsequent frames in a motion picture, can be used to represent a variety of activities such as building a snowman, constructing a home or planting a garden. Try other punched shapes or small die cuts to fit your page theme. Create the punched border and title as shown on the facing page. Mount border on left side of navy background. Fold photo corners from ¾ x 1½" navy strips. Slip corners onto photo and mount on a 6¼ x 4¼" evergreen mat. Mat again with white. Print and cut out caption. Double mat photo and caption together with navy and white paper. Add mini and small punched snowflakes embellished with glitter. Mount title centered above photo. Stamp letters for "fresh" on white paper and double mat.

MATERIALS

- Two sheets of navy solid-colored paper
- One sheet each of white and evergreen solid-colored paper
- Scraps of yellow and tan paper
- Super jumbo contemporary tree punch (Emagination Crafts)
- Mini snowflakes from snowflake corner rounder punch (Family Treasures)
- Tiny stars from bunting border, small circle and small snowflake punches (Marvy/Uchida)
- Lettering template (Provo Craft)
- Glitter glue (Ranger)
- Letter stamps (PSX Design)
- Navy stamping ink

1 Punch four evergreen and three white trees. Cut four 2¼ x 2½" navy rectangles. Freehand cut wavy strips of brown and white paper for the earth, snow and clouds.

2 Use scissors to trim off the bottoms of the white trees—about two thirds of the first tree, half of the second and a quarter of the third to represent the snowfall progression.

3 Layer trees with earth, snow and clouds on each navy rectangle. Punch yellow moons and stars and mini snowflakes. Mat each rectangle with white paper. Mount the rectangles in order on a 2¾" evergreen strip.

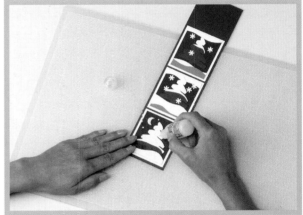

4 Use glitter glue to add sparkle to snow, stars and snowflakes.

5 To create the title, mount a wavy white strip at the bottom of a navy strip. The widths of the strips depend upon the desired height of each letter. Use a lettering template to cut out each letter, positioning the snow at the bottom of each character. Accent with punched and trimmed mini snowflakes. Embellish with glitter. Mat each letter with evergreen and mount on a 7 x 2" strip of vellum.

Window Shaker Box

ENCASE GLITTERY SNOWFLAKES

Jodi Amidei, Lafayette, Colorado
Inspired by Teresa Magill

MATERIALS

- Window pattern on page 313
- One to two sheets each of cream and dusty blue solid-colored paper
- One sheet of patterned paper (MiniGraphics)
- Background stamp (Magenta)
- Black stamping ink
- Colored pens
- Glitter glue (Duncan Enterprises)
- Double-sided foam tape (3M)
- Scraps of vellum paper
- Mini snowflake punch (Family Treasures)
- Small plastic snowflakes (Jesse James Co.)
- Clear Mylar or poly page protector
- White paint
- Mini framed photos (Joshua's)
- Lettering template (EK Success)
- Colonial corner pocket punch (Marvy/Uchida)

Regardless of the subject, window shaker boxes add whimsy and fun to any scrapbook page. Any small objects can be used in a shaker box. Try seashells for a beach theme, tiny confetti notes for a music theme or mini punched leaves for autumn. To replicate this page, build the window shaker box following the steps on the facing page; mount at the top of solid-colored background paper along with mini framed photos. Use a similar technique to create the shaker box for the initial title letters. Cut remaining title letters using template. Print caption. Mount photos on cream rectangle. Create cream photo corners using corner pocket and mini star punches. Draw details around title shaker box, title letters, photo corners and caption with blue pen.

1 Cut a 4 x 12" cream strip. To create the village scene, stamp two images side by side. Embellish scene with colored pens and glitter glue for snow.

2 Cut a 4 x 12" patterned strip. Make two photocopies of the window pattern on page 89. Center the first pattern on the patterned strip and use it to cut out the windowpane openings. Use the second pattern to cut out the window frame from the same color as the background.

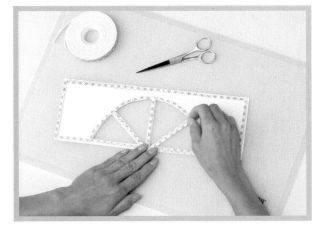

3 Trim strips of double-sided foam tape the same width as the window grids. Adhere strips to the back of the patterned window. Outline the outer edges of the entire strip as well as the window and panes.

4 Remove the tape backing and mount the patterned window on the stamped village scene. Fill each window pane with punched vellum snowflakes and small plastic snowflakes.

5 To mimic the window glass, trace the outside edge of the solid-colored window frame onto a rigid piece of Mylar or plastic page protector and cut out. Mount this piece beneath the window frame. Add "frost" by brushing white paint on the back of the plastic. Then mount the window frame over the patterned window to seal the shaker box.

Sticker Reflections

CREATE AN ILLUSION WITH MIRROR-IMAGE STICKERS

Megan Schoepf, Panama City, Florida
Photos Kelly Angard, Highlands Ranch, Colorado

MATERIALS

- One sheet each of dark green, purple and lavender solid-colored paper
- One sheet of light blue solid-colored ribbed paper
- One sheet each of white and blue vellum paper (Karen Foster)
- Penguin and Winterscape stickers (Mrs. Grossman's)
- Glitter (Magic Scraps)
- Alphabet stickers (C-Thru Ruler)
- Black pen

You can use this technique with any sticker images that are mirror images along any line, whether vertical, horizontal or even diagonal. First create the penguin border as shown on the facing page. Use the same technique to create the title and an additional penguin accent. Mat border with purple paper and mount on left side of dark green background. Crop photos and mat with light blue ribbed paper. For corner accents, cut lavender triangles and embellish with glitter. Write caption on lavender rectangle.

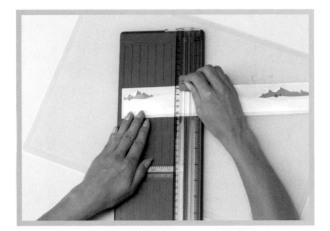

1 Cut a 3½ x 11½" rectangle of blue ribbed paper. Trim two 3½" sections of the Winterscape border sticker for the upper and lower parts of the border. Freehand cut additional vellum strips.

2 Cut a 3½" strip of blue vellum to overlay the border background; attach at lower edge using a snowy section of border sticker. Mount a white vellum strip over this sticker section. Pull back the vellum overlay and adhere mirror-image penguin stickers to the border background.

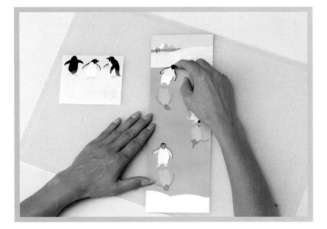

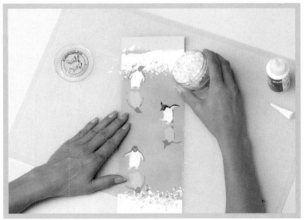

3 Attach the top of vellum overlay to the background using a mountain section of border sticker layered with a white vellum strip. Adhere matching penguin stickers on the vellum overlay to create the illusion of a reflection.

4 Use glue and glitter to accent snowbank and lake edges.

VARIATION

For a terrific take on a familiar fairy tale, assemble a princely reflection for a plain 'ol frog die cut (Ellison) using a Paperkins paper doll kit (EK Success) layered beneath blue vellum paper.

Megan Schoepf, Panama City, Florida

Peek-a-Boo Window

PEER THROUGH FROSTED PANES

There are no buddies like SNOW buddies

Deana, Sarah, Amanda, and Griffin
These four kids have been friends since 1984.
They have celebrated birthdays, build snowmen,
shot fireworks, and attended school together.

Linda Cummings, Murfreesboro, Tennessee

You can illustrate any season or activity using this window technique. Simply fill the window with the appropriate scene—a bunny for Easter, fireworks for the Fourth of July, a jack-o-lantern or ghost for Halloween or lighted trees for the holidays. For this wintry scene, first assemble the window as shown on the facing page. Mat photo with brown paper; cut triangles for corner accents and embellish with punched snowflakes. Print and mat caption and title, leaving extra space beneath the first title phrase. Use lettering template to cut larger title letters from patterned paper. For the letter mats, cut another set of brown letters. Layer letters slightly askew and mount with self-adhesive foam spacers.

MATERIALS

- Snowman, window and curtain patterns on page 313
- Scraps of white and orange solid-colored paper
- One sheet each of cream, brown and red solid-colored paper
- One sheet each of pine tree and brown check patterned paper (Frances Meyer, Rocky Mountain Scrapbook Co.)
- One sheet of patterned vellum paper (EK Success)
- Colored chalk
- White opaque, brown and black pens
- Large snowflake and small spiral punches (All Night Media, Family Treasures)
- Lettering template (C-Thru Ruler)
- Curlz MT computer font (fonts.com)
- Self-adhesive foam spacers

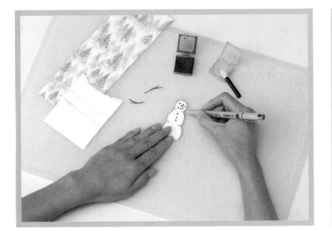

1 Use the pattern on page 89 to cut snowman shape. Draw details with black pen and shade with colored chalk. Cut brown twigs for arms and orange carrot for nose.

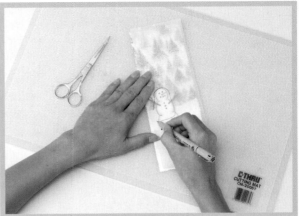

2 Cut a 3 x 9" rectangle of pine tree paper. Cut a matching rectangle of patterned vellum paper for the overlay. Lay the snowman in the desired position beneath the patterned vellum and on top of the pine tree background. Trace an oval around the snowman's face and part of his body. Cut out the oval opening.

3 Mount a scrap of plastic page protector or transparency film beneath the oval opening. Use an opaque white pen to add frost details to the back of the vellum overlay. Draw swishes and dots to simulate a frosted window. Mount vellum overlay over snowman on top of background.

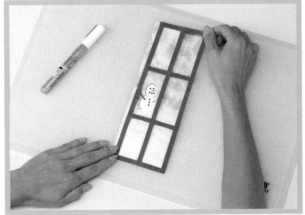

4 Cut ¼" brown strips for the window frame. Draw details with brown and black pens. Use the pattern to layer strips for the window frame.

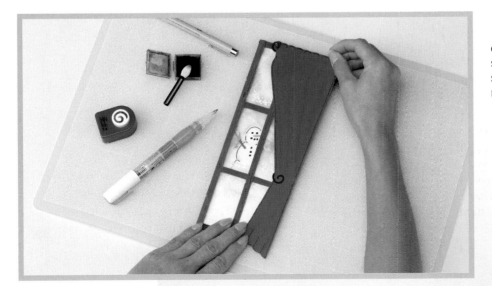

5 Use the pattern to cut the red curtain. Draw details with black pen and shade with chalk. Punch small black spirals for curtain rod and tie-back hardware.

Embossed Ornaments
IMPRESS RAISED IMAGES IN MYLAR SHEETS

how the boys **trim** the **tree**

1. Colt (14) reluctantly builds the tree.
2. Hunter (1½) test drives empty box.
3. Colt pulls stray needles from feet.
4. Jake (8½) and Dylan (12) decorate it!

MaryJo Regier, Littleton, Colorado

Take the garland idea to new "lengths" with different beads, buttons, bows and other embellishments. If you poke a hole in it, you can string it on a garland. Simply use different-themed shank buttons to fit your page theme. To create the embossed ornament garlands, follow the steps on the facing page. Position garlands on the left edge and lower right corner of trimmed plaid paper; tape ends on the backside. Double-mat plaid paper with white and evergreen. Crop and mat photos. Print and adhere captions. Print title, leaving space for large letters. Trim title to a ½" strip and mat with evergreen. Use templates to cut letters and numbers from Shimmer Sheetz; mat with evergreen; mount with self-adhesive foam spacers.

1 Use an embossing heat gun to heat Shimmer Sheetz. Move the heat gun in a circular motion for 10 to 15 seconds to evenly heat the material, which will become soft and pliable.

2 Lay the warmed Shimmer Sheetz on a mouse pad or three sheets of craft foam. Firmly push the patterned side of a Christmas button into the Shimmer Sheetz to emboss the button's design. Remove the button and allow the Shimmer Sheetz to cool.

3 Repeat Steps 1 and 2 until all desired images are embossed. Use small, sharp scissors to trim around the edges of each embossed ornament.

4 Use beading thread and a beading needle to string garlands of embossed ornaments and bugle beads.

MATERIALS

- One sheet plaid patterned paper (Hot Off The Press)
- Two sheets green solid-colored paper
- One sheet white solid-colored paper
- One sheet each of red and white iris Shimmer Sheetz (Sulyn Industries)
- Embossing heat gun
- Mouse pad or 3 sheets craft foam
- Christmas buttons (Blumenthal Lansing)
- Red and green bugle beads (Westrim)
- Beading thread and needle
- Lettering template (C-Thru Ruler)
- Self-adhesive foam spacers

Vellum Stained Glass

PIECE A LUMINOUS DESIGN

For me, the Christmas tree is really the heart of our Christmas celebrations. We choose it as a family, we decorate it as a family, we enjoy the lights, again as a family. We all take turns removing Tolstoy the cat from the tree and straightening it. Of course, the most magical parts of Christmas take place there: the quiet before bedtime on Christmas Eve, when Earl and I can bask in the glow of the lights and the quiet of sleeping children, the joy and confusion of Christmas morning, with grown ups as excited as the kids and the cats attacking stray wrapping paper. Our tree stands for so much laughter, so much love and so much joy at Christmas. December, 1998

Jenna Beegle, Woodstock, Georgia

MATERIALS

- Pattern on page 312
- One sheet each of white and black solid-colored paper
- Scraps or small sheets of red, light green, dark green and yellow vellum paper
- Glue pen (Zig Two-Way from EK Success)
- Pebbles in My Pocket lettering template (EK Success)
- Black pen

Using a simple geometric design to create a border saves time without losing impact. Check your local library for thousands of different stained-glass patterns. To re-create this stained-glass border, follow the steps on the facing page. Mount border at bottom of white background. (If you choose a dark background, back the border with white paper.) Use the same technique to create stained-glass corner accents for caption and stained-glass letters for title. Double-mat photo with two shades of vellum paper. Pencil lines for caption and write with pencil; trace with thin black pen.

1 Make two photocopies of stained-glass window pattern. Place the first pattern over black paper on a cutting mat. Hold the pattern in place or secure it with removable tape. Cut out the window frame using a craft knife and a metal-edge ruler as needed.

2 Lay the second pattern beneath a piece of colored vellum paper. Trace the window panes you wish to fill with that color, making each pane slightly larger than the frame opening. Repeat for each color vellum. You can also use craft punches to punch rectangles and squares.

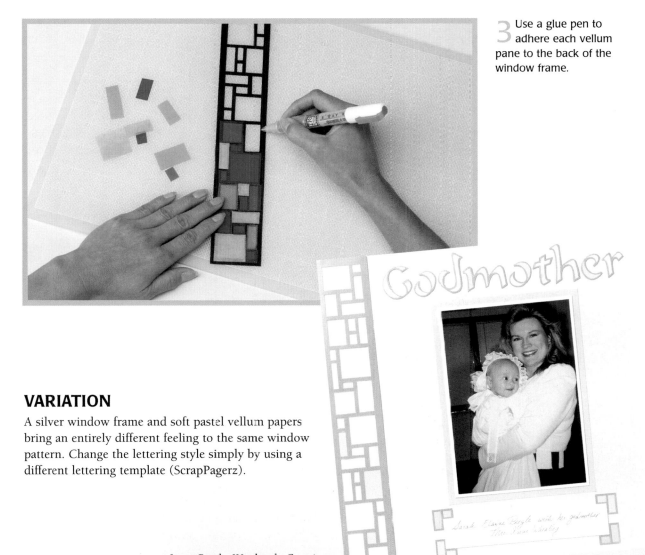

3 Use a glue pen to adhere each vellum pane to the back of the window frame.

VARIATION

A silver window frame and soft pastel vellum papers bring an entirely different feeling to the same window pattern. Change the lettering style simply by using a different lettering template (ScrapPagerz).

Jenna Beegle, Woodstock, Georgia

Frosted Letters

DECORATE SATISFYING SWEETS

Betsy Bell Sammarco, New Canaan, Connecticut

This title idea is perfect for those with an incurable sweet tooth. You'll have no trouble thinking up ways to embellish dozens of cookie letters for any holiday baking—including Valentine's Day, Easter and Halloween! For this Christmas title, cut and double mat a 2" strip of silver metallic paper; mount at top of red flecked background. Create cookie letters following the steps on the facing page. Snip the lower right corner of the letter S using Ripple scissors. Mount letters on title strip. For the large cookies, punch large hearts, stars and trees from brown and white Diamond Dust paper; trim white pieces and layer over brown. For the border design, cut six 1" silver squares and mount on left edge of page. Punch small stars, snowflakes, hearts and gingerbread men from brown paper; "frost" punched shapes by coloring with white opaque pen, leaving a brown border. Write caption on brown rectangle; shade with brown chalk. Crop and mat photos and caption. Accent photo corners with triangles and mini cookies. Embellish with additional seed beads.

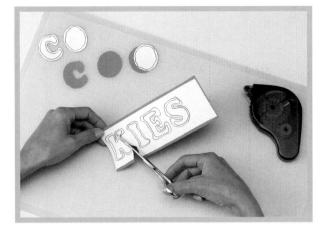

1 Make two photocopies of the lettering pattern. Lay the first pattern over a 2" brown strip. Hold pattern in place with removable tape. Cut out letters following the outer lines on the pattern.

2 Use brown chalk to shade the letter edges to resemble baked gingerbread cookies.

3 Place the second pattern over a 2" strip of white Diamond Dust paper. Hold pattern in place with removable tape. Cut out letters, this time following the inner lines of the pattern to form the frosting layer.

4 Mount white letters over brown letters. Use tweezers and a fine-tipped glue pen or bottle to adhere green and red seed beads to each letter.

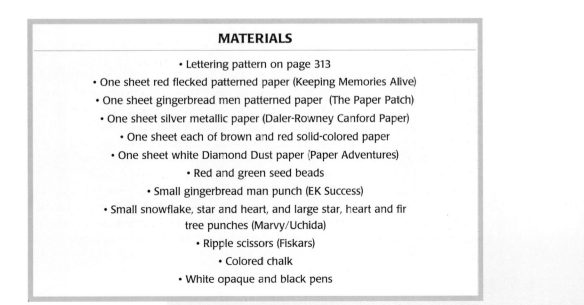

MATERIALS

- Lettering pattern on page 313
- One sheet red flecked patterned paper (Keeping Memories Alive)
- One sheet gingerbread men patterned paper (The Paper Patch)
- One sheet silver metallic paper (Daler-Rowney Canford Paper)
- One sheet each of brown and red solid-colored paper
- One sheet white Diamond Dust paper (Paper Adventures)
- Red and green seed beads
- Small gingerbread man punch (EK Success)
- Small snowflake, star and heart, and large star, heart and fir tree punches (Marvy/Uchida)
- Ripple scissors (Fiskars)
- Colored chalk
- White opaque and black pens

Threaded Accents

STITCH AND WRAP PAGE EMBELLISHMENTS

Anissa Stringer, Phoenix, Arizona

This border and title idea takes little time but makes a big design impact. Best of all, it's easy to adapt to any theme. For the background, crumple a sheet of gold mulberry or handmade paper and flatten several times to achieve the desired texture. Create the wrapped tree, corner accents and title following the steps on the facing page. Write caption with gold pen on evergreen rectangle; wrap in the same manner as the tree. Crop photos. Mat all elements with dark red mulberry and arrange on gold background.

MATERIALS

- Tree pattern on page 313
- One sheet gold mulberry paper (source unknown)
- One sheet evergreen solid-colored paper
- One sheet dark red mulberry paper (PrintWorks)
- Scrap of brown paper
- ¾" square punch
- Star-shaped brad fasteners (HyGlo/AmericanPin)
- Gold metallic thread
- Sewing needle
- Gold metallic pen

1 Photocopy tree pattern. Cut tree from evergreen paper and trunk section from brown paper. Punch evergreen squares for corner accents. Adhere star brad fasteners to tree and squares.

2 Wrap tree and evergreen squares with gold metallic thread. Secure ends on the backside with tape.

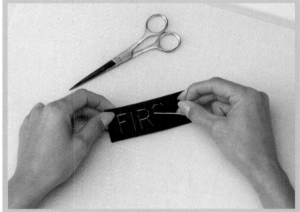

3 Freehand draw letters for title on 1¼" evergreen strips. Following the lines, use a sewing needle to pierce holes for stitching.

4 Thread sewing needle with gold metallic thread and stitch gold letters. Secure ends with tape on the back of the title strips.

VARIATION

Adapt the wrapped and sewn concept to a spring theme with a freehand-cut floral topiary and a "bunny pink" title stitched with embroidery floss. For fall, try leaves wrapped in bronze thread and orange stitched letters.

Anissa Stringer, Phoenix, Arizona

Spring

Memorable events fill our spring days—from the budding of green leaves that are brighter than any other time of the year and egg-painting to honoring Mother and dressing little girls in delicate dresses. Create the perfect page accents for your springtime photos with:

• Raffia lacing • Folk hearts • Layered shapes • Stamped paper clay
• Cracked glass • Pierced die cuts • A shadow box • Decorative edges

Once you've tried these simple scrapbook projects, you'll be racing to apply the ideas to your winter, summer and fall pages as well!

Raffia Lacing

WHIP STITCH TEXTURED EDGES

Little Girls are Heaven's

F L O W E R S

Gabby is such a beautiful baby! She brightens up the world around her.

Gabrielle Lilly
May 2002

Terri Davenport, Toledo, Ohio

These laced borders, titles and corner accents are reminiscent of old-fashioned lacing cards, and they couldn't be easier to create. Just punch holes and stitch with paper raffia. Change the punched shape and the raffia color to fit your page theme. Refer to the instructions on the facing page to create the title, border and corner accent. Computer print the caption on white paper; trim and mat with pink. Punch two holes at the bottom of the caption and lace with white raffia. Mat photos with white paper. Arrange elements on a light pink background.

MATERIALS

- One sheet each of white, pink and light pink solid-colored paper
- Large flower punch (Family Treasures)
- Letter punches (EK Success)
- ⅛" hole punch
- White Twistel paper raffia (Making Memories)

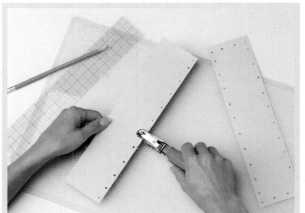

1 Cut four 2" white squares. Punch centers with large flower punch. Cut a 1½ x 7" white strip for the title; punch letters, saving the centers of the O and R.

2 Print black title words on pink paper; trim to 3½ x 8". Cut two additional pink rectangles in these sizes: 3 x 11½" for the border and 2¾ x 3¼" for the corner piece. Use a pencil and a graphing ruler to mark dots along the edges of each rectangle. They should be about ¼" in from the edges and spaced about ¾" to 1" apart. Punch holes with ⅛" hole punch.

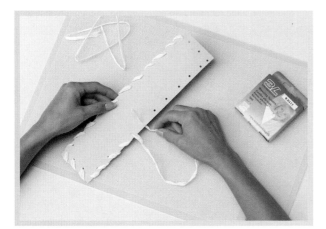

3 Lace the edges of each rectangle using a whip stitch. Simply pull the raffia up through one hole, wrap it around the edge of the rectangle and pull it up through the next hole. Be sure to lace through each hole in the same direction.

4 Use additional raffia to secure the title and white punched flowers to the pink rectangles. Use tape to secure all loose ends to the back of each rectangle. Mount the centers of the O and R on the title.

VARIATION

Lace up a little boy page by combining bright blue and pale sage paper with punched dragonflies (McGill). Use a lettering template (EK Success) to create the whimsical letters.

Terri Davenport, Toledo, Ohio

Folk Hearts
CONTRAST TEXTURED RAFFIA WITH SIMPLE GRAPHIC ELEMENTS

Nicole Hinrichs Ramsaroop, Horst, The Netherlands

Accented "banners" make for quick and easy page embellishments. To change the theme from "love", simply change the hearts to a different shape such as Easter eggs, flowers, leaves or Christmas trees and apply them to the banners. Start with a cream scrapbook page or a solid-colored background. For the background, mount a 10 x 12" sheet of plum paper next to a 2" strip of tan raffia. (Dampen the raffia to make it easier to untwist it.) For the border background, mount a 1½" strip of untwisted tan raffia in the center of a 4 x 11½" red strip. Follow the steps on the facing page to create the hearts and banners. Mount banners on the border as shown. Cut a 4" red square in half to create the lower right triangle. Mount large heart over triangle. Use the computer font as a template for the large title letters; cut out and mat with plum mulberry. Write remaining title words with thick black pen on dark red strips; mat with tan paper. Crop and mat photos and printed caption. Draw details with black pen.

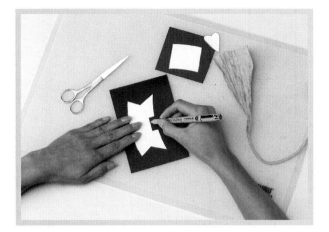

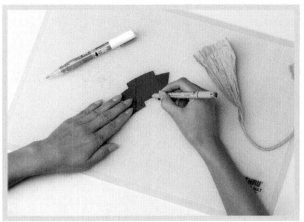

1 Photocopy and cut out heart and banner patterns (enlarge or reduce heart as needed; banner pattern has two pieces). Trace around each pattern piece onto the appropriate colors of paper and raffia. Cut one large heart, three small hearts and three of each banner piece.

2 Mount each rectangular piece onto each banner. Draw banner details with black pen.

3 Use a small paintbrush and water to lightly dampen mulberry paper. Place a raffia heart over the dampened mulberry and hold in place. Following the edges of the raffia heart, tear mulberry paper into a slightly larger heart shape. Repeat for each heart. Mount hearts onto mulberry mats.

4 Adhere hearts to banners. Punch a hole in the center of one small heart, punching through all layers. Punch a hole in the center of the large heart. Insert brad fasteners through holes and flatten ends on the backside.

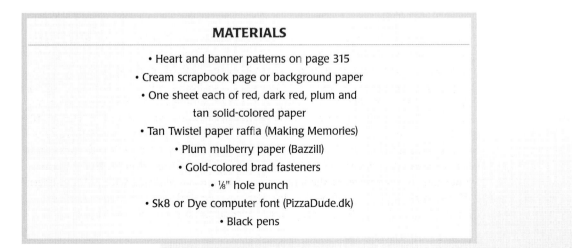

MATERIALS

- Heart and banner patterns on page 315
- Cream scrapbook page or background paper
- One sheet each of red, dark red, plum and tan solid-colored paper
- Tan Twistel paper raffia (Making Memories)
- Plum mulberry paper (Bazzill)
- Gold-colored brad fasteners
- ⅛" hole punch
- Sk8 or Dye computer font (PizzaDude.dk)
- Black pens

Layered Shapes
COMBINE PUNCHED SHAPES AND OPENINGS

Pam Klassen, Westminster, Colorado
Photos Patricia Hymovitz, Torrance, California; Michele Rank,
Cerritos, California; JoDee Yamasaki, Torrance, California

All you need are a few geometric or organic-shaped punches to create striking page elements with depth and dimension. Here's your chance to experiment with different patterns, textures and color combinations for a truly one-of-a-kind look. Create the title and border following the steps on the facing page; mount on a bright pink background. Crop photos and mat using lime vellum and light pink paper. Write caption on light pink vellum rectangle; mount over white rectangle. Create corner accents using the same punching and layering technique as the border.

MATERIALS

• One sheet each of light green, lime green, bright pink and light pink solid-colored paper

• One sheet each of bright yellow, pink, dark pink and lime green vellum paper

• Medium flower and gigantic flower, groovy flower and 2¾" circle punches (Family Treasures)

• Medium daisy punch (Carl)

• Small flower and 2" circle punches (Emagination Crafts)

• Small flower punch (EK Success)

• Personal die-cutting system and letter dies (QuicKutz) or lettering template or letter punches

• Colored pens

1 Cut a 3⅝ x 11" light green strip. Punch gigantic groovy flower and 2" circle openings toward the right side.

2 Cut a 3⅜ x 10¾" bright pink strip. Punch gigantic flower and 2¾" circle openings so that they partially overlap the openings in the light green strip.

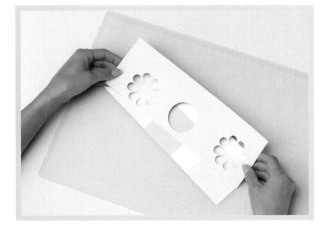

3 For the border backing, cut a white strip the same size as the light green strip. Mount squares of bright yellow vellum and pink paper beneath the openings in the light green strip. Mount the light green strip on the white backing.

4 Punch additional flowers from colored vellum and layer on the bright pink strip, trimming as necessary. To complete the border, mount the bright pink strip over the light green strip.

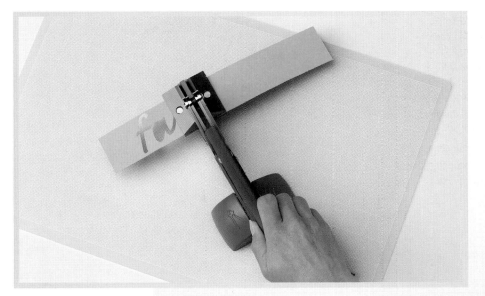

5 Follow the manufacturer instructions to die-cut the title letters in a 10¼ x 1¾" bright pink strip; mat with lime green; embellish with punched and trimmed vellum flowers and circles.

Stamped Paper Clay
REVERSE-EMBOSS WHIMSICAL IMAGES

Erikia Ghumm, Brighton, Colorado
Photos Catherine Medlin, Brighton, Colorado

MATERIALS

- One sheet of speckled green patterned paper (Provo Craft)
- One sheet of cream solid-colored paper
- Paper clay (Creative Paperclay Co.)
- Easter stamps (PSX Design)
- Watercolor paints
- Embroidery floss
- Purple pen

These paper tiles are created with Paperclay, an acid-free product that air dries in about a day. It is lightweight and can be rolled thin and embedded with beads or other embellishments. The product comes in a natural white color but can be painted when dry. Besides stamping, you can also use push molds, cookie cutters or form objects freehand. To create the reverse-embossed images, follow the steps on the facing page. To create the corner accents, simply roll out Paperclay to ⅛" thickness, cut into triangles, allow to dry, and paint with watercolors. Mount the paper-clay elements on a patterned background. Crop and mat photos. Write captions and draw details with purple pen.

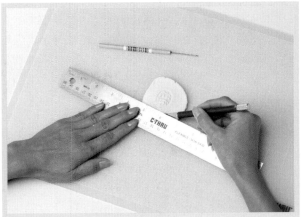

1 Use a small rolling pin or dowel to roll out paper clay to ⅛" thickness. Firmly press stamp into clay without rocking. Lift stamp straight up from clay. Repeat for each design. The clay now has reverse-embossed images.

2 Use a craft knife and metal ruler to cut the images into tile shapes. Use an awl to pierce a hole at the top and bottom of each title. Pierce a single hole in the *Happy Easter* tile.

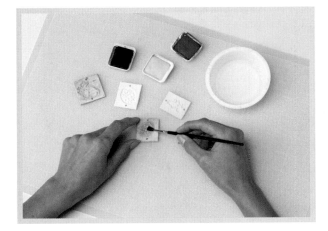

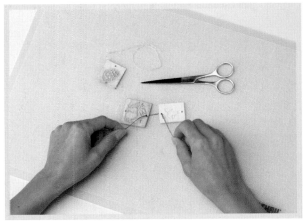

3 Let the paper clay dry overnight. Paint with a light coating of watercolor paint and allow to air dry.

4 Create a garland by tying the tiles together with colored strands of embroidery floss. String floss through the Happy Easter tile and tie a bow.

VARIATION

Change the look of this technique by inking the stamps before pressing them into the paper clay. Then tear the edges of each image. (School stamps by PSX Design, Stampcraft by Plaid Enterprises and Stampin' Up; papers by Scrapbook Wizard)

Erikia Ghumm, Brighton, Colorado
Photos Lora Mason, Orlando, Florida

Cracked Glass
HEAT AND BEND ULTRA THICK EMBOSSING ENAMEL

Erikia Ghumm, Brighton, Colorado
Photos Sally Scamfer, Bellvue, Nebraska

MATERIALS

• Heart pattern on page 314
• One sheet of patterned paper (Anna Griffin)
• One sheet each of cream and tan solid-colored paper
• Journaling block (Anna Griffin)
• Purple pen
• Suze Weinberg's Clear Ultra Thick Embossing Enamel (Ranger)
• Clear embossing ink pad
• Embossing heat gun
• Pressed flowers (Nature's Pressed)
• Tweezers

Ultra thick embossing enamel is similar to regular embossing powder except that the grains are larger, which results in a thicker coating. This embossing technique can be used with any flat object such as stickers, duplicate photos, die cuts, punched shapes, stamped images and printed designs that coordinate with your page theme. Follow the steps on the facing page to create the cracked hearts. Use the same technique to create the photo corner accents and the title strip, which incorporates both pressed flowers and a handwritten label sticker. Double mat photo and center on patterned background. Adhere cracked glass accents with a strong adhesive.

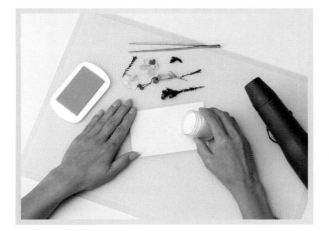

1 Stamp cream paper with clear embossing ink pad. Apply a layer of ultra thick embossing enamel (UTEE). Tap off excess. Heat with embossing gun about 2" from the surface until it melts.

2 Gently press a dried flower into the melted UTEE using tweezers. Allow to cool several minutes.

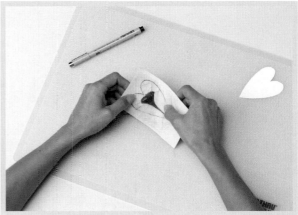

3 Stamp surface with clear embossing ink, apply another layer of UTEE, and heat surface again. Apply additional layers of UTEE while the previous layer is still hot until the image is the desired thickness.

4 Place heart pattern over the flower image and trace. Carefully holding the flower image in both hands, gently bend the paper to create the cracked-glass effect.

5 Cut out heart shape, cutting just inside the traced heart outline.

Pierced Die Cuts

OUTLINE SIMPLE SHAPES WITH TINY PINPRICKS

Sandi Genovese for Ellison Craft & Design
Photos Vicki Krum, Redmond, Washington

Paper piercing is an easy technique that adds texture and pattern to basic shapes and solid colors. First cut and piece vellum rectangles to fit on a white background. Adhere vellum corners at page center. Attach remaining vellum corners by punching holes and inserting mini brad fasteners. Print title on pink vellum; trim and mount over solid blue strip using mini brad fasteners. Silhouette-cut photo and mount with self-adhesive foam spacers. Print captions; accent with punched hearts and carrots. Follow the steps on the facing page to create the pierced title letters and eggs. Use self-adhesive foam spacers to mount letter die cuts; adhere vellum line stickers. Arrange eggs using self-adhesive foam spacers as desired.

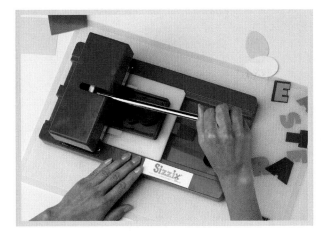

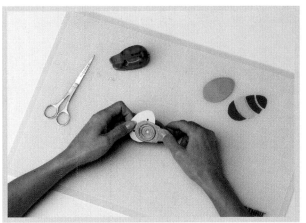

1 Follow the manufacturer instructions to die cut letters and eggs from various shades of solid-colored papers. Select two shades of the same color for each egg.

2 Choose one color for the top layer of each egg; punch various sizes of holes or cut apart into strips.

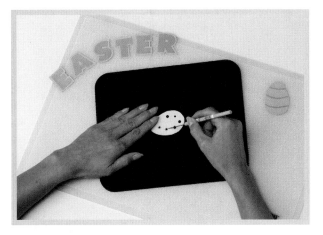

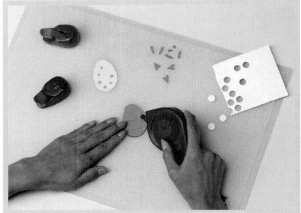

3 Use a sewing needle or straight pin to pierce designs around each punched hole. For the striped eggs, pierce holes along the edges of each stripe or in the lower layer between stripes. For the letter die cuts, pierce holes in the larger letter mats around the smaller letters.

4 Assemble egg layers and accent with punched carrots and hearts. Pierce additional holes as desired.

MATERIALS

- One sheet white paper for background
- One sheet each of yellow, green, blue and pink colored vellum (Hot Off The Press)
- Shades of yellow, green, blue, pink and orange solid-colored paper
- Mini brad fasteners (Making Memories)
- Sizzix personal die-cutting system, alphabet and eggs dies (Ellison/Provo Craft), or letter and egg templates
- Large egg die cuts (Ellison)
- $\frac{7}{16}$" and $\frac{3}{16}$" hole punches
- Heart and carrot punches (EK Success)
- Needle or straight pin
- Vellum line stickers (Mrs. Grossman's)
- Self-adhesive foam spacers

Shadow Box

CONNECT SOLID STRIPS FOR A DIMENSIONAL EFFECT

Nicole Hinrichs Ramsaroop
Horst, The Netherlands

It's not difficult to imagine all sorts of treasures to place in these shadow box designs. How about seashells, potted plants, Christmas ornaments, paper dolls or actual dollhouse miniatures? For this baby theme, first layer patterned paper on a cream background. Follow the steps on the facing page to create the shadow box for the border. Use the same technique to create the title shadow box, blocks for sticker letters and a corner embellishment. Crop and mat photos, tearing lower mat edges and shading with colored chalk. Write titles and caption; shade with chalk; cut out and mat. Punch holes in titles and connect with blue twine. Attach solid blue eyelet at top loop of twine.

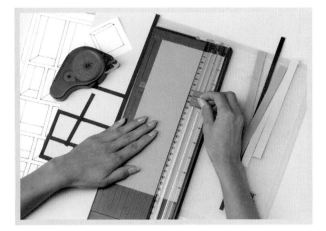

1 Transfer shadow box patterns to gray paper, or trace patterns onto gray paper using a light box. Cut ½" dark blue strips for the face, ½" light blue strips for the sides and ½" medium blue strips for the shelves.

2 Using the pattern lines as a guide, trim and mount strips to create the shadow box. Miter the corners as shown to give the illusion of depth.

3 Trim additional ½" strips for the top and right sides. Arrange these pieces with the shadow box on the page background. Shade the right side with blue chalk.

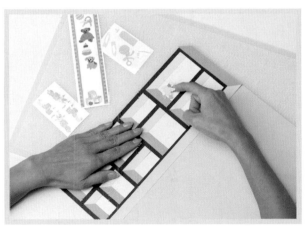

4 Decorate the shadow box with stickers.

MATERIALS

• Shadow box patterns on page 314

• Cream scrapbook page or background paper

• One sheet of blue patterned paper (Current)

• One sheet each of gray, dark blue, medium blue, light blue, pink, lavender and mint green solid-colored paper

• Colored chalk

• Various stickers related to page theme (Mrs. Grossman's)

• Black pens

• ¹⁄₁₆" hole punch

• Blue twine

• Solid blue eyelet

Decorative Edges
LAYER PERFECTLY MATCHED STRIPS

Mother's Day

Every Mother's Day,
I bring Mom lilacs from
my yard. She loves them,
but doesn't have any bushes
of her own. This year I also
made her a card, and gave her
a pretty box containing a
"certificate" for my help with
organizing her craft room.

2002

Pamela Frye, Denver, Colorado

This technique is so versatile that it's difficult to think of a theme with which it won't work. Vary the look by changing the style of decorative scissors and patterned papers. For this spring page, follow the steps on the facing page to create the border. Crop and mat photos. Cut triangles for corner accents; trim with decorative scissors and layer as shown. Print title, year and caption. Trim lower edges of title and year with decorative scissors. Double mat title with printed vellum and white paper. Embellish caption and title with purple fiber.

1 The key to lining up decorative edges is to cut the paper layers together. To do so, use removable tape to adhere a 6" strip of white paper to the back of a sheet of patterned paper. Use a pencil and ruler to draw a cutting guideline about 2" from one edge. Cut along the guideline with decorative scissors. Lay aside the larger piece and use the remaining border strip for Step 2.

2 Draw a second cutting guideline on the border strip parallel to the first cut line and about ½" from the straight edge. Cut along this second guideline with decorative scissors. Save the strips with two decorative edges for the corner and title accents.

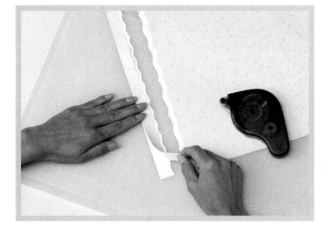

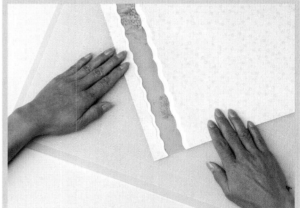

3 Remove tape and separate layers of white and patterned paper. Mat cut edge of narrow patterned strip with matching white strip. Mat cut edge of patterned page with matching white strip.

4 Cut a 2' strip of printed embossed vellum. Using a full sheet of white paper as a base, layer this strip between the decorative edges to complete the border design.

MATERIALS

- One sheet white paper for the background
- One sheet yellow patterned paper
  (Scrapbook Wizard)
- One sheet each of white, lavender and
  purple solid-colored paper
- One sheet of Juliana Lilacs printed embossed vellum
  (K & Company)
- Decorative scissors
- Purple fiber (On the Surface)

Summer

The sun is out, the breeze is warm, and there's tons to do outdoors! Family vacations, tending the garden, water play, and trips to the zoo are the joys of summer. Capture the frolicking activities on film and preserve them on pages that include:

• Marbled designs • Fancy vegetables • Tied tags • Intaglio shrink art
• Knotted twine • Twisted wire • String-tie and brad fasteners • Layered scenes
• Embellished edges

These clever and oh-so-cute concepts will provide you with hours of seasonal scrapbook fun. The hard part will be determining to which season you want to apply the concepts next!

Marbled Designs

GLUE TINY GLASS MARBLES FOR A BUMPY EFFECT

One Sunday afternoon my sweet little daughter was playing in the backyard. It was quite. Maybe too quiet! So I went to check on her. She was playing in soaked potting soil. I'm not too sure what notions were sprouting, but for whatever reason she smeared her face with the moist soil. Instead of getting angry, I saw the humor and seized the moment with my camera. Her delightful expression still brings smiles to her Mothers face. April 2002

Little Miss Bailey

Suzee Gallagher, Villa Park, California

The texture of these marbled embellishments is so appealing that you just have to rub your fingers over the smooth yet bumpy surface. This is a great technique for bringing dimension to pre-printed punch outs and die cuts, stickers and clip art. For the background of this summer theme, mat a trimmed sheet of green paper with yellow. Print caption. Triple mat photo. Create the title and border as shown on the facing page. Apply letters, bugs and other designs to title, border, caption and photo corners using self-adhesive foam spacers as desired.

1 Punch out the desired printed designs. Select the areas that you wish to embellish with tiny glass marbles. Apply clear crystal lacquer to these areas and sprinkle with marbles. Gently tap off excess.

2 Apply a coat of clear crystal lacquer to the remaining areas of each design. Allow to dry thoroughly.

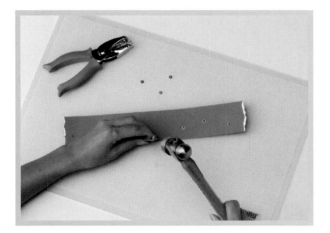

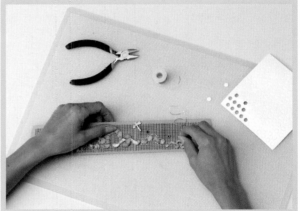

3 Cut a 2" blue strip for the border and a 5½ x 3½" rectangle for the title. Trim and apply self-adhesive screen. Randomly punch holes for eyelets. To set each eyelet, insert an eyelet on the mesh side and turn over to the backside. Insert an eyelet setter into the eyelet tube and tap several times with a small hammer. Turn back to the front side, cover eyelet with a soft cloth, and tap again with a hammer. Repeat until all eyelets are set.

4 Cut a length of thin craft wire twice the length of the border or title. Randomly lace the wire in and out of the eyelets as desired. Curve and loop the wire between eyelets. Secure the wire ends beneath an embellishment or tape to the back of the title or border.

MATERIALS

- One sheet each of white, yellow, green and periwinkle solid-colored paper
- Bugs paper punch-outs (Creative Imaginations)
- Clear crystal lacquer (Sakura Hobby Craft)
- Clear Micro Beedz (Art Accents)
- Self-adhesive mesh screen (Magic Mesh by Avant 'Card)
- ⅛" hole punch
- Colored eyelets (Impress Rubber Stamps)
- Eyelet setter
- Small hammer
- Thin craft wire (Artistic Wire)
- Self-adhesive foam spacers

Fancy Vegetables
EMBELLISH PAPER PIECINGS

Jodi Amidei, Lafayette, Colorado
Inspired by Dana Swords, Fredericksburg, Virginia

The next time you're at the craft store, pick up a few decorative items such as glitter, beads, fiber, sequins, squiggle eyes, doll hair, confetti, yarn and embroidery floss. These items come in handy when you want to add sparkle and texture to die cuts, punched shapes, template shapes, printed designs or any page element. For this garden page background, mat a trimmed sheet of light green paper with dark green. Create the embellished vegetables as shown on the facing page. For the title, mat a 6¾ x 1¾" patterned rectangle with green; adhere carrots for each letter part; complete each letter with green pen. Crop and mat photos with cream, green and patterned paper. For the left photo, accent punched and folded cream photo corners with carrots. Print and mat caption. For the border, mat a 3" patterned strip with green, tearing one long edge of each piece. Arrange vegetables on border using self-adhesive foam spacers as desired.

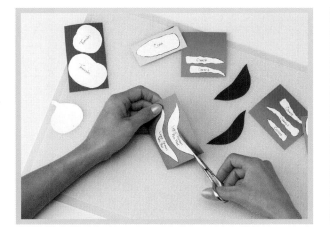

1 Use the vegetable patterns to cut out each vegetable piece from various solid-colored papers.

2 Shade each piece with colored chalk and draw details with black pen.

3 Use liquid adhesive to embellish vegetables with color-coordinated sequins, seed beads, glitter and tiny glass marbles.

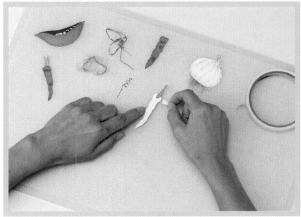

4 Tape strands of green embroidery floss to the back of the carrots. Accent onion with tan fiber. Tape spiraled lengths of green craft wire beneath the ends of the string beans.

MATERIALS

- Vegetable patterns on page 314
- One sheet each of green, light green and cream solid-colored paper
- One sheet leaf patterned paper (Keeping Memories Alive)
- Scraps of orange, red and yellow solid-colored paper for vegetables
- Colored chalk
- Black and green pens
- Orange seed beads (Westrim)
- Green sequins (Westrim)
- Red Micro Beedz (Art Accents)
- Yellow glitter (Magic Scraps)
- Green embroidery floss
- Funky Fibers™ (Lily Lake Crafts) for onion
- Green craft wire (Artistic Wire)
- Corner pocket punch (Marvy/Uchida)
- Self-adhesive foam spacer

Tied Tags

CONNECT DESIGNS WITH COLORFUL FIBER

Marpy Hayse, Katy, Texas

Use any kind of fiber or paper strips to tie together similar elements such as journaling blocks, stamped designs, stickers, die cuts, punch art or even vintage color clip art. To create the seed-packet border, follow the steps on the facing page. Mount border on left side of rust patterned background. Crop photo and mat with sage. Stamp and embellish cream mat and small tags using the same technique as for the large tags. Cut 7 x 2½" sage strip for the title; wrap fiber around right side; layer over ⅜" sage strips; adhere letter stickers. Stamp and cut out angel; shade with colored pencils. Mount angel and small tags using self-adhesive foam spacers. Mount seed label beneath vellum tag and arrange below title.

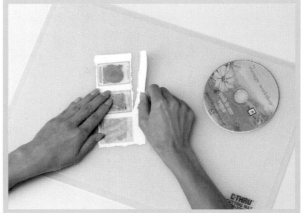

1 Stamp tags using decorative stamp and brown stamping ink.

2 Print CD-ROM seed-packet graphics sized to fit on the tags. Tear along the edges of each seed packet.

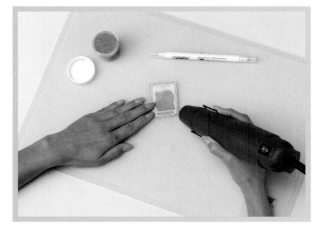

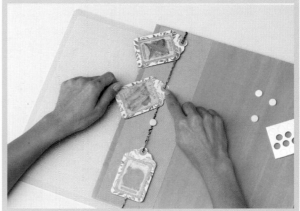

3 Emboss torn edges of seed packets using an embossing pen, embossing powder and a heat gun. Mount packets on tags. For the eyelets, punch a ⅛" hole in the center of a small punched circle. Insert copper eyelet through circle and then through tag. Set eyelet. Repeat for each tag.

4 String tags onto fiber. Mount vertically on a 3½ x 12" sage strip using self-adhesive foam spacers. Tape fiber ends to back of border strip.

VARIATION

Stamped, colored and torn seashell designs are united in this beach theme with cream-colored paper raffia. (Paper and letter stickers by Creative Imaginations, stamps by Hero Arts)

Marpy Hayse, Katy, Texas

Intaglio Shrink Art

WATCH THE MAGIC OF INCREDIBLY SHRINKING PLASTIC

Pam Hornschu for Stampendous

Shrink plastic is just plain fun. You just never get tired of watching a thin sheet of plastic shrink into a design half the size and more than twice as thick. And the design possibilities are limitless. For this zoo page, first stamp brown cheetah spots on a 9½" tan ribbed square. Crop photos and mat with pumpkin paper. Print caption on brown vellum; tear edges as well as orange and cream vellum accents. Punch ⅛" holes and adhere eyelet stickers. For the background, stamp black zebra stripes around edges of 11½" brown square; punch two ¼" holes in upper left and upper right corners. Tie together pieces of natural raffia, tying ends through punched holes. Mount tan square on brown square; mat with black background sheet. Create the shrink plastic letters as shown on the facing page. Tie each letter to the raffia with black twine and mount with self-adhesive foam spacers. To create the corner accents, stamp triangles of ivory shrink plastic; shrink and cool, flattening with the back of a stamp.

MATERIALS

- One sheet tan, ribbed solid-colored paper
- One sheet each of black, brown and pumpkin solid-colored paper
- One sheet each of orange, cream and brown vellum paper
- Zebra Stripes, Cheetah Spots, Prancing Zebra, Giraffes and Kenya Montage stamps (Stampendous)
- Black, brown, orange and white stamping inks (Stampendous)
- Class A' Peel eyelet stickers (Stampendous)
- Natural raffia
- Lettering template (Provo Craft)
- Black and ivory shrink plastic (K & B Innovations)
- Stabilo pencil
- ¼" and ⅛" hole punch
- Talcum powder
- Black twine
- Self-adhesive foam spacers

1 Trace letters from template onto scrap paper. Use a photocopy machine to enlarge letters about twice the size, keeping in mind that the letters will shrink to nearly one-half their original size when heated. Trace letters onto shrink plastic with a Stabilo pencil and cut out.

2 Punch ¼" holes at the top of each letter. Dust the front and back of each letter with talcum powder to prevent sticking during shrinkage. Before shrinking each letter, ink the stamp you want to use in Step 3. One at a time, heat each letter with an embossing gun for about 30 seconds, holding it down with an embossing stylus or other heat-safe tool. The letter will curl during heating and flatten when shrinkage is complete.

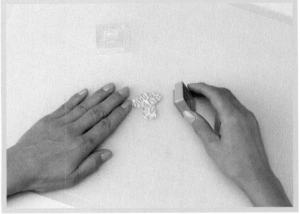

3 While the letter is still warm, immediately press an inked stamp into the shrunken plastic to reverse-emboss the image, creating an "intaglio" or carved look.

4 When the stamped letter images have dried and cooled, accent each letter by brushing it with another ink color.

VARIATION

Experiment with shrink plastic silhouette shapes (Stampendous) to create shaped and curved seashells and sea glass that look amazingly realistic. (Stamps by Stampendous on frost shrink plastic, shell stickers by Stampendous)

Pam Hornschu for Stampendous

Knotted Twine
STRING BUTTONS AND PUNCHED SHAPES

Jenna Beegle, Woodstock, Georgia

If you can tie a knot, you can easily assemble these star and heart designs. Vary the look by changing the embellishments. For example, connect hearts with pink thread for Valentine's Day, or tie balloons to a bow for a birthday theme. For this all-American page, write the title and caption with a blue pen on 1½" cream strips; shade edges with brown chalk; mat title with navy. Triple mat photo with navy, cream and burgundy. Create frayed fabric border and heart and star accents as shown on the facing page; layer with page elements on tan background.

1 Trim star printed fabric to 2½ x 11½" rectangle and fray edges. Use a Xyron machine or double-sided sheet adhesive to apply adhesive to the back of the fabric.

2 Use star pattern to cut out two burgundy stars. Punch primitive hearts and stars. Shade star edges with brown chalk. Draw heart and star details with black pen.

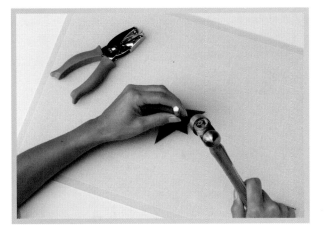

3 Punch a ⅛" hole in the center of each large star. For each star, insert a silver eyelet through the hole from the front, turn over, insert eyelet setter, and tap with a hammer. Turn to the front and tap eyelet again.

4 Thread several strands of thin white twine through each eyelet. Tie a knot on top of each star to connect the strands and prevent them from slipping through the eyelet. Punch ¹⁄₁₆" holes in the centers of the small hearts and stars. String loose ends of twine through punched shapes and buttons. Secure ends with slipknots.

MATERIALS

- Star pattern on page 315
- One sheet each of tan, burgundy, navy and cream solid-colored paper
- Navy and black pens
- Brown chalk
- Strip of star printed fabric (source unknown)
- Medium primitive star and heart and super jumbo primitive heart punches (Emagination Crafts)
- ⅛" and ¹⁄₁₆" hole punches
- Silver eyelets (Impress Rubber Stamps)
- Thin white twine or embroidery floss
- Two- and four-hole buttons

Twisted Wire
COIL AND SPIRAL COPPER WIRE

Torrey Miller, Westminster, Colorado

Craft wire is a blast. With just wire cutters and pliers you can bend, coil, twist and crimp all sorts of artistic embellishments and fasteners to hold memorabilia or photos. For this travel page, trim a sheet of pumpkin paper for the background and mat with black. Mount sheet of textured paper. Trim and punch 1¼" black strip for belt. Print caption; cut into tag shape and punch hole. Cut and punch an additional blank tag. Shade caption, blank tag and tag die cuts with brown chalk. Write year on round tag. Create and attach wire holders as shown on the facing page. Use a similar technique to bend and attach wire letters and tag accents. Adhere poster stickers to scrap paper; trim ends with stamp scissors. Mount poster stickers and photos by slipping between wire coils and mounting to page with self-adhesive foam spacers.

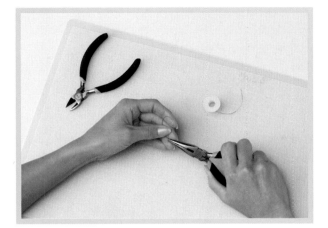

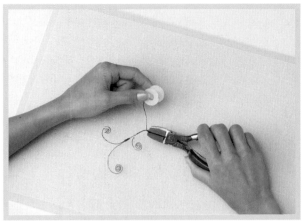

1 For each wire holder, start with a long piece of wire for the base. Cut several 3 to 4" lengths of wire for the "branches." Curl one end of each piece into a round, square or triangular flat coil. For the round coils, curl wire around the tip of round-nose jewelry pliers or a thin round object such as a nail or toothpick. For the square or triangular coils, use flat pliers to bend each wire corner.

2 Take the uncoiled end of each piece of wire and wrap it tightly around the base wire. Trim ends with wire cutters. Repeat for each coil. To keep the coils from sliding up and down the base wire, put cloth between a pair of flat pliers and pinch each coil firmly.

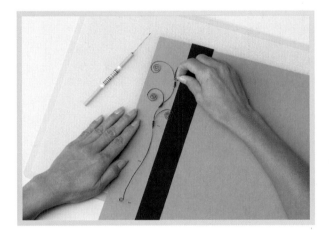

3 To attach wire holder to the background, place it in the desired position. Use a needle or straight pin to punch pairs of holes on each side of the wire. Cut 1" lengths of wire and fold in half to form U-shaped fasteners. Insert fastener ends over wire piece into two holes. Repeat for each fastener.

4 Turn page over and press fastener ends flat. Cover ends with tape.

MATERIALS

- One sheet each of tan and mustard solid-colored paper
- One sheet plus one strip black textured paper (Bazzill)
- One sheet faux reptile skin textured paper (source unknown)
- Tag die cuts (DMD Industries)
- 24-gauge copper craft wire (The Beadery)
- Wire cutters and round pliers
- Travel poster stickers (Stampa Rosa)
- Stamp decorative scissors (Fiskars)
- ¼" hole punch
- Self-adhesive foam spacers
- Brown pen

String-Tie Brad Fasteners
WIND UP A FOLDOUT BORDER

Kelly Angard, Highlands Ranch, Colorado

Re-create the string and button closure of "inter-departmental" business envelopes with a string-tie fastener for a simple foldout border. It's a fun look that also increases your page real estate. For the background, mat a trimmed sheet of olive paper with brown strips. Create the foldout border as shown on the facing page. Tear the long edge of a 5" strip of stamp patterned paper; mount at page bottom. For the pocket, mount cut and torn brown strips around the edges of an 8¼ x 5" cream vellum rectangle; adhere to page along left, bottom and right edges. Create brad fasteners for pocket using the same technique as for the foldout border. Crop and mat photos and printed captions; slip into pocket.

MATERIALS

- Fold-out pattern on page 315
- One sheet each of olive, dark olive, tan and brown solid-colored paper
- One sheet marble patterned paper (Scrap Ease)
- One sheet postage stamp patterned paper (Anna Griffin)
- One sheet cream vellum
- Lettering template (EK Success)
- Letter stickers (Creative Memories)
- Vintage Travel printed page accents (Fresh Cuts by EK Success)
- Brass brad fasteners (Creative Trends)
- Silver to Black jewelry oxidizer (source unknown)
- Cream cotton string (Making Memories) or embroidery floss
- Gold photo corners (Canson)

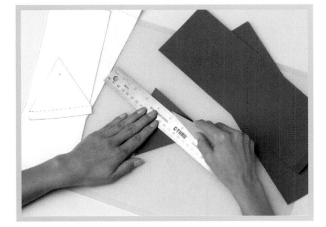

1 Transfer foldout patterns to brown paper and cut out. Use a metal ruler and bone folder to score and fold along the fold lines on the triangular and one rectangular piece.

2 Assemble the foldout border by mounting the remaining rectangular piece over the folded tabs of the other two pieces. Close the foldout border and adhere marble patterned paper to the fronts of the front flap and the triangle.

3 Embellish the front flaps with dark olive title letters, printed page accents and stamps cut from patterned paper. Prepare each brad fastener by dipping it in a jewelry oxidizer to give it an antique look. For each brad fastener, punch a ¼" small tan circle. Punch a ¼" hole in the center of each circle. Punch holes in the front flaps where you want to fasten each brad. Attach each brad through a punched circle and hole, flattening the ends on the back and taping down if necessary. Cut lengths of string and tie ends in a slipknot; wind around brad fasteners beneath punched circles.

4 Open the foldout border. Trim and mat photos; mount with gold photo corners.

This brad-fastened foldout border opens to reveal four rectangular photos. You can adapt the idea for extended journaling, panoramic photos or memorabilia.

Layered Scenes

TEAR SAND, WATER, HILLS AND SKY

Beth Rogers, Mesa, Arizona

This quick and easy idea makes a huge design impact. Change the scene to fit the venue, whether snowy hills, mountains and trees, streams and rivers or gorgeous sunsets. For this beach theme, start with a tan background. Tear blue and navy strips to layer beneath title letters. Create title letters and border as shown on the facing page. Write remaining title words with silver metallic pen. Crop and mat photos. Use similar tearing and layering technique to create photo corner accents. Print caption on white vellum paper; layer over photo and blue mat.

MATERIALS

- One sheet each of tan, navy and blue solid-colored paper
- One sheet each of blue, light blue and white vellum paper
- One sheet each of cloud (Hot Off The Press) and sand (Sandylion) patterned paper
- Block Upper lettering template (EK Success)
- Jumbo and super jumbo square punches (Marvy/Uchida)
- Silver metallic pen

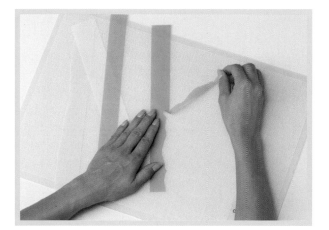

1 Cut several 11 x 1½" strips of vellum and sand patterned paper. Tear long edges of each strip.

2 Cut two 11 x 1½" strips of cloud patterned paper, one for the border and one for the title letters. Layer, overlap and adhere torn strips atop cloud strips to create scene.

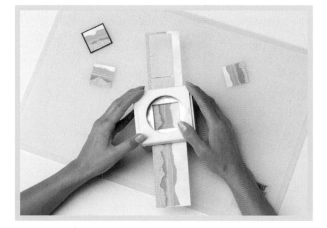

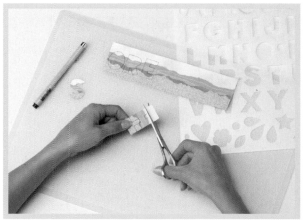

3 Insert border strip face up into upside-down jumbo square punch. Punch squares from border with minimal waste between squares. Punch super jumbo navy squares to mat each square.

4 Use template to trace letters onto second border strip. Cut out each letter using a craft knife and cutting mat.

VARIATION

Recall camping fun by punching tiny trees and layering with torn brown hills. Match the colors to the photos. (Tree punch by McGill)

Beth Rogers, Mesa, Arizona

Embellished Edges
TEXTURIZE TORN STRIPS

Brandi Ginn, Lafayette, Colorado
Inspired by Kathleen Aho, Rochester, Minnesota

The fancy edges in this beach scene not only add sparkle and texture but also mimic the high tide line at the beach. Pull colors from your photos to embellish torn edges to match your page theme. For this project, start with a light blue background. Tear and embellish strips for border following the steps on the facing page. Layer strips at page bottom. Crop and mat photos. Tear and embellish strips for the page title and photo corner accents using a similar technique, however cut out the title letters before embellishing. Write remaining title words with black pen on tan strips. Print caption. Accent border with tiny seashells and starfish.

MATERIALS

- One sheet each of blue, light blue, tan and light tan solid-colored paper
- One sheet each of light blue and dark blue patterned paper (Paper Adventures, Magenta)
- Copper embossing powder (Stampin' Up)
- Silver Micro Beedz (Art Accents)
- Blue glitter (Art Institute Glitter)
- Clear/silver seed beads (Westrim)
- Glitter glue
- Liquid adhesive
- Tiny seashells and starfish (Magic Scraps, U.S. Shell)
- Black pen

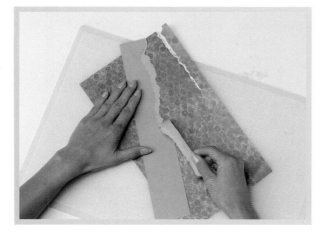

1 Tear top edges of solid and patterned strips for the border.

2 To emboss a torn edge, brush with an embossing pen, sprinkle with embossing powder, and remove excess. Heat with an embossing gun until set.

3 To embellish with tiny glass marbles, seed beads or glitter, apply liquid adhesive to torn edges. Use a generous amount of adhesive for beads. For glitter, use glitter glue, which spreads more evenly and allows the glitter to adhere without clumping. Sprinkle glued areas with embellishment and press lightly with fingertips. Gently shake off any excess.

VARIATION

Monochromatic embellishments add further elegance to this torn-edge technique. (Shaved Ice glitter by Magic Scraps)

Brandi Ginn, Lafayette, Colorado
Photos Brian Cummings, Aliso Creek, California

Fall

The leaves dance in the crisp air while pumpkins smile their silly jack-o-lantern grins and the aroma of roasted turkey wafts through the house. There's much to be thankful for with these handmade page notions and ideas!

• Vellum pockets • Stamped leaves • Lacquered stamping • Metallic leafing
• Tab-top curtains • Fancy gift bags • Paper cord mosaic • Border collage
• Aged tag art

There you have it: a year-round smorgasbord of delightful scrapbooking techniques that you can apply to any scrapbook page—regardless of its theme!

Vellum Pockets

STITCH BEADED CORNERS

Brandi Ginn, Lafayette, Colorado

Pressed flowers, punched snowflakes, movie ticket stubs and postage stamps are just a few of the things you can put in these vellum pockets. For this leafy version, start with a patterned background. For the title, stamp brown letters on tan paper and color letters with gold pen. Cut out each word; brush edges with brown ink; mat with rust paper. Mount title over fiber using self-adhesive foam spacers. Create the border as shown on the facing page. Mat photos with sage paper. Embellish photo corners in the same manner as the lower corners of the vellum pockets. Print caption; tear edges and color with brown ink; attach with mini brad fasteners.

1 Cut a 2½" sage strip and five 1¾ x 1" vellum rectangles. Adhere the first leaf sticker at the top of the border. Holding a vellum rectangle in place over the sticker, use an awl or straight pin to pierce four holes at each lower corner—two holes on the side and two holes on the bottom to form an asymmetrical X. Pierce two holes near each upper corner. Pierce through both the vellum and the sage background. Repeat this step for each leaf sticker and vellum rectangle. Pierce two additional sets of holes at the bottom of the border for the wire accent.

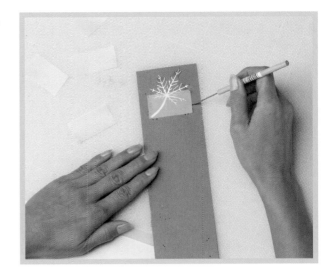

2 Thread three strands of embroidery floss on a beading needle and knot ends together. Stitch Xs across the vellum pocket corners, stringing three seed beads onto the top stitch of each X. Stitch the upper corners, stringing one bead onto each stitch. Secure loose ends to the back of the border. String seed beads onto a short length of craft wire; slip ends through pierced holes at the bottom of the border; curl ends. Mat border with rust paper; tear edges.

MATERIALS

- One sheet stripe patterned paper (Frances Meyer)
- One sheet each of rust, sage and tan solid-colored paper
- One sheet white vellum
- Letter stamps (Stampin' Up)
- Brown stamping ink (Colorbök)
- Gold metallic pen
- Adornaments fiber (K1C2)
- Self-adhesive foam spacers
- Leaf stickers (Stickopotamus)
- Awl or straight pin
- Beading needle
- Brown embroidery floss (DMC)
- Seed beads (Magic Scraps)
- Gold-colored craft wire (Darice)
- Mini brad fasteners (HyGlo/AmericanPin)

Stamped Leaves

AIR-BRUSH AN AUTUMN THEME

Terri Davenport, Toledo, Ohio

A spray bulb ink applicator is just one way to texturize a solid-colored background. You can "faux finish" any page element to add texture, depth and dimension. Try sponge painting, chalking, watercolors, or adding stripes or polka dots. Find inspiration in the patterns and theme of the photos. For this autumn page, create the border, title background and leaf accents following the steps on the facing page. Use a similar technique to splatter, stamp and wrap the title letters. Print and trim caption; splatter with ink. Mat photos and caption with rust paper.

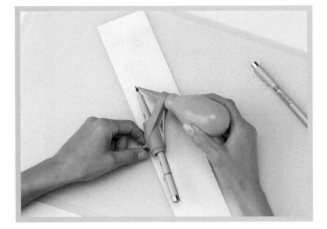

1 Cut 2¾" tan strips for the title and border and 2" tan strips for the smaller leaf accents. Insert a brush pen into a spray bulb applicator and splatter tan strips with various colors.

2 Randomly stamp leaves using brown and green stamping ink. Stamp off the edges of the title and border strips. Stamp a leaf in the center of each smaller strip. When you are finished stamping, mat each strip with rust paper.

3 Wrap border with jute. Use a craft knife to cut slits in the smaller leaf accents; wrap jute through slits and around edge. Secure all loose ends to the backside of each piece.

MATERIALS

- One sheet each of tan and rust solid-colored paper
- Inkworkx spray bulb applicator (EK Success)
- Brush-tip colored pens
- Leaf and letter stamps (Stampin' Up)
- Green and brown stamping inks
- Jute

Lacquered Stamping
CREATE GLOSSY, DIMENSIONAL IMAGES

MaryJo Regier, Littleton, Colorado
Inspired by Jan Monahan, Dayton, Ohio

Color crystal lacquer adds a subtle hint of dimension to stamped images, stickers and pre-printed die cuts or punch outs. Embossing before lacquering raises the image just enough to "corral" the paint. You can also color theme clip art by first tracing with an embossing pen and then embossing with powder. For the background, trim a sheet of cream paper and mat with orange. Mount a 10½" evergreen square at an angle on the background. Print words for title and caption mat on cream paper. Trim title to 2¼" strip and caption to 7 x 4½" rectangle. Mount photo over caption mat. Wrap raffia strips around ends of title strip and left edge and right corner of page; secure loose ends to the back with tape. Follow the steps on the facing page to stamp, lacquer and cut out pumpkins. Use a similar technique to create title letters. Mount pumpkins and letters with self-adhesive foam spacers, tucking edges beneath raffia as desired.

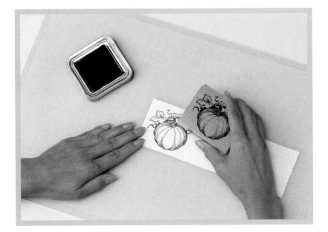

1 Stamp pumpkins on cream paper with embossing ink.

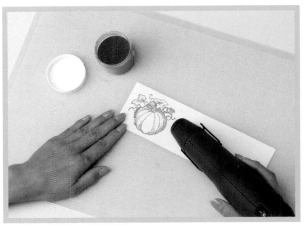

2 Sprinkle each image with gold embossing powder and tap off excess. Heat with an embossing gun to set powder.

3 Color image with 3-D color crystal lacquer, shading as desired. For added dimension, let the first coat dry and then apply a second coat. Allow each coat to dry at least 30 minutes.

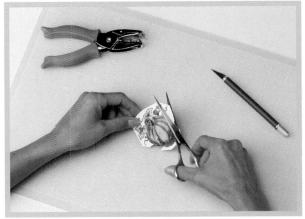

4 Silhouette-crop each stamped image. Use a craft knife to cut around vines and a small hole punch to cut holes in vines.

MATERIALS

- One to two sheets each of orange, cream and evergreen solid-colored paper
- Natural raffia
- Pumpkin stamp (PSX Design)
- Letter stamps (Close To My Heart)
- Embossing ink pad
- Gold embossing powder
- Embossing heat gun
- Small hole punch
- 3-D colored crystal lacquer (Sakura Hobby Craft)
- Self-adhesive foam spacers

Metallic Leafing
GILD STAMPED IMAGES

Jodi Amidei, Lafayette, Colorado

Metallic leafing is available in a variety of colors, so you can easily find colors to coordinate with any theme. Start with a black background. Create the border and title as described on the facing page. Crop and double mat photos with cream and rust paper. Punch and fold black photo corners. Use tape adhesive to embellish photo corners with metallic leaf. Cut an additional cranberry mat for the photo with corners. Print and double mat caption. Stamp, gild and cut out an additional leaf; mount with self-adhesive foam spacers.

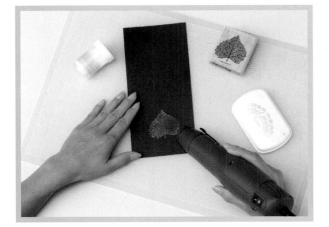

1 Stamp leaves with clear embossing ink on black paper. Sprinkle powder adhesive over the image and shake off excess. Heat with embossing gun until image becomes shiny and tacky. Do not overheat.

2 Use a medium stiff brush to apply metallic leaf until image is completely covered. Brush off excess.

3 Gently buff each image with a soft cloth or old sock to polish and remove loose flakes.

4 Cut a 2' black strip for the border. Apply tape adhesive to both long edges. Apply metallic leaf in the same manner as Steps 2 and 3. Mount gilded leaves on border strip using self-adhesive foam spacers for every other leaf.

5 For the title, trace the first letter using a lettering template and glue pen. Let the glue dry to a tacky stage and then apply metallic leaf as described in Steps 2 and 3. Repeat for each remaining letter. Trim title and mat with rust paper.

Tab-Top Curtains
BUTTON DOWN PAPER FLAPS

Torrey Miller, Westminster, Colorado
Photos Tracy Johnson, Thornton, Colorado; MaryJo Regier, Littleton, Colorado

This whimsical design, based on the popular curtain style, can also be embellished with beads, flowers, tassels, snaps, eyelets, ribbons and bows—whatever best suits your page theme. For this button version, trim and mat a patterned sheet for the background. Write title word at top left corner. Follow the steps on the facing page to create the tab-top section. For the title, cut evergreen letters using template. Double mat each letter with punched squares, mounting every other letter at an angle; draw letter highlights in white ink. To form hanging loops for each letter, punch two holes and thread ends of a 6" piece of yarn through each hole from the back. "Hang" letters over buttons and mount on background; tie knots and trim yarn ends. Mat photos with cream. Trim opposite corners of turkey photo; mat again; fold corners; adhere buttons; mat again. Print and mat caption.

1 Transfer tab-top pattern to the back of evergreen pat-terned paper and cut out. Mount a 3" evergreen strip over the lower part of the tab section on the wrong side.

2 Mount a second 11½ x 9½" sage patterned square so that it covers all but about ¾" of the evergreen strip. Mount a ⅜" wood-grain patterned strip at the top of the evergreen strip with self-adhesive foam spacers. Bend tabs down over dowel and adhere points to sage patterned square.

MATERIALS

- Tab-top pattern on page 316
- One sheet each of cream, sage, evergreen and dark evergreen solid-colored paper
- One to two sheets each of sage and evergreen patterned paper (Anna Griffin)
- One ⅜" strip of wood-grain patterned paper (Frances Meyer)
- Green pen
- Self-adhesive foam spacers
- Buttons
- Glue dots (Glue Dots, Int'l)
- Lettering template (Scrap Pagerz)
- Square punches (EK Success, Marvy/Uchida)
- ⅛" hole punch
- Yarn

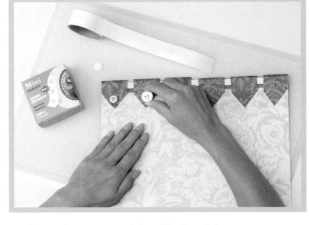

3 Mount buttons over tabs with glue dots.

VARIATION

For a softer, "less dimensional" version of the tab-top design, select coordinating shades of solid, printed (Doodlebug Design) and vellum (Paper Adventures) papers. Attach the tabs and folded photo corners with white flower and lavender eyelets (Making Memories).

Torrey Miller, Westminster, Colorado
Photo Pam Klassen, Westminster, Colorado

Fancy Gift Bags
WRAP UP YOUR HOLIDAY SHOPPING

Nicole Hinrichs Ramsaroop
Horst, The Netherlands

You can adapt these holiday bags for any gift-giving occasion from birthdays and anniversaries to weddings and baby showers. Create the gift bags as shown on the facing page. Mount two bags on a 3½" matted strip of brown corrugated paper. Mount border on left side of brown background. Cut 4" brown corrugated square in half for lower right corner; mount last shopping bag over triangle. Cut title letters using computer font as template; layer with fiber and untwisted paper raffia on brown rectangle; tear edges; double mat with white and gold foil tissue. Print and mat caption. Crop and arrange photos. Color bag and photo labels as shown on the facing page; use the same technique to color handwritten date for title. Mat labels with brown paper or white mulberry.

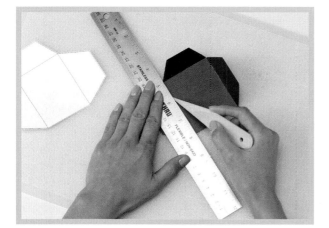

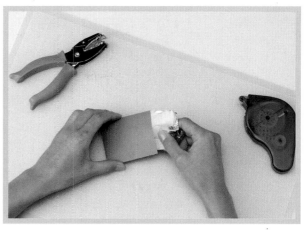

1 Use bag pattern to cut out three brown bags. Before folding bags, use a metal edge ruler and a bone folder or embossing stylus to score along fold lines.

2 Punch small holes at the upper edge of each bag for the handles. Gather and crumple together two 3" foil and mulberry squares; tuck inside bag. Secure on the backside with tape.

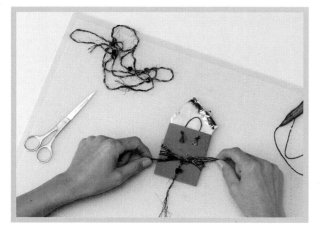

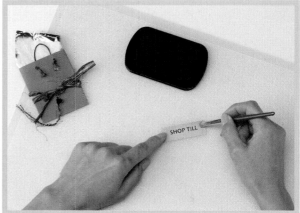

3 For the handle, insert ends of untwisted paper raffia into punched holes; tie knots and trim ends. Combine lengths of untwisted paper raffia with fiber; tie around bag and knot on the front side; trim ends.

4 Print labels for bags and photos and cut out. Use a small stiff brush and brown stamping ink to stipple color onto each tag with an up and down pouncing motion.

VARIATION

Four birthday candles light up this colorful birthday page. Torn pieces of colored and patterned paper and chunky, textured fiber lend a festive look to the gift bags.

Nicole Hinrichs Ramsaroop, Horst, The Netherlands

Paper Cord Mosaic
REARRANGE STAMPED AND PATTERNED STRIPS

Tricia Morris for Club Scrap

These mosaics are simply gorgeous and the colors can be changed to fit any page theme. You build them using strips of paper rather than cutting and arranging tiny squares. Follow the steps on the facing page to learn the technique. For the background, use eyelets to attach an 8½" square of patterned vellum diagonally to a sheet of mustard paper. For the corners, cut mosaics into triangles and double mat long edges. For the photo, cut another mosaic strip in half and double mat outside edges. Arrange strips above and below photo on mustard and brown mats. Cut, stamp and mat large tag; adhere eyelet and fiber; write caption; mat with mosaic strip and brown paper. Write captions on mini tags; shade with yellow ink; adhere with mini brad fasteners and self-adhesive foam spacers. Sew beads to shaded yellow scrap; write year.

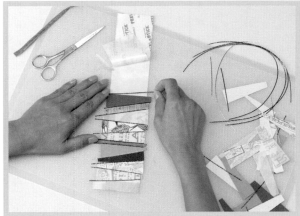

1 Randomly stamp solid-colored paper to create custom designs. Choose coordinating patterned papers. Cut stamped and patterned paper strips at least 2½" wide at random angles.

2 Cut a strip of double-sided tape at least 2" wide. Remove one side of the backing and lay on a flat surface, sticky side up. Starting at one end of the tape strip, adhere a paper strip, then a piece of paper cord, then a different paper strip. Continue this process until the tape strip is covered.

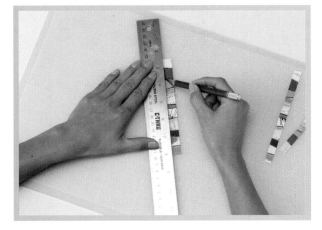

3 Using a metal edge ruler and a craft knife, trim excess paper and cord from both edges of the tape. Then cut the border into long strips approximately ½" wide.

4 Alternate the direction of every other strip so that the colors are rearranged and produce a mosaic effect. Mount the cut strips on another piece of double-sided tape, alternating strips with lengths of paper cord, trimming as needed. Mat each completed design.

MATERIALS

- One sheet each of mustard, light brown and dark brown solid-colored paper (Club Scrap)
- One sheet patterned vellum (Club Scrap)
- Coordinating solid and patterned papers for mosaic
- Miscellaneous stamps and stamping ink for mosaic
- Various colors of Mizuhiki paper cord (Yasutomo and Company)
- Gold-colored eyelets (Making Memories)
- Fiber
- Black pen
- Mini tags
- Mini brad fasteners (Creative Impressions)
- Letter and amber beads (Westrim)
- Self-adhesive foam spacers

Border Collage
BLEND PHOTOS AND MEMORABILIA

Pam Klassen, Westminster, Colorado
Tree by David Cobb, Thornton, Colorado

MATERIALS

- Tree pattern on page 316
- One sheet each of cream and black solid-colored paper
- Black pen
- Colored chalk
- Color-copied photos, memorabilia, pressed flowers, etc. for collage
- Skeletonized leaves (All Night Media)
- Lettering template (Wordsworth)

The collage technique is a great way to use up extra photos and memorabilia from any occasion. Layer Christmas cards, ticket stubs, airline tickets, birthday confetti or whatever elements fit the theme. For the family tree design, use the pattern to trace the tree onto cream background paper. Outline tree and write names with black pen. Shade tree and background with colored chalk. Create the top and right collage borders as shown on the facing page. To mount the title, trim around the uppermost leaves on the tree through the background paper; slip title border beneath leaves and mount on top edge of page. Write caption on cream strip and mat with brown.

1 Gather collage elements such as color photocopies of heritage photos, memorabilia, skeletonized leaves, pressed flowers and ribbon. Collect enough material for two collages—one for the side border and one for the title.

2 Arrange and layer items as desired to form collage on right side. Mount items and trim edges as necessary.

3 For the title, arrange and mount a second collage on a 3" strip of paper, trimming edges as necessary. Use template to pencil letter outlines on collage. Using a craft knife and cutting mat, cut out each letter through all layers. Mount a 2" black strip beneath the letter openings.

Aged Tag Art
SHADE WITH COLORED CHALK

Grandma Mary in the 1930's - on the farm in a dress she made herself and in a beautiful formal portrait.

Betsy Bell Sammarco, New Canaan, Connecticut

MATERIALS

- Tag pattern on page 316
- One sheet green patterned paper (Anna Griffin)
- One sheet each of cream, lavender, sage and brown solid-colored paper
- ¾" square punch
- ¼" and ⅛" hole punches
- Black brush pen and journaling pens
- Colored chalk
- Floral stickers (Debbie Mumm)
- Cream embroidery floss (DMC)

This simple aging technique works well not only for heritage photos but also for outdoor, western and masculine themes. Add the technique to any layout for a vintage or old-fashioned effect. Create and "age" tags for title as shown on the facing page. Wrap lengths of cream embroidery floss through each tag hole and tie bows. Mount tags at top of green patterned background. Use the same technique to create and age narrow ¾" tags for the border, cutting small brown rectangles and punching ⅛" holes at each end; tie together with embroidery floss. Write and age caption; adhere flower sticker. Crop and mat photos, using an aged mat for right photo. Cut out and age cream corner accents and adhere stickers.

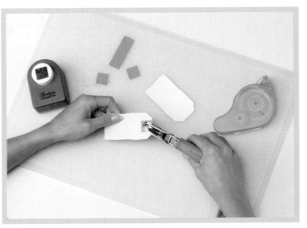

1 Use pattern to trace tags onto cream paper. Cut out tags.

2 Punch ¾" brown squares and adhere to top of each tag. Punch ¼" holes through the center of each square.

3 Color tag edges with

edges with brown chalk. Adhere stickers.

VARIATION

Shade stamped tags (stamps by Stampin' Up) with brightly colored chalk for a contemporary take on the aging technique. The torn edges on the patterned border background (All My Memories) are slightly curled up for added texture.

Brandi Ginn, Lafayette, Colorado

Project Patterns

Use these reproducible project patterns to complete scrapbook pages featured in this book. Enlarge patterns on a photocopier by the percentage shown. When transferring patterns to your paper of choice, be sure to note solid, continuous lines for cut lines and dotted lines for fold lines.

Row houses, pages 228–229 (200%)

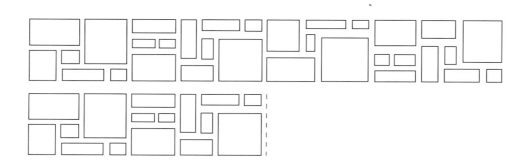

Vellum stained glass, page 248 (200%)

312

COOKIES

Frosted letters, page 250 (200%)

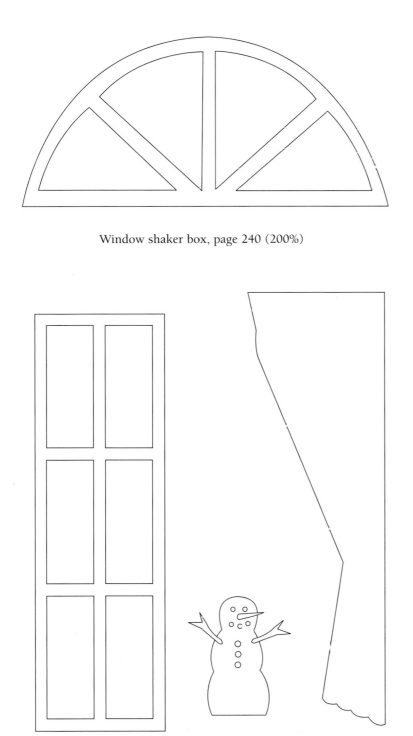

Window shaker box, page 240 (200%)

Peek-a-boo window, page 244 (200%)

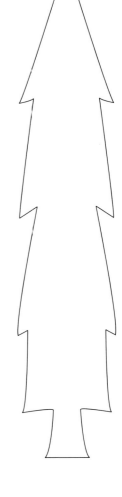

Threaded accents, page 252 (200%)

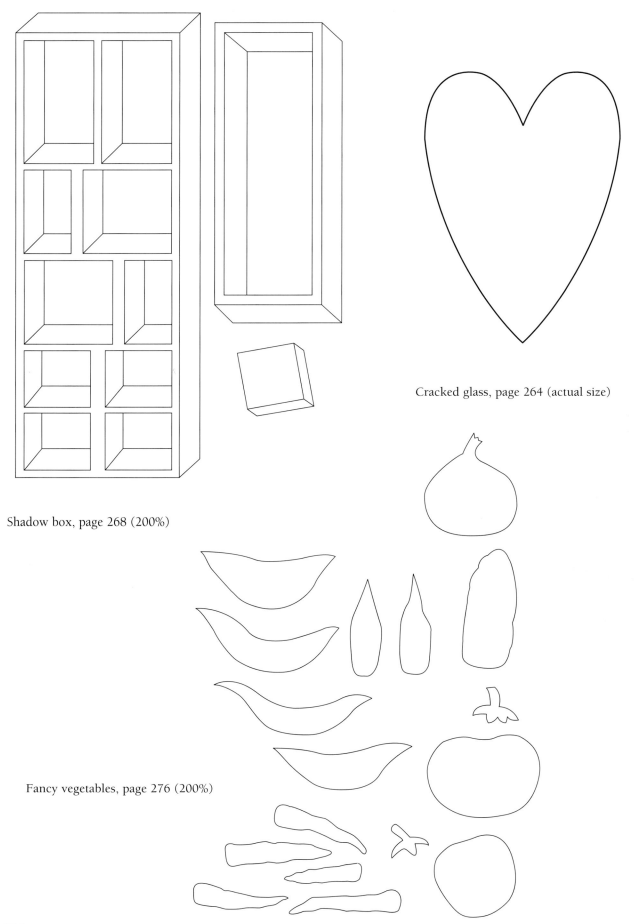

Shadow box, page 268 (200%)

Cracked glass, page 264 (actual size)

Fancy vegetables, page 276 (200%)

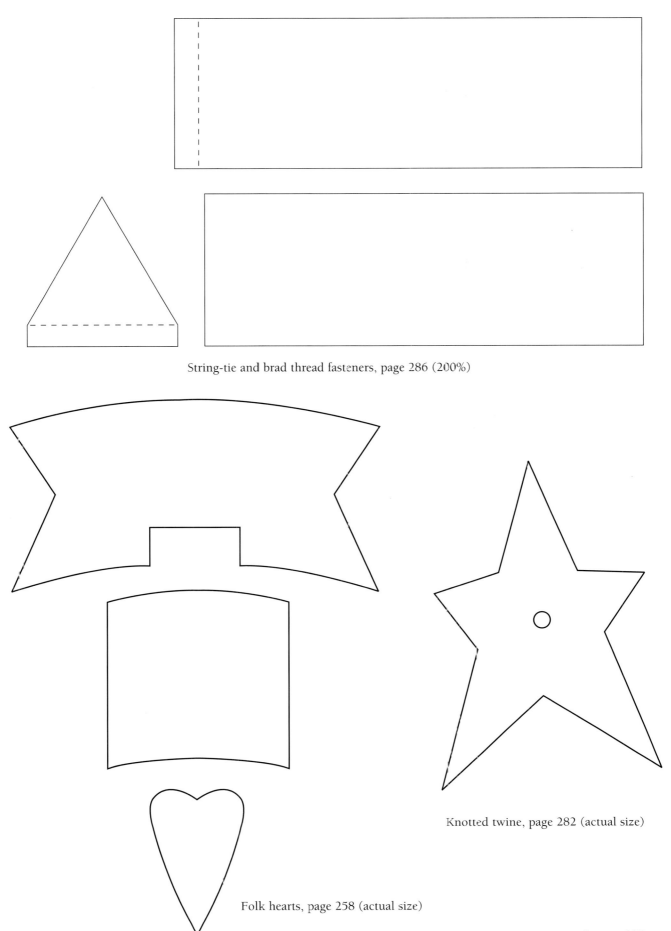

String-tie and brad thread fasteners, page 286 (200%)

Knotted twine, page 282 (actual size)

Folk hearts, page 258 (actual size)

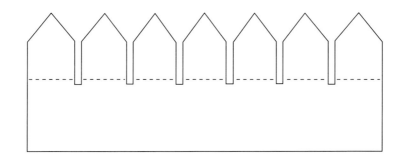

Tab-top curtains, page 302 (200%)

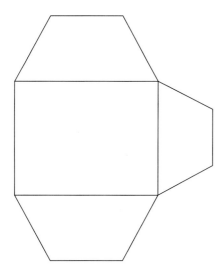

Fancy gift bags, page 304 (200%)

Border collage, page 308 (200%)

Aged tag art, page 310 (actual size)

316

Additional Instructions & Credits

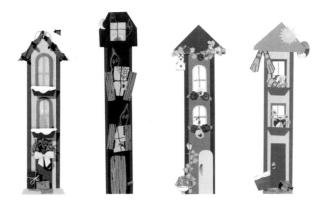

Row Houses
Start with the pattern on page 312. Transfer pattern pieces to papers of choice; cut out. Reassemble pieces to form row house, using vellum or cut apart page protectors for window "glass." Place seasonal or theme-appropriate stickers or punched shapes behind glass. Accent house with additional seasonal or theme-appropriate embellishments such as punched shapes, stickers, curled wire, eyelets, fasteners, buttons and embroidery thread. Adhere accents with self-adhesive foam spacers for dimension, if desired. Torrey Miller, Westminster, Colorado, Inspired by Lynn Schwiebert, Osceola, Wisconsin

Summertime is Family Time
Begin with a color-blocked background of red, white and blue patterned papers (Keeping Memories Alive). Then follow the instructions above to create a patriotic row house; mount on left side of page. Double mat photo, accent with curled wire and punched stars; adhere. Create matted title using a lettering template (Scrapbook Specialties), accent in same manner and mount atop decorative-scissor cut paper strip with self-adhesive foam spacers. Create a journaling block and corner accent to finish the page. Photo Greg Baron, Broomhall, Pennsylvania

Sources

The following companies manufacture products featured in this book. Please check your local retailers to find these materials. In addition, we have made every attempt to properly credit the items mentioned in this book. We apologize to any company that we have listed incorrectly or where the sources were unknown to us, and we would appreciate hearing from you.

3L Corp.
(800) 828-3130
www.3lcorp.com

3M Stationery
(800) 364-3577
www.3m.com

All My Memories
(888) 553-1998
www.allmymemories.com

All Night Media
(800) 782-6733

Anna Griffin, Inc.
(888) 817-8170
www.annagriffin.com

Art Accents
(360) 733-8989
www.artaccents.net

Art Institute Glitter Inc.
(877) 909-0805

Artistic Wire Ltd.™
(630) 530-7567
www.artisticwire.com

Avant 'Card
www.avantcard.com.au

Bazzill Basics Paper
(480) 558-8557
www.bazzillbasics.com

Beadery®, The/Greene
Plastics Corp.
(401) 539-2432

Biblical Impressions
(877) 587-0941
www.biblical.com

Blumenthal Lansing
Company
(563) 538-4211

Canson®, Inc.
(800) 628-9283

Carl Mfg. USA, Inc.
(800) 257-4771
www.carl-products.com

ChartPak
(800) 628-1910
www.chartpak.com

Close To My Heart®
(800) 655-6552
www.closetomyheart.com

Club Scrap™, Inc.
(888) 634-9100
www.clubscrap.com

Colorbök™, Inc.
(800) 366-4660
www.colorbok.com

Craf-T Products
(507) 235-3996

Creative Imaginations
(800) 942-6487
www.cigift.com

Creative Memories®
(800) 468-9335
www.creativememories.com

Creative Paperclay® Co.
(805) 484-6648
www.paperclay.com

Creative Trends
(877) 253-7687

C-Thru® Ruler Co., The
(800) 243-8419
www.cthruruler.com

Current®, Inc.
(800) 848-2848
www.currentinc.com

Daler-Rowney USA
(609) 655-5252

Darice, Inc.
(800) 321-1494
www.darice.com

Debbie Mumm®
(888) 819-2923
www.debbiemumm.com

Delta Technical Coatings,
Inc. (800) 423-4135

DMC Corp.
(973) 589-0606
www.dmc.com

DMD Industries, Inc.
(800) 805-9890
www.dmdind.com

Doodlebug Design Inc.™
(801) 966-9952

Duncan Enterprises
(559) 294-3282

EK Success™ Ltd.
(800) 524-1349
www.eksuccess.com

Ellison® Craft & Design
(800) 253-2238
www.ellison.com

Emagination Crafts, Inc.
(630) 833-9521
www.emaginationcrafts.com

Family Treasures, Inc.®
(800) 413-2645
www.familytreasures.com

Fibers By the Yard
www.fibersbytheyard.com

Fiskars, Inc.
(800) 950-0203
www.fiskars.com

Frances Meyer, Inc.®
(800) 372-6237
www.francesmeyer.com

Glue Dots International
(wholesale only)
(888) 688-7131
www.gluedots.com

Hero Art® Rubber Stamps,
Inc. (800) 822-4376
www.heroarts.com

Hot Off The Press, Inc.
(800) 227-9595
www.paperpizzaz.com

Hyglo®/AmericanPin
(800) 821-7125

Impress Rubber Stamps
(206) 901-9101
www.impressrubber-
stamps.com

Indygo Junction
(913) 341-5559
www.indygojunctioninc.com

Jesse James & Co., Inc.
(610) 435-0201

Joshuas (wholesale only)
(972) 423-1827

K1C2, LLC
(805) 676-1176

K & B Innovations
(262) 966-0305

K & Company
(888) 244-2083
www.kandcompany.com

Karen Foster Design
(801) 451-9779
www.karenfosterdesign.com

Keeping Memories Alive®
(800) 419-4949
www.scrapbooks.com

Lily Lake Crafts
(480) 659-5616
www.lilylakecrafts.com

Magenta Rubber Stamps
(800) 565-5254
www.magentarubber-
stamps.com

Magic Scraps™
(972) 385-1838
www.magicscraps.com

Making Memories
(800) 286-5263
www.makingmemories.com

Marvy® Uchida
(800) 541-5877
www.uchida.com

Photo Contributors

Artist Index

We took these photos on our trip to the island of Kauai in November 2001

ALOHA!

SCRAPBOOK LETTERING

50 classic and creative alphabets from the
nation's top scrapbook lettering artists

**MEMORY
MAKERS
BOOKS**

CONTENTS

ntroduction Do you remember when you first learned to write your name in cursive? After much practice, you mastered a new way of connecting letters. Once you grasped the basics, you spent hours doodling your name, experimenting with different ways of writing it. It seemed essential that your signature perfectly convey your style or personality.

By now your signature is so familiar that you can write it without thinking. With a little effort, you can become equally adept at any lettering style in this book. It's not a matter of artistic talent. It's simply a matter of practice.

Why make the effort? Because creative lettering, is the best and least expensive way to unify a scrapbook page design. Your lettered title can make or break a finished page, and your journaling is essential when telling the stories behind the photos. Lettering adds a personal, artistic and homemade touch that is custom-tailored to your page theme and colors.

This book is designed to be used in a number of ways. You may wish to freehand draw the lettering styles seen on these pages. Mastering the technique may take some practice, but will result in a sense of accomplishment and unique titles. You may also choose to photocopy your selected alphabet, enlarging or reducing it as desired. Cut out individual letters and use them to form eye-catching titles. Or trace the letters, using one of the techniques shown on the following pages, onto your paper to create your page title. Cut and adhere them to your scrapbook page.

This book contains 50 different lettering styles. It includes the best alphabets published in *Memory Makers* over the past few years as well as innovative new styles developed by some of the nation's top scrapbook artists. For each lettering style, you'll find a complete set of characters, how-to instructions and scrapbook page illustrations. Use this multitude of design ideas as a starting point for customizing a style to fit your own specific theme or purpose.

Once you discover the creative possibilities, you'll find that the joy of creative lettering is making it truly your own, just like your signature. Happy lettering!

Michele

Michele Gerbrandt
Founding Editor, *Memory Makers®*

TOOLS AND SUPPLIES

Practicing the art of creative lettering requires a few essential tools that you may already have on hand.

Pencils

Use a comfortable, easy-to-erase pencil for light tracing and drawing freehand. Choose from standard pencils that can be sharpened or mechanical pencils with lead refills available in different lead weights.

Ruled notebook or graph paper

Keep plenty of ruled notebook or graph paper on hand for practicing different lettering styles, whether tracing or drawing freehand.

Graphing ruler

Use the lines and grid marks of a graphing ruler (see page 327) to help you keep lettering straight and evenly spaced.

Pens and markers

Use archival quality pigment ink pens, which are fade-resistant, waterproof and colorfast. The chart on the right illustrates the variety of pen styles and the results each one creates. A black fine-tip pen is good for journaling and tracing letter outlines. A black bullet-tip pen lets you draw bolder letters and thicker outlines.

Non-abrasive eraser

Non-abrasive erasers safely remove pencil marks without tearing the paper. They are available in different sizes, as well as retractable, pen-styles with refillable eraser sticks.

Paper for title and journaling blocks

Unless you're writing directly on the scrapbook page, you'll need solid-colored, acid-free scrapbook paper on which to pen your lettering for page titles and journaling blocks.

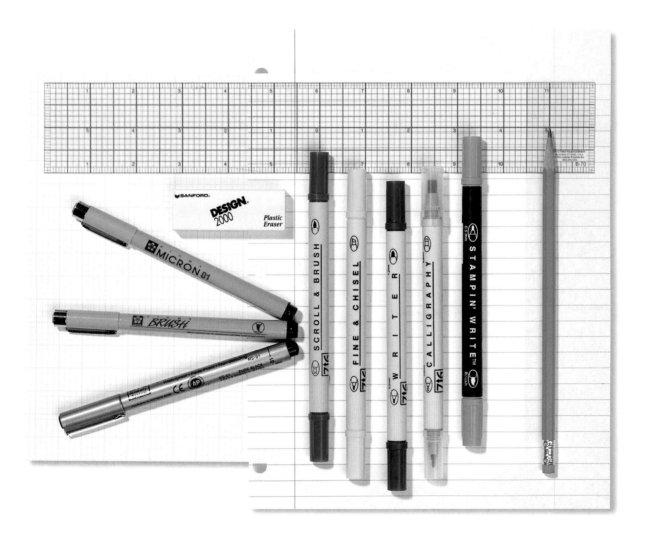

Tools for transferring and tracing lettering

These optional items help make it easier to trace the lettering shown (see page 326 for tips on using these items) in this book and to work with the lettering once it is traced.

- Access to a photocopier for enlarging or reducing letters

- A sunny window or a light box for tracing

- Removable artist's tape to anchor photocopies and paper while tracing

- White typing or copier paper

- Transfer paper

- Translucent paper or vellum

- Embossing stylus

- Scissors, a craft knife and a cutting mat

- Photo-safe adhesives for mounting

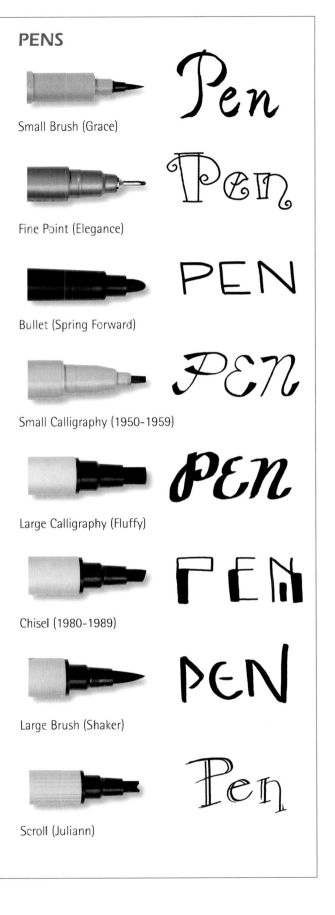

PENS

Small Brush (Grace)

Fine Point (Elegance)

Bullet (Spring Forward)

Small Calligraphy (1950-1959)

Large Calligraphy (Fluffy)

Chisel (1980-1989)

Large Brush (Shaker)

Scroll (Juliann)

METHODS FOR REPRODUCING LETTERING

You can re-create the lettering styles in this book through either tracing or freehand drawing. Tracing letters can help you make beautiful titles and will also help you develop the skills needed to more easily and confidently draw the characters. Several tracing methods are detailed below.

How to trace letters

Before attempting any of the illustrated tracing methods photocopy the alphabet you wish to reproduce, enlarging or reducing it to suit your needs. If the alphabet shown in this book is the perfect size for your project, simply trace it onto white scrap paper. Once you have a complete alphabet on white paper, you're ready to trace the letters to create scrapbook titles.

Light box or sunny window

For light-colored papers, use artist's tape to attach your selected alphabet to a light box, sunny window or an underlit glass table. Lightly pencil guidelines on the paper on which you wish to create your title. Tape this paper atop the alphabet. Trace letters one at a time, in appropriate positions, until your message is complete.

Translucent paper or vellum

Trace any lettering style through translucent paper such as vellum, tracing paper or thin white paper. Lightly pencil guidelines on the paper and lay it over the copy of the selected alphabet. Trace letters one at a time, in appropriate positions, until your message is complete.

Transfer paper

Use white or yellow transfer paper to trace onto heavy, dark-colored paper. Before transferring lettering, trace it onto scrap paper, using any of the described methods. Place traced lettering atop transfer paper. Layer both sheets of paper (traced and transfer) over a sheet of dark-colored paper. Trace. Use graphite transfer paper for tracing onto light-colored paper.

Embossing stylus

If you don't have transfer paper and want to trace onto dark paper, use an embossing stylus. First trace the lettering onto scrap paper, then place the lettering over dark paper on top of a soft surface such as a cutting mat. When you trace the lettering with an embossing tool, it leaves an indentation that may be traced over with an opaque pen.

How to draw letters freehand

If you are relatively new to freehand lettering, create your title on vellum paper. Place the transparent sheet over lined notebook or graph paper, then follow the underlying grids and lines to maintain consistent letter heights and spacing. Curvy, more arbitrary lettering styles are a good choice for novices because they require less precision and are more forgiving of errors.

Following, are the basic steps for drawing letters freehand. Once you recognize the different components of a lettering style, it becomes much easier to re-create. Drawing letters freehand takes practice, practice, practice!

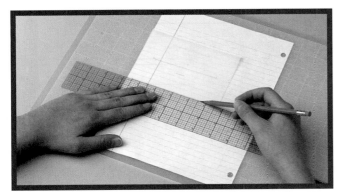

1 Use a ruler to lightly pencil any necessary guidelines, including those for spacing.

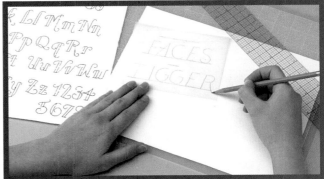

2 Sketch the basic shape of each letter without any stroke embellishments.

3 Outline in pencil any wide, thick or fill-in areas as desired.

4 Add any stroke embellishments such as curves, swirls, flowers or other details.

5 Erase and revise as necessary until you're satisfied with each letter.

6 Outline letters with an appropriate pen, then color and embellish if desired (see pages 330–331).

PAGE DESIGN TIPS FOR LETTERING

A great scrapbook page is a work of art. It showcases photos, journaling and embellishments in a way that conveys a message and pleases the eye. Use these tips to help guide you through the process of pulling together your completed page or spread. Remember that a strong scrapbook page is made even more powerful with the appropriate, beautifully lettered title.

2 Match your page theme or style

Choose a lettering style that fits the theme and mood of the page but don't overdo it. Use elaborate letters only for very short titles, or for specific words or letters within a title. Too many elaborate letters draw attention from your photographs. If your page is formal, use a formal lettering style. If your page is whimsical, use a whimsical lettering style.

1 Plan ahead

Determine your page layout and design before you start lettering. Consider photo selection, page theme, paper colors, embellishments and text blocks. Before permanently mounting elements, loosely arrange them on your page. Use scrap paper placeholders for the title and journaling blocks.

3 Determine size, design and placement

If a title is too large, it will overwhelm your layout. If it is too small, it will get lost on your scrapbook page. When designing a title, sketch it in different sizes and styles. Select a title that will work in proportion to the other page elements.

If you have a large space to fill with a short title consider matting the title several times. Or separate the letters that make up the title and mat each individually. String them across the page, inserting small embellishments such as beads, if you wish. If your title is too large for the available space, create it on vellum and mount it so it overlaps other page elements..

4 Disguise your mistakes

We all make mistakes. When it's an "oops" with a permanent pen, you can either live with it (after all, it adds character!), or disguise it. Turn a mistake into a pen stroke embellishment—such as a flower, star or other theme-related doodle—or hide it beneath a theme-related sticker or punched shape.

HOW TO ADD COLOR AND EMBELLISHMENTS

There are dozens of ways to add color and embellishments to your lettering. You can color, shade, paint or chalk lettering. Doodle on it, or in it. Add shadows or enhance finished lettering with stickers, punch art, glitter, stitching. embossing and more. How you add color and embellishments depends upon the lettering style and the look that you wish to achieve. The possibilities are limitless.

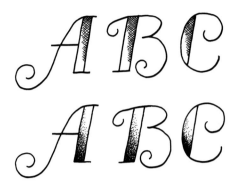

Shading with pens and pencils

Black and colored pens generally produce a solid and saturated effect that is great for shading. Simply draw dots, lines or "cross hatches." Use two different colors for a more complex look.

Graduating pencil color

A "fill-in" lettering style has wide open portions that scream to be filled with color and shading. Try graduating the pressure used when applying color to create the illusion that a light source is falling upon the letter. Use less pressure or a blender pencil to soften the transition from dark to light color.

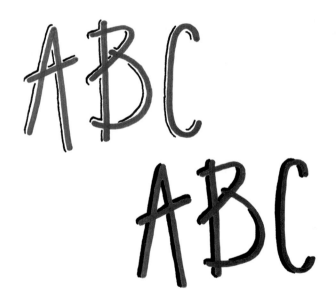

Shadowing

Pencils, chalks and pens are ideal for adding simple shadows to lettering. Simply trace along the edges of your colored lettering. The wider your traced line, the more significant and dramatic the shadow will look.

Shading with chalk

For a subtle look, try adding color with chalk, using a small, sponge-tip applicator for more control. You can shade around each letter as well as color any fill-in areas.

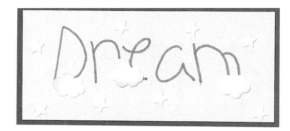

More colorants to try

Colorants such as stamping inks, embossing inks and powders, glitter and glitter glue can be used to accent lettering.

Using stickers, die cuts and punched shapes

Embellishments are the icing on the cake of creative lettering. Stickers, small die cuts and punched shapes are great letter accents, and can also be used to hide pen mistakes.

Freehand or patterned paper "fill"

Create fill patterns by drawing lines, plaids, polka dots or stars. Or use patterned paper to fill in letters.

More embellishments to try

Fabric, embroidery thread, ribbon, fibers, raffia, jute, beads, buttons, sequins, eyelets, wire, brad fasteners, pressed flowers and leaves—virtually any craft supply—can easily be used to enhance your lettering!

A TOUCH OF CLASS

Trends may come and go, but elegance never goes out of style. Like a slender silver candlestick, a flawless black sheath, a gracefully shared compliment, elegance is recognized and appreciated for its classic appeal. A classic lettering style is also universally embraced. Whether it sports sweet little loops, the vulnerable simplistic lines of a child's printing, the confident, smooth curves of a femme fatale or a tailored pinstripe masculine look, you're sure to find a place and a purpose for it within your scrapbook.

BOW TIE

If a scrapbook page is a wrapped present, then this flowing cursive alphabet is the ribbon. You can almost imagine curling different lengths into each casually elegant letter. The widened points even mimic the snipped ends of a pretty bow.

Although it looks fancy, this script is easy to master because it doesn't require perfection. You can replicate the general feel of each letter without having to copy exactly. Starting with penciled guidelines, draw the basic shape of each letter. Connect letters if it seems natural, such as the letter m flowing into the letter a. If the connection seems awkward, as in the letter w followed by the letter e, just end the first letter and start the next one beside it.

When you're happy with the overall flow of each word, add extra swirls and curves where needed. The transitions from thin lines to thick are an important element in this lettering, so be sure to outline the thicker parts of each letter. Note that all lines in this alphabet are curved except for the widened letter ends, which are blunt.

Now it's time to color. Dress up this style with a metallic pen on dark paper, or go more casual with bright colors. Add fancy embellishments or let the letters stand alone. Whatever your preference, this beautiful script is versatile enough for almost any purpose.

FLUFFY

Write the alphabet using your fanciest printing. Then write it again with your best cursive. Now choose the characters from each set that you like the best. What do you get? The handwriting you've always wanted—a sophisticated cross between fancy printed and cursive characters.

This lettering requires consistent heights and even lines, so be sure to pencil guidelines before you start. After lightly drawing each letter, decide whether you want any characters to be connected as in a cursive style. Then draw the connecting lines. When you're satisfied, trace each letter with a medium to thick pen. The pen tip should be uniform because the lines in each character are the same width and don't vary.

To fully master this style takes some practice. Start out by tracing it several times on inexpensive ruled notebook paper. Once you get the feel for each character, try drawing words freehand. You'll be glad you invested the time because Fluffy is a terrific look to add to your repertoire of lettering styles for both captions and titles.

ABCDEFG
HIJKLM
NOPQRST
UVWXYZ
abcdefghi
jklmnopqr
stuvwxyz
1234567890

Debbie and Sande
BEST FRIENDS

·My Best Friend·
we share many things
there is lots of laughter
and sometimes tears
as our days together
turn into years.

VARIATIONS

Reminiscent of old-fashioned cursive typewriters, Fluffy lettering is ideal for formal or heritage themes. When using this style exclusively, write the more significant title words with a heavier weight pen to make them stand out. For a less formal look, use Fluffy for the title alone and write the captions in a more casual style. Because this lettering is simple and uncluttered, you can match the letter colors to your page without compromising impact.

mom and Perry Como

Now—More Dates—More Fun!

In the winter of 1946, my mom, Barbra Whittemore, won a contest after participating in the DuBarry Success Course. She won a brand new wardrobe and a trip to New York to do some modeling and to meet Perry Como. She also appeared in the February 10, 1947 issue of Life Magazine.

ELEMENTARY

Do you remember learning to print? Lips pressed together in concentration, eyes focused on blue rule lines and a small fist squeezing a freshly sharpened #2 pencil, you carefully tried to copy perfectly printed letters. The result was always less than perfect but reflected your individuality. Elementary lettering captures this charming personality.

Unlike grade-school printing, this style is deliberately imperfect. The letters only loosely follow guidelines. Vertical and diagonal lines start and stop at different heights, avoiding that too-straight look. Not all loops are closed, as in the letters B and O, suggesting that the characters were written quickly. And just to add to the cuteness, the letters g and y have sweet little loops.

You really can't make a mistake with this style if you're able to leave your perfectionist tendencies behind. Draw guidelines only if you want the letters to casually line up. Then pencil each character and trace with the pen color and thickness of your choice.

Use this lettering as a starting point for creating your own personal style of printing. Customize each letter with little idiosyncrasies that make it your own. The greater the imperfection, the greater the charm!

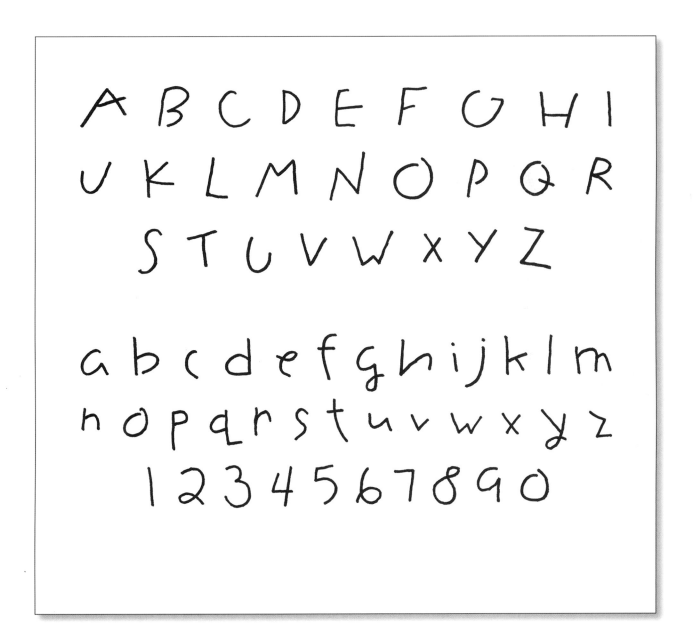

VARIATIONS

Elementary lettering is simple enough for captions as well as titles. Because it's quick and easy to write, you have more time to get creative. Decorate characters with themed stickers, punched shapes and other embellishments. For added whimsy, replace an entire letter with a graphic element, such as a soccer ball for the letter O.

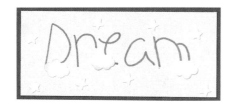

SIGNATURE

It's the contemporary yet classic cursive handwriting you've always dreamed of. Confident lines, smooth curves, simple flourishes. Before you say, "I can't write like that," give it a try. With some lined paper and a little practice, you'll soon be the envy of your scrapbooking friends.

To get the feel of each letter, lay ruled notebook paper over a photocopy of the letters and trace each character. Use the lines as a guide to keep the letters a consistent height. Draw each letter until you feel comfortable with its shape. You may notice that this style draws its contemporary as well as classic feel from the combination of mostly printed uppercase letters with cursive lowercase letters.

Now practice words and phrases, starting with your name and short titles. Note that while the uppercase letters are often unconnected, the lowercase letters are usually joined, whether directly or by gently touching edges. Lowercase letters may be unconnected when the first letter ends low and the second letter starts high, as in the word "an." Rather than relying on rigid rules to determine which letters should connect, focus on the overall visual flow, striving for movement throughout the word.

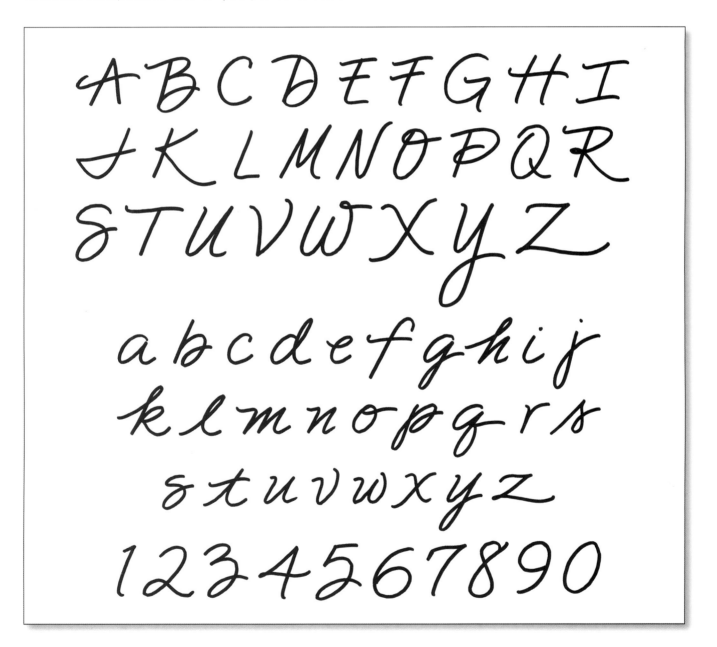

VARIATIONS

In Signature's uppercase letters, most of the horizontal lines cross over the verticals. This detail gives the style a feeling of movement. To further accentuate this sensation, embellish the title with a thin shadow line and freeform swirled lines as seen in the *Falling for Fall* page at the right. You can almost sense the breeze moving over the page.

PINSTRIPE

Who says that pinstripes are just for men's fashion? They perfectly "suit" these contemporary, masculine letters, resulting in a tailored style that emphasizes vertical lines.

Start with guidelines to keep your letter heights even. Then pencil the basic letter shapes with single lines. Outline the wider parts of each character by drawing additional lines on either side of your base lines. If the line is straight, then the outlines should be straight and squared off at the top, as in the letter H. If the line curves, then the outlines should narrow and blend into the curve as it turns horizontal, as in the letter C. When a letter does not have a vertical line, such as the letter X, then widen one diagonal line and leave the other line single. Note how the inside lines became the pinstripes!

A few sketching notes: Most of the uppercase characters are the same height except Y, which drops down below the baseline. Also, for variety, the lowercase g and j drop down lower than p and q.

The fun part is deciding how to colorize your letters. Consider black outlines and colored pinstripes, leaving the fill-in areas empty. Or draw all lines black and color the fill-in areas. Whatever you choose, you'll like the clean, crisp look of a well-tailored suit.

VARIATIONS

Pinstripe lettering offers multiple design options. For a more translucent quality, color the pinstripes while leaving the letter outlines black. To give the characters more weight, color each stripe, adding horizontal lines to change colors within each stripe. For a bold graphic element, use a single Pinstripe character as the first letter of a title or caption.

SAMPLER

The needle arts provide a wealth of ideas for creative scrapbookers. Quilting, appliqué and cross-stitch patterns, among others, can be easily adapted for scrapbook designs. The same holds true for needlepoint alphabets. This traditional lettering, inspired by the look of hand-stitched letters, yields the same effect without a needle and thread.

When arranging these letters, it's helpful to use graph paper as a grid, similar to a cross-stitch pattern. You can pencil a grid directly on paper or place graph paper on a light box so the grid shows through. The grid ensures uniform letter heights and spacing and makes it easy to draw diagonals. To determine the size of the grid, decide how wide you want the thicker parts of each letter. Make the grid the same size. If, for example, you want the line width to be ¼", use a ¼" grid.

Begin by outlining the thickest part of each letter. Then draw the thin lines, ending with the curved embellishments. Note that the thin lines may be straight and diagonal, as in the letter M, or more curved, as in the letter A.

When you're satisfied with the letters, color the outlines and fill with either a matching or contrasting color. Although this lettering style has a traditional look, you don't have to use conventional scrapbook supplies to create it. How about fabric and embroidery floss?

VARIATIONS

Sampler letters provide an uncluttered, old-fashioned look when simply penned in a solid color. Machine-sewn borders and frames tie in the stitched theme. For an even more homespun look, fabricate the letters from embroidery floss and bits of calico, gingham and denim.

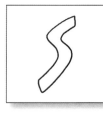

SHAKER

Sometimes your lettering just needs some space. Space to make a statement, stretch out and relax. Shaker does just that, and then some. It's casually sophisticated, elegantly whimsical and quietly bold.

Creating Shaker can take no time at all, which means you can quickly move on to the fun part—filling in all those letters. Spread out your supplies because there's lots of room for variation. You'll find many uses for this versatile style that works for most contemporary themes. Just give it some space!

Like the famous Shaker style, less is more, so be selective when choosing words to feature using this style. If you want the letters to roughly line up, pencil guidelines. Then sketch the basic shape of each character with a single line. Leave adequate space between letters. Now outline the letters so they are transformed into block-style characters.

The exaggerated widths of letters such as h, m and n are a key element of this style, so be sure to stretch them out. Note that most of the letter loops are wide open, especially in the letters a, b and g and that the middle line in the letters E and F are not connected to the rest of the character.

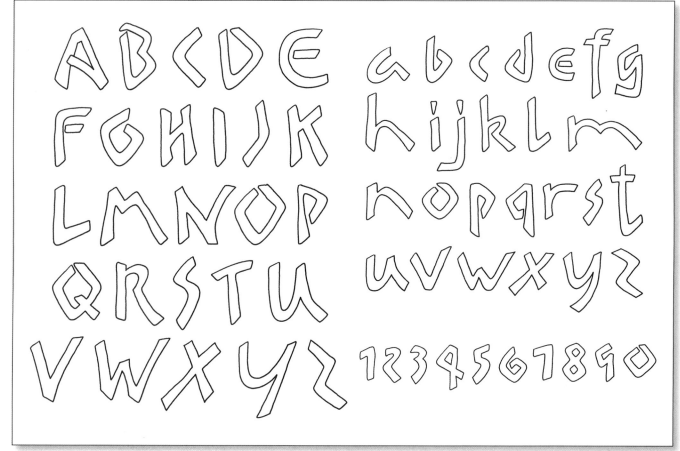

VARIATIONS

Shaker letters are quick and easy to outline, so you have plenty of time to get creative with color. Try painting polka dot and plaid designs with colored pens. Integrate the outlines into a graphic element such as a blazing sun, and color everything shades of yellow and orange. Or simply cut each letter from softly patterned paper.

SLANT

Here's a fast lettering lesson. Start with a basic printed alphabet. Drop the lowercase f and s and every uppercase letter slightly below the baseline. Slant all horizontal lines and have them cross over the verticals. Leave the loops open. Now you have Slant, a tall, narrow style that allows you to fit a lot of words in a small space.

Of course there are more nuances to this lettering, but Slant teaches a valuable lesson: By changing a few details of an alphabet, you can come up with your own personalized lettering. All it takes is a little experimentation.

To re-create this lettering, start with guidelines to keep things generally straight. Pencil each character and finish with the pen color of your choice.

Notice that this style is meant to look like handwriting, so the lettering is not precise. Vertical lines in letters such as H and N are different heights. The crossovers extend beyond the vertical lines, like a quick scrawl. And the letters a, b, d and p are not perfectly joined, which adds to its casual feeling.

Aa Bb Cc Dd Ee Ff Gg

Hh Ii Jj Kk Ll Mm Nn

Oo Pp Qq Rr Ss Tt Uu Vv

Ww Xx Yy Zz

1 2 3 4 5 6 7 8 9 0

VARIATIONS

Slant works equally well for both titles and captions. The letters are even simple enough to re-create with craft wire. In the *My Girls* page, both the white craft wire and small seed beads are held in place by white sewing thread. The center border design adds further embellishment with gray metal shapes and buttons attached with embroidery floss.

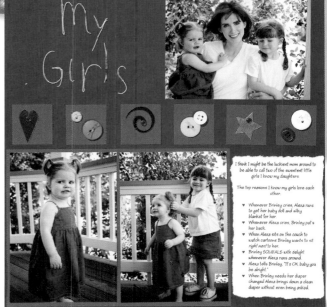

ALL FOR ONE

If you disliked grade-school grammar, here's your chance to break all the rules. Begin a sentence with a lower-case letter. Don't capitalize a proper noun. Even put uppercase letters in the middle of words. Shocking! And delightful.

If you can draw two parallel lines, you can write All for One lettering. Just choose a letter height, draw two lines that distance apart, and pencil the characters between the lines. The greater the distance between your guidelines, the taller the letters appear.

Keep the letters as straight as possible. Emphasize the exaggerated elements such as the small half circle in the letter e and the tall ovals in the letters a, b and d. Variety is created by charming inconsistencies. For example, some curves, such as in the letters a and e and the number 6, are completed, while other curves in letters like g, j, s and t seem to stop short before they've completed the turn.

The best thing about All for One is its simplified approach. You only need one set of characters to convey the message, so why mess with upper- and lowercase? Just don't tell your English teacher.

abcdefghijkLM
nopqrstuvwxyz
1234567890

VARIATIONS

All for One is an easygoing linear style that looks good in any size, large or small. When using this lettering for a title and caption on the same page, add emphasis to the larger letters by drawing them with a thick pen and outlining them with a dark color.

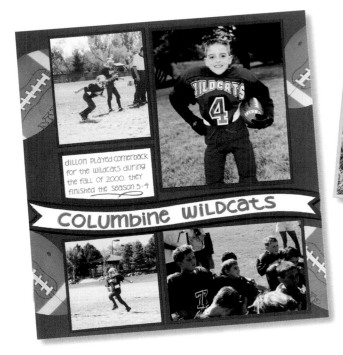

CONTEMPO

Ever spin a yarn, tell a tall tale or stretch the truth? As this lettering style illustrates, exaggeration can be an art. Stretching letter widths and vertical lines creates a classic, elegant look, and the lowercase letters provide a sophisticated understatement. With a few embellishments, however, this style easily adapts to a more whimsical theme.

This lettering can be easily mastered by practicing with a calligraphy pen. To keep the letters a consistent height, first lightly pencil guidelines. Holding the pen tip at a 45-degree angle, draw the lines of each letter using separate strokes.

For example, for the letter b, first draw the tall vertical line from the top to the bottom. Lift the pen from the paper and place the tip slightly up from the bottom. To complete the letter, draw the oval in a clockwise direction until it meets the bottom of the first stroke.

In general, draw the vertical lines from top to bottom, the curved lines from left to right and the round parts in a clockwise direction. Pay attention to exaggerating the widths of the letters h, m, n, s, u, v, w and x to capture the look of this alphabet. This style works particularly well when lettered along an arc or a curve. Simply use a journaling template to draw guidelines.

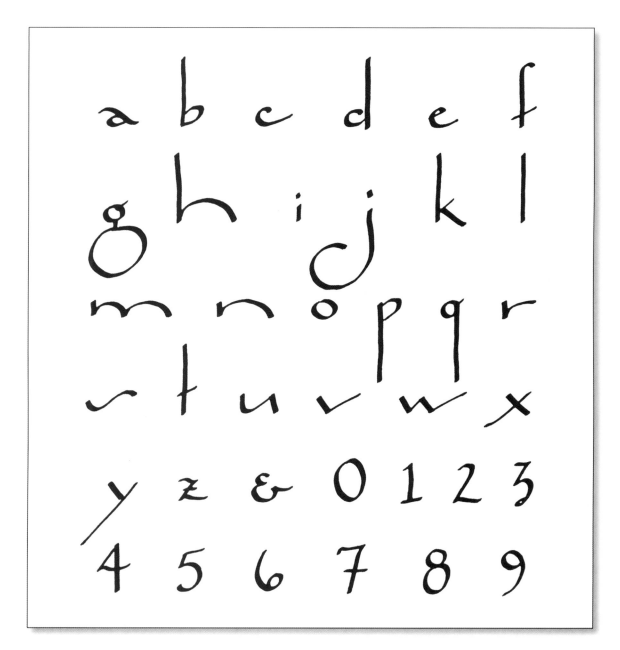

carde & harrison
dewegeli
dec. 20, 1958

to have and
to hold,
from this
day forward

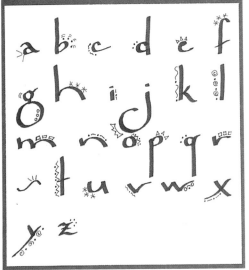

VARIATIONS

To convert the classic look of Contempo to a fun and whimsical theme, simply doodle small embellishments with a fine-tip pen. Try squiggles, swirls, stars, zigzags, sun rays, circles, squares, dots and dashes. Use these samples as a starting point for your own unique embellishments.

a work of heart

ELEGANCE

They say that opposites attract. Perhaps that's why the straight, asymmetrical fill-in areas of Elegance pair so well with its thin and curly lines. It's the contrast that appeals, like black and white, smooth and bumpy, sweet and salty.

If you think of Elegance as two distinct or opposite parts, it's much easier to create. In most cases you start with the fill-in area and then draw the curly lines. However, for round letters like C, G and O, and numbers such as 3, 6 and 9, draw the curved lines first and then the straight line for the fill-in space. The number 8 is simply one big double swirl.

Use penciled guidelines for both upper- and lowercase letters. For each columnar fill-in space, pencil-draw two straight and slanted lines, using a ruler as necessary. Close off the space with two horizontal lines that extend beyond the corners. Note that these asymmetrical areas taper up or down depending upon the letter. Complete each letter by drawing the thin curly lines.

Trace each penciled letter with a dark pen and color the fill-in areas as desired. Your page theme might suggest a coloring scheme or a variation for the swirls. Consider decorating with contrasting colors, patterns and textures.

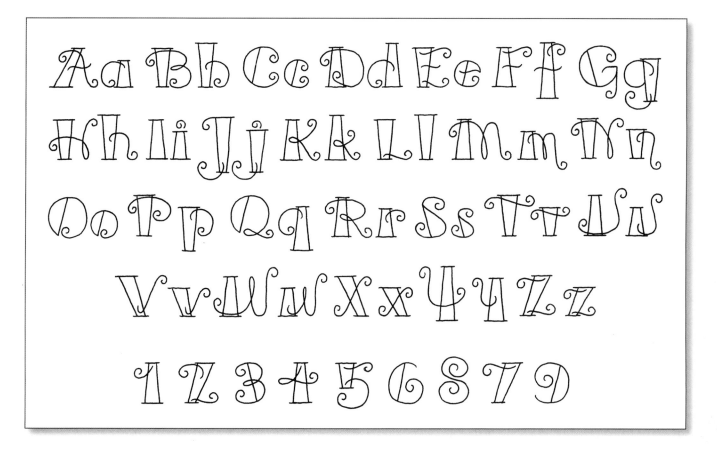

VARIATIONS

The individual boxes on the *Spring* page mimic the shapes of the letters' fill-in areas. Strung on a length of red craft wire with swirled ends, the curved design adds a touch of whimsy. For variety, transform the curls at the ends of each letter into other shapes such as leaves, teardrops, flowers, balloons, knots, stars or whatever fits the theme.

WHIMSICAL BLOCK

There's nothing symmetrical about this alphabet. The characters are different heights. The lines in each character are different lengths. In fact, this lettering is perfectly imperfect. But that's what gives it personality and gives you freedom to make mistakes. You can goof and nobody will notice. In fact, the more you tilt and slant, the better the look.

You can trace these block letters or easily draw them free-hand. Using a pencil, draw each letter with single lines, varying the tops and bottoms so nothing appears to line up.

Leave adequate space between each character. Next, outline each letter, adding rectangular shapes at the ends of each line. When you are satisfied, trace each letter outline with a thin dark pen.

Perfect for contemporary photos or any page with a light-hearted theme, block letters like Whimsical Block beg for color, whether saturated hues from colored pens or the soft shades of colored pencils and watercolors. Experiment with different blending and shading techniques. If you make a mistake, no one will be the wiser, because it's supposed to be imperfect!

VARIATIONS

One way to tie a title to a page theme is to add graphic elements to the title that reflect the action in the photos, such as the acorns in *Nuts Over Acorns* and the waves in *Jet Skiing Fun*. To add even more whimsy, embellish with dimensional items such as wire, beads and stars.

JULIANN

If you've ever tied a locket of baby hair in a pretty ribbon and safely encapsulated it on a baby page, you'll instantly recognize the inspiration for this lettering. As wispy as those soft, strawberry blonde curls, Juliann letters almost look like they could be formed from individual strands.

Juliann has a casual, sketchy look that is designed to look imperfect. So your only challenge is to emulate the free-form style, not copy it exactly. Start with guidelines if you want the letters to loosely line up. Then sketch each letter, adding short crossbars and double lines where necessary. Notice that few of the lines meet; they either cross over or don't touch at all.

Trace the penciled letters with the pen color of choice and add color between the double lines if desired. You can get creative with the materials you use to create Juliann lettering, but make sure the locks continue to look light and feathery as infant curls!

VARIATIONS

Whether it's a sophisticated graduation page or a delightful page featuring a child's "first," Juliann lettering adds just the right touch. Coloring this style can be as easy as smudging chalk around a title, embellishing with colored pens or adding free-form strokes with a watercolor brush.

CHARITY BALL

Dress it up. Dress it down. Fill it in. Leave it empty. With its clean lines and gentle swirls, Charity Ball is versatile enough to adapt to a variety of page themes.

The consistent heights and straight fill-in areas of this style make guidelines a necessity. Start by sketching each character with single lines. Note that the lowercase letters are extra tall, which gives the entire style a feeling of height. Also, some uppercase letters like A, B, D, R and S drop below the baseline, almost like dropped capitals.

To create the fill-in areas, simply draw one or two lines following the initial lettering guidelines. You might prefer to use a ruler for this portion. Notice that each fill-in space is slightly tilted to the right. Look at the letter A, for example. If you connected the top left corner to the bottom right corner of the fill-in area, you'd end up with a straight line. This image may help you determine how steeply to slant each letter.

When you're happy with the sketched characters, trace them with a dark pen. Then color the fill-in areas, adorn them with texture and pattern, or simply leave them blank. Charity Ball works just about any way you design it.

The many
FACES
of
TIGGER

For all her attitude and orner-
iness, Tigger is quite the pretty,
photogenic girl! For whatever
reason she's also finally mel-
lowing out around Jim. She'll
even climb up on him for pets.

VARIATIONS

Charity Ball's clean lines and pretty swirls call for simple
embellishment. You might opt to leave the fill-in spaces
empty or just fill them with a single color. Add texture with
an easy pattern such as a wavy line. As illustrated in *Auntie's
Shower*, apply glitter over colored pencil for added sparkle.

The
Aunties Shower

My Mother threw me a beautiful dessert shower
at her house on Friday night. I helped her make
the desserts that day, and had beautiful flowers were
the perfect decoration. All the schooner "aunties" were
there and the baby and I felt truly celebrated!

I Believe...

FALL FUN

ARCHITECTURE

Those domestic goddesses who've had their share of laundry disasters know that the only way to salvage a favorite yet shrunken sweater is to dampen it and play tug-of-war with the now preemie-sized sleeves. Imagine doing the same with a basic uppercase alphabet and you've created Architecture lettering.

Every letter is expanded horizontally as if someone tugged and stretched each character as wide as it could go. For added flair, the S is stretched vertically. Because of its simplicity, this style works as well for captions as it does for titles. Its lack of embellishment also makes it a good choice for fast pages and masculine themes.

With the exception of the letter S, Architecture's uppercase letters fit between two parallel guidelines. Just determine the letter height and draw each character with exaggerated widths and angles. Note how the diagonal lines are stretched out in letters such as N and Y. The horizontal lines in the letters A, E and H are also lowered almost as far as possible.

To keep the letter widths consistent, try to match each width to the almost triangular letter A. Think about stretching that tiny sweater and you're on the right track.

VARIATIONS

Quickly enhance Architecture's horizontal, masculine style with a variety of shadowing techniques. Shadow thick letters with a thin black pen, or reverse the idea and draw thin black letters shadowed by a thick colored pen. Embellish with random dot clusters, sophisticated stickers or even a banner-flying airplane.

SIMPLE STRETCH

Remember the popular childhood game Pick-Up Stix? You'd drop a wad of what looked like giant colored toothpicks on the floor, creating a random design. If that design actually formulated into letters of the alphabet, you'd see something that looked an awful lot like Simple Stretch.

The key to this alphabet is that each character is drawn with separate lines that cross each other at junctions. For example, the letter A is composed of three straight lines and three crossovers. The letter B includes one straight line, two curved lines and four crossovers. Notice that letters such as J and Y droop down noticeably below your baseline. The beauty of these characters is that the more crooked they are, the better they look.

If you focus on each line or curve rather than each letter, re-creating this style is a cinch. Just pencil in each letter and trace with black pen. Because it is not overly embellished, Simple Stretch works for both journaling and titles. Use this style alone for a simple, childlike effect, or dress it up with added decorations, like Easter eggs in the corner of each letter, to create something decidedly more festive.

VARIATIONS

Try shadowing Simple Stretch characters with light gray or a lighter shade of the letter color. For added dimension, draw each letter on a separate square and pop every other letter off the page with self-adhesive foam spacers. Combine Simple Stretch with letters in a different style, coloring the alternative letters and setting them against a pastel background, while writing the Simple Stretch-lettered words in plain black ink.

CURVED CLASSIC

Look closely. You won't find a single straight line. Although it seems too fancy to be easy, this lettering style is surprisingly simple because there's no perfect version of each letter. Nothing needs to be straight with this romantic, curvy style.

If you want the letters to generally line up, start with some guidelines. First lightly sketch or trace each letter with a pencil. Remember, all the lines are curved, so draw with a relaxed, loose hand.

Next, draw over the letter outlines with a thin dark pen. Color the fill-in parts of each letter with markers, pencils, watercolors, chalk or other supplies.

This style works well with a variety of themes from classic heritage to toddler antics. Keep the letters upright, or tilt them for fun and flair. Design the fill-in colors, patterns or textures to suit your page. Accent with decorative embellishments such as quilling, wire and beads. However you create these curvy characters, you'll enjoy the freedom from sticking to the straight and narrow.

VARIATIONS

Curved Classic letters look terrific when shaded with colored pencils. For added dimension, shade the lettering background with colored chalk and gold leaf the fill-in spaces. Accentuate the letter curves by bending and beading craft-wire embellishments.

GRACE

"Seemingly effortless beauty or charm of movement, form or proportion." There you have it—a definition of the word, "grace." It certainly applies to this lovely manuscript writing. The gentle curves and flowing lines of Grace lettering are equally appropriate for both titles and captions.

Mastering this style takes practice, but is well worth it. Begin by tracing the alphabet and numbers repeatedly on ruled notebook paper. Use the lines as a guide to keep the letters a consistent height. Notice how lowercase letters such as b, d and h are actually taller than the uppercase characters. The uppercase letters N, V, W and X have matching tall flourishes.

When you feel confident enough to create your own titles and captions, begin writing on penciled guidelines. Draw each character, revising as necessary. When finished, trace over the letters with a pen. The pen tip should be uniform because the lines in each character do not vary in width.

You'll find Grace an appealing style for any theme or time period. Its classic, handwritten look gives the impression that the words were worth the time it took to scribe them beautifully...gracefully.

Aa Bb Cc Dd Ee Ff Gg
Hh Ii Jj Kk Ll Mm
Nn Oo Pp Qq Rr Ss Tt
Uu Vv Ww Xx Yy Zz
1234567890

VARIATIONS

Tired of the same old adhesive? *Dunsmuir House* illustrates the use of brass brads holding vellum titles in place. Another idea: Tie together two phrases by slipping craft wire through metal eyelets and twisting into a curly bow. Want a more floral look? Embellish any lettering with tiny punched leaves.

The embossed title above takes lettering to new "heights." To re-create, use a stylus to emboss the copper from the back side, writing each letter backwards. Hold the copper piece with kitchen tongs over a gas stove or candle to discolor it. When it's cool, trim around the title. Punch a square and a small hole to attach the heart charm. Write the remaining words on metallic gold vellum and tear edges. Attach the vellum with copper-embossed brass brads.

PUTTIN' ON THE RITZ

"High hats and narrow collars, white spats and lots of dollars." Irving Berlin's lyrics perfectly describe these tall, narrow letters with their elegant style and cool sophistication. These particular characters must be puttin' on airs, however, because they can dress down as easily as they can dress up.

Puttin' on the Ritz is easy to reproduce as long as you use a ruler and guidelines to keep the letters the same height and each character standing straight and tall. Start by penciling each character with a single line. Notice that horizontal lines are either "shoulder" high, as in the letters E, F and H, or "knee" low, as in the letters A and G. The lowercase t is also exaggerated in height.

Once you've sketched each letter, draw the outlines, taking care to keep the letter widths consistent. Use a ruler, as necessary, to keep the lines straight. Then trace and color each letter.

Puttin' on the Ritz is especially well-suited for cutting letters from solid or patterned paper. The lack of detail makes the cutting go faster, and the paper choice determines whether you end up with a simple, uncluttered caption or a fancy, sophisticated title. For extra glitz, outline each patterned letter with gold pen or sprinkle with glitter. A la Berlin, "you'll declare it's simply topping."

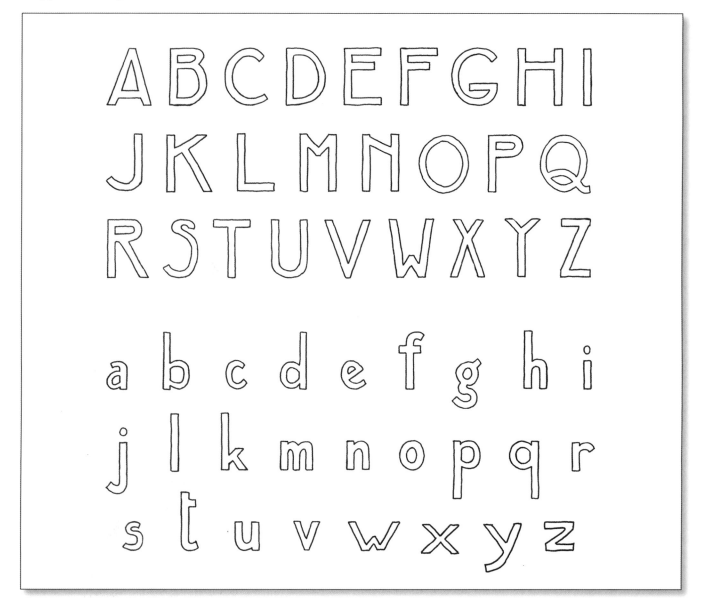

VARIATIONS

A streamlined style reminiscent of the Art Deco era, Puttin' on the Ritz is appropriate for a variety of occasions, from casual bathtime fun to elegant vintage portraits. If you can't get enough color and pattern, cut the letter shapes out of printed vellum and layer patterned paper beneath the letter openings. As illustrated in *Happy New Year*, the result is amazingly sophisticated.

FUN & FUNKY

RYAN, RYAN, ISAIAH, AUSTIN, MARSHALL AND JOSH.

HO Boy Scout

RYAN

HO Party

JOSH AND MARSHALL

WE PLAYED A FUN GAME AT THE SCOUT CHRISTMAS PARTY! EACH BOY HAD TO ANSWER A CHRISTMAS TRIVIA QUESTION. IF THEY GOT IT RIGHT, THEY ROLLED THE DICE, AND GOT THE SAME NUMBER OF COTTON BALLS. THEY DIPPED THE COTTON BALLS IN LOTION TO MAKE A SANTA BEARD. THE SCOUT WITH THE FULLEST BEARD WON!

ISAIAH

HO

Creative, entertaining and simply oozing with personality, these center-stage lettering styles are distinct enough to share the spotlight with your most vibrant photos. Each alphabet has been designed to add that certain "je ne sais quoi" to your scrapbook page, not only supporting, but also carrying forward, your page theme. Whether bursting with sunflowers, decked out with holly leaves, mimicking Roman columns or emulating cross-stitch, all these alphabets are compellingly unique. Add your own embellished or drawn modifications, and most of these alphabets can be used on a variety of pages. Draw ideas from our variations or let your imagination run free and applaud as your titles steal the show.

HOLLY

Just try not to hum "Deck the halls with boughs of holly" as you decorate these letters with handmade holly boughs. These simple printed characters entwined with festive garlands are sure to put you in the holiday spirit, whether it's July or December.

Start by penciling each character using guidelines if desired. Then decide which characters to decorate. Follow the lettering guide to pencil swirling lines around each letter.

If desired, extend a long swirling line behind a group of unadorned letters, as shown on the facing page. When you're satisfied with the placement of the lines, pencil in the holly leaves and berries.

Now pull out your box of colored pens, because using different pen tips really adds to the look of this lettering. Outline the leaves and berries and color the swirling lines with a thin pen. Use a thicker point to draw the letters, highlighting with a thin black pen if desired. Finally, color in the leaves and berries. Now your letters are officially "decked."

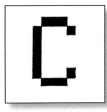

CROSS STITCH

If you've ever tried your hand at counted cross-stitch, you'll recognize the inspiration for these handmade letters. The building blocks for each character are tiny squares that mimic the X-shaped stitches of the popular craft. Stacked vertically or horizontally, the squares form straight lines. Arranged diagonally, the squares touch corner to corner to form rough diagonals.

The easiest way to re-create this style is with graph paper or a checkerboard grid drawn with a ruler and pencil. When using graph paper, make sure the grid is the appropriate size. You can reduce or enlarge it using a photocopy machine. Lay a sheet of vellum or tracing paper over the sized grid so the lines show through. Then fill in the appropriate squares for each letter. If you happen to have some cross-stitch patterns for inspiration, try designing embellishments using the same tiny squares in various colors.

As seen on the page below, you can add a touch of whimsy by slightly tilting the grid for each character. This style is perfect for adding a homemade touch to any page, especially those quilt-style layouts. Refer to *Memory Makers Quilted Scrapbooks* for gobs of inspiration but, beware, you might get bit by the quilting bee.

Babies dream of clean diapers, warm milk, snuggling close to Mom and soft kisses from a two-year-old sister. Mothers dream for their daughters to grow happy healthy and strong, to follow their hearts, remember who they are and expect to be treated like a Queen. Our Heavenly Father dreams for his children to Return with Honor.

Aa Bb Cc Dd Ee Ff Gg
Hh Ii Jj Kk Ll Mm Nn
Oo Pp Qq Rr Ss Tt Uu
Uu Ww Xx Yy Zz

VARIATIONS

If you're more of a seamstress than a cross-stitch enthusiast, create titles using a variety of decorative sewing techniques. Add pen stroke dash and dot "stitched" lines to handwritten, sticker or template letters. Create "fabric" letters by penciling in swirls, stars and other shapes. Tear or overlay paper pieces to make homey quilted letters and warm and friendly titles.

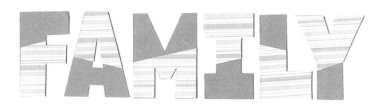

HEARTS ENTWINED

Hearts for love, holly for Christmas, apples for school days, flowers for spring, snowflakes for winter. Whatever the theme, you can always create a matching design. Apply the idea to lettering and the result is this elegant, versatile style.

The Hearts Entwined concept is simple. Start with basic lettering and add themed doodles. These letters are fancy enough to use in separate letter boxes or as the featured first letter of a word or journaling paragraph.

When drawing or tracing these letters, start with guidelines to keep everything straight. Draw each character with single lines. Then go back and widen the thicker vertical parts. Once you're satisfied with the basic letters, draw over them with a dark pen, adding small triangles, or serifs, at the ends of each line.

For the doodled embellishments, pick up your pencil again. Combine swirls and dots with hearts, apples, holly leaves, snowflakes, flowers or whatever fits your theme. Color over the thin lines with a dark pen and fill in the other shapes as desired.

VARIATIONS

Hearts Entwined lettering can be easily adapted to fit any theme. Draw your inspiration from symbols associated with the events featured on your scrapbook pages. Wrap your title letters in decorative vines, allow the embellishment to sprout, twine and fill up the hollows within the letters.

SUNBURST

"You are my sunshine, my only sunshine, you make me happy when skies are gray." You might be humming this familiar song as you outline the triangular rays of these sunny letters.

Perfect for the little sunshines in your life, a bright day in May or a hot afternoon at the beach, Sunburst literally glows with warmth and energy.

Don't bother with guidelines because these letters are designed to go up and down so that you can nestle each letter next to the previous. Just pencil the basic shape of each letter with single lines including the small crossbars, or serifs. Almost every letter has a little swirl to represent the sun, although you don't have to draw sun rays on each letter. Note that in the lowercase alphabet, the vertical lines stretch extra high and low, as in the letters h, l, g and j.

When you're satisfied with the letter placements and shapes, draw the outlines to create fill-in characters. Add little triangles around the swirls and an extra dot or swirled shape inside. Trace each letter outline with dark pen and color in. Then brighten each sunburst with vivid yellow, glowing orange, fiery red or any hot colors from your arsenal.

VARIATIONS

Sunburst is a whimsical lettering style designed for pages featuring upbeat events. You can vary the look by changing the graphic element. For example, *Lake Mead* depicts a hot day at the lake with squiggly orange heat waves emanating from each letter. The feeling is further emphasized by blending orange and yellow pencils when coloring in each letter.

SWIRL

Draw it, box it, doodle it. That's all there is to these simple box letters. They're fast, they're easy, and best of all, they make you look exceedingly creative. Choose a lettering style, choose a doodle and the hard part's done.

Start with any basic lettering style such as the Roman characters shown. You can trace or draw them or use a lettering template, alphabet stickers or computer-generated lettering. Just leave enough room between each character to cut or punch them into box shapes. This style looks best when all the boxes are the same size, so be sure to center each letter in the box.

Now it's time to doodle. Thin colored pens are a great place to start, but if you prefer, branch out with geometric or textured stamps, ink splatters, watercolor swirls, little stickers, mini punches and even patterned paper backgrounds. When finished, mat each letter with multiple layers of colored and patterned paper to match your theme and colors.

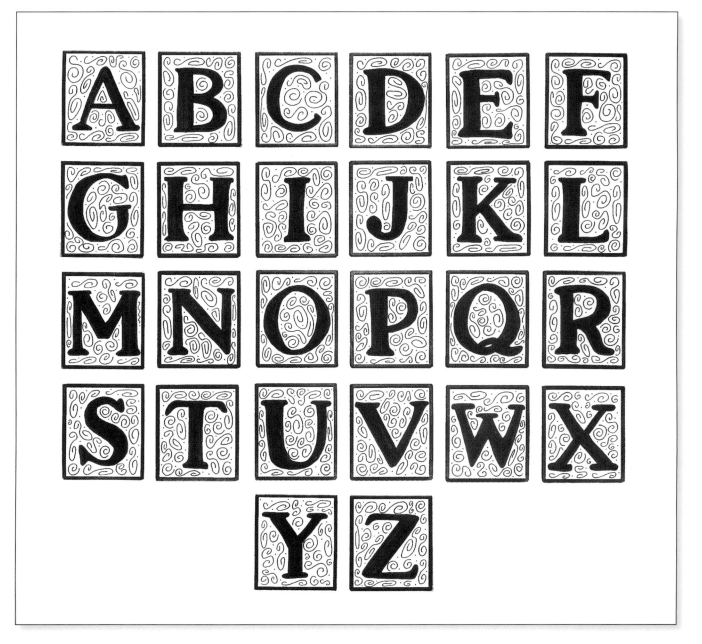

JONATHAN COE · NOVEMBER 2000

VARIATIONS

With Swirl lettering, the fun is in the doodling, so get creative and match the doodles to the theme. How about splashes for water play, stars and stripes for the good ol' USA, multicolored balls for playtime fun or curly hearts for teenage loved ones?

COLOR BLOCK

Do you like to color inside the lines, or would you rather stray outside them? If you scribble without restraint, you'll like how Color Block defines a new shape for each letter with its free-form ovals and curvy triangles and rectangles. If you are more tidy ('fess up, perfectionists), you'll be satisfied with how each vivid color neatly conforms to its defined space.

Regardless of your style, Color Block is simple to create. Start by penciling each letter with plenty of surrounding space. Because the curvy letters have few embellishments, they show up clearly against their colorful backgrounds.

Using the lettering guide for reference, pencil an oval, triangle, diamond or rectangle over the letter so that it creates different areas to color. To match the letters, keep the lines curved and deliberately imperfect.

Trace each letter with a medium to thick pen. Outline the shape with a thin pen. Now it's simply a matter of coloring each section with colored pens, pencils or the tools of choice. This time, stay inside the lines!

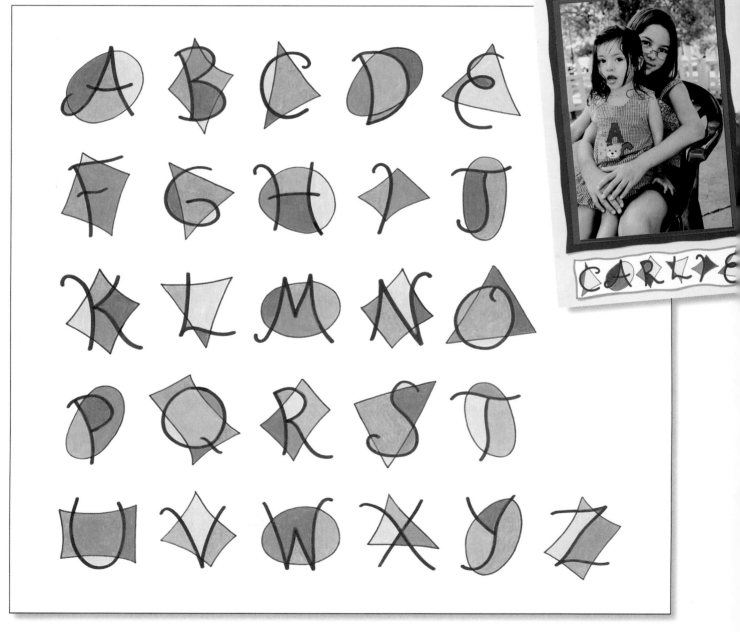

VARIATIONS

Vary the look of Color Block letters by changing the background shapes. For example, try using circles exclusively or using a shape template to draw flowers and butterflies. For added interest, use a decorative ruler to create a coordinating border.

ROMAN HOLIDAY

Quick Quiz: What do the words abacus, capital, keystone, shaft, springer and voussoir have in common? Answer: They're all parts of Roman columns and arches. Fortunately, you don't have to pass a quiz to build these letters from classic architectural elements. But you do need a little time and patience. After all, Rome wasn't built in a day!

Start by drawing pencil guidelines to keep the letter heights consistent. Then lightly pencil each character with single lines, leaving adequate space to turn each one into an architectural wonder. First transform the straight lines into columns, using a ruler to draw parallel outlines. Draw details at the column tops and bottoms (capitals and bases for you architecture buffs) and then fill in with more freeform lines to create fluted columns.

Next, transform the curved parts of each character into arches. Draw two curves to outline each arch and then fill in with short lines. Add swirls and other embellishments to complete each character.

This style looks beautiful when colored in and is ideal for special occasions such as weddings, anniversaries and proms. Use it to create an architectural statement for any page, especially those "monumental" vacations. Then, when at home, draw as the Romans!

VARIATIONS

Not just for Italian vacation pages, Roman Holiday lettering adds impact to university names, dates, official titles and more. To save time, use this style for just the first letter of a word. Also experiment with different coloring techniques such as shading with a single color or blending with two or more colors.

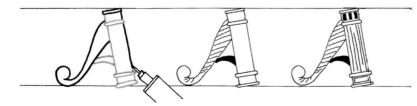

COLLEGIATE

If you ever lettered in high school or bought a sweatshirt with your alma mater's name emblazoned across the front, you'll quickly recognize this block lettering. Almost universally used for school names and athlete numbers, Collegiate is a timeless style that works equally well for vintage photos of a '50s high-school class or contemporary snapshots of youth soccer and college football.

The fastest way to re-create these letters is to trace them. First photocopy the lettering in the desired size. Starting with a guideline to keep your letters straight, trace the appropriate characters. Outline with pen, and color as desired.

You can also draw these letters using graph paper, a checkerboard grid or parallel guidelines. When using graph paper, which helps keep the lines straight and the widths consistent, make sure the grid is the appropriate size. Lay a sheet of vellum or tracing paper over the grid so the lines show through. Then sketch each character using the lettering guide as a reference.

With Collegiate lettering, it's easy to show your school spirit. Dress it up with gold or silver mats for a formal graduation. Combine it with logos and mascots for college snapshots. For whimsical pages of grade school or youth sports, sketch simple stick figures and outfit them to fit the theme.

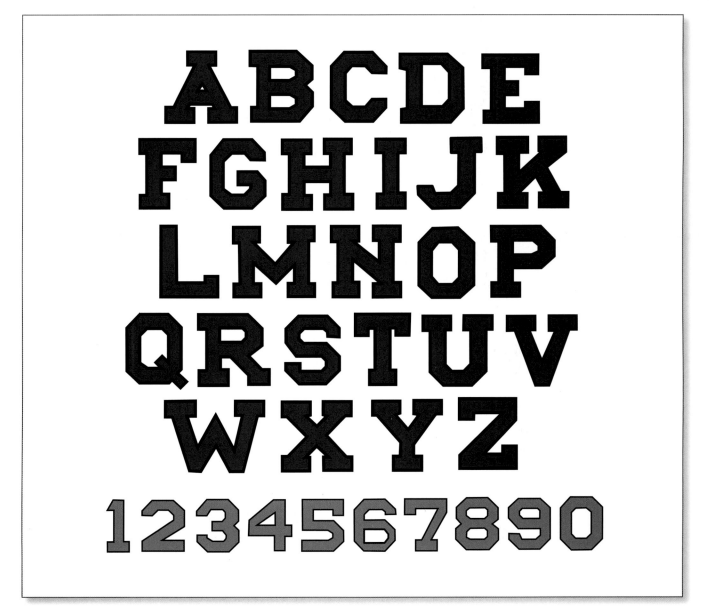

VARIATIONS

Stacking a smaller word on a larger word not only keeps this Collegiate title from overwhelming the page but also adds an interesting design element. Simple stick figures provide a playful decoration, or a perfect page border, as seen on the right. Sketch each figure with a pencil, drawing a round head, triangle body and stick arms and legs. Add an outfit, shoes, hair, face and other details. Color to match your photos or theme.

WORLDWIDE

The more you travel, the more you want each travel scrapbook to be as unique as the place you visited. But you don't have to design a new lettering style each time. Simply fill in these Worldwide letters with the sights, colors, textures, patterns, themes and symbols of your destinations.

You can decorate any fill-in lettering using these ideas. To draw the Worldwide outlines, begin with two parallel guidelines the desired height of the letters. Use a ruler to sketch the straight or angled fill-in areas first. Be sure to keep the fill-in widths consistent. Then pencil in the curved lines. Add the short crossbars, or serifs, at the ends of each line or fill-in area. Trace the letter outlines with black pen.

Now comes the creative fun. Draw flag designs, animal prints and southwestern designs with colored pens and pencils. (If you have flag stickers on hand, simply cut them to fit each space.) Trim lovely shades of tropical printed paper for an Asian title. For wintry themes, stamp white snowflakes on a blue-colored background. Or just cut tiny pieces from a road map for your latest travel adventures.

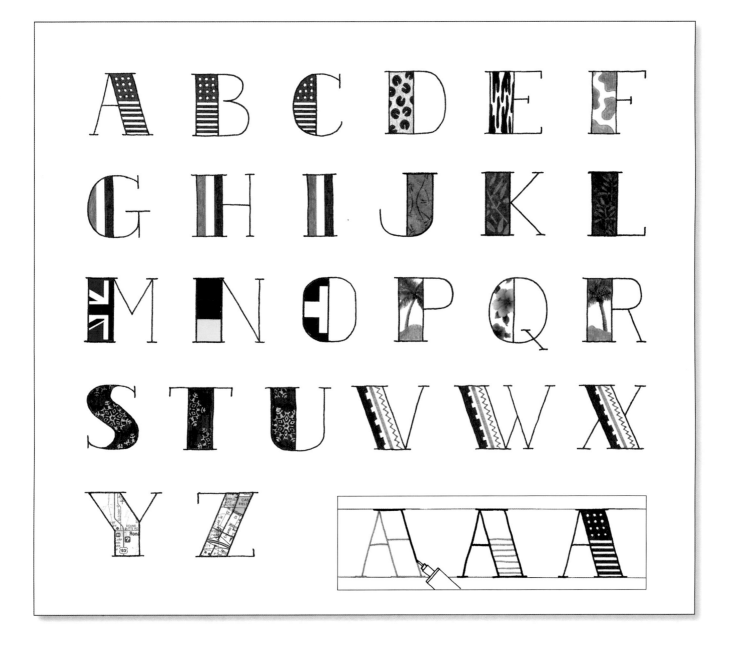

VARIATIONS

Trimmed palm tree and floral stickers along with penciled details fill the Worldwide letters in this *Aloha* page. For variety, the letters were outlined with slightly squiggled lines. As illustrated by *"Our Global Adventure,"* another quick way to fill these letters is to outline them on vellum, cut out the fill-in parts and mat with patterned paper. Once you've designed your fill-in pattern, it's easy to use the same technique to design a matching border. Just draw a rectangle and fill it in.

IN BLOOM

Tulips for spring, daisies for summer, mums for fall and poinsettias for winter. Whatever the season, your titles will always be freshly blooming with these beautifully embellished letters. To grow your own, simply choose your favorite flower and unearth a calligraphy pen. Absolutely no green thumb required!

Before you begin, decide which letters to embellish, perhaps the first letter of each word or the first letter of a title or caption. Starting with penciled guidelines, sketch or trace the basic shape of each letter. For the embellished letters, sketch the flower on the left side of the character. When drawing a tulip, sketch a U shape, add a small peak at the top, and connect the peak to the sides of the U.

Color in the flower as desired. Holding a calligraphy pen at a 45-degree angle, draw the wide letter lines using separate strokes, taking care to start and stop around each flower. Complete the remaining letters and add leaves if desired. To further define each letter, highlight with a thin black pen, accenting with dots. Embellish each flower with additional details such as leaves and vines until they're blooming with color.

IT'S FALL AGAIN... AN...
PICTURES! ASHLEY IS...
LEE FRESHMAN. SHE...
ABELL JR. HIGH AT 8...
AT 8:40. AUSTIN IS...
BOWIE ELEMENTARY...
FROM PARKER ELEM...
AT 7:40. SCHOOL B...
THIS IS AUSTIN'S...

HAPEL HILL, NORTH
CAROLINA... THE
LOCATION OF 'FOR
GARDEN'S SAKE, A GARDEN
CENTER AND NURSERY TUCKED
AWAY IN THE WOODS. WALTER
AND JOANN DAVIS PURCHASED
THE NURSERY IN 1999 AND
THE WORK CONTINUES AS THE
BUSINESS DEVELOPS AS THE
AREAS OF COMMERCIAL AND
RESIDENTIAL LANDSCAPE AND
DESIGN ARCHITECTURE.

VARIATIONS

Apply the In Bloom concept to any title by incorporating a themed icon into a letter or word. Whether flowers or kites, pansies or paw prints, these embellishments add a graphic pop. If you don't want to draw, try stamps, stickers, punch art or whatever you pluck from your toolbox.

FISHBONE

If your cat were asked to design the purrfect alphabet, Fishbone, comprised of tiny fish skeletons, would be the result. You can almost imagine him licking his chops!

To draw these feline-friendly letters, first pencil the basic shape of each character with single lines. Draw triangles at the ends of the appropriate lines to represent the fish heads and tails. Refer to the lettering guide for the orientation and placement of each triangle. Erase the guidelines from inside the fish heads and tails.

Now add details. Draw the bones on each skeleton with 5 to 8 lines that vary in length. Sketch tiny black lines sprouting from the corner of the tail. Add a dot inside the fish head for the eye. When your lettering is adequately appetizing, at least to a cat, color in the triangles and trace the skeleton with a thin black pen.

Notice that letter Q and the number 2 use little fish hooks to form part of the character. Also, the number 0 is designed to look like a cat face. To sketch, narrow the bottom half of the 0 to look like a chin. Add whiskers, eyes, nose and ears. Meow!

Jake came to us in San Antonio from the Humane Society. We had forgotten how goofy kittens are!

~ Just Another Kitty Cat ~

Variations

Take the Fishbone concept and apply it to any title. Think of something that represents your page theme and incorporate it into the lettering. For example, add tiny horseshoes to a horse-themed title.

GIDDY-UP

FLOWER GIRL

BUTTERFLY
beauty

FANCY FELINE

FLEAS

Oh my, Fido lost his flea collar and those pesky bugs have invaded your scrapbook. Wait, they're not real. Thank goodness, because this lettering style almost makes your skin crawl.

If you can keep from scratching, use a pencil to sketch each letter, adding the small crossbars, or serifs, wherever necessary. This lettering style is designed to feel loose and freeform, so the letters vary in size, height and width. The lines within the same character are different heights and widths and purposefully crooked. The more variety, the more whimsy.

Once you've completed each word, trace the letters with a colored pen. Next, pencil bouncing dotted lines that connect each letter. Where the lines come to a point, draw a larger dot to represent each flea. Place the dots wherever you want or follow the lettering guide for suggested placement. When you're satisfied with the design, draw over the dotted lines and flea dots with a dark pen. Now, stop that scratching!

Quinn and Allison Remund enjoy eating their food while their youngest little girl sleeps and their two-year-old sits quietly. Moments to treasure!

Ferrera Family brought friends and everyone ate lots of food.-Yummy

Everyone loves a picnic! The

Memorial Day Picnic

The Evans Early's and Brasier's enjoy the picnic together and wait for the food to come for her Abram Early saved the day when he got the frisbee off the roof!

and lots of desert. The Cook family shows everyone just how much they love to eat!-Especially Layne!*Looks good!

We ate hot dogs, hamburgers, chips

VARIATIONS

Fleas lettering complements pages of perky puppies or any canine companions. To adapt this style to a completely different theme, simply change the insect. Try ants or flies for picnic pages, ladybugs and caterpillars for spring and summer themes or butterflies for flower-filled gardens.

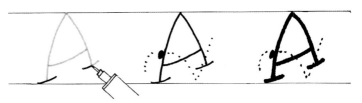

GRIN

Gimme an F! Gimme a U! Gimme an N! What's that spell? FUN! Inspired by cheerleading contortionists, these stick-figure letters add playful personality to scrapbook layouts. With a ruler and some colored pens anyone, regardless of artistic talent, can draw these animated people. Best of all, you can easily dress them up to match any occasion from A to Z.

To create your own characters, pencil top and bottom guidelines if you want the words to be straight. Using a ruler as necessary, sketch the basic shape of each letter person.

Draw the heads by tracing a small circle template or a small punched circle. The size of the circle depends upon the letter height you've chosen. Freehand draw the smaller circles for the hands or use a tiny circle template.

Trace each character with a colored pen and add faces, clothing and other accessories to match your theme. Try playground toys for summer fun, Santa hats and boots for holiday memories, angel wings and halos for your lil' darlings, bunny ears and carrots for Easter and a bride and groom for, well, you get the idea.

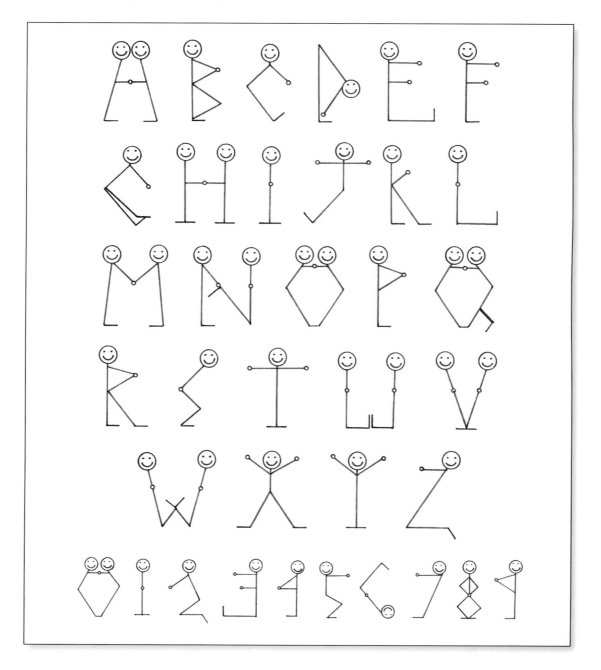

VARIATIONS

The stick people in Grin lettering can be dressed up for any occasion. Decorate all or just a few letters from your title to ft your page theme. Add a border using the same concept as illustrated by the Santa heads border. As an alternative, punch small circles for each head.

CHICKEN SCRATCH

It's fast, fun and possibly even thera-peutic. Best of all, it requires absolutely no handwriting skills. All you need to create these letters are random, reckless pen marks. This lettering is a perfect fit if you're tired of being neat and tidy.

This alphabet works well with colored pens. For a different effect try glitter or metallic pens on a dark background or bright colors on complementary papers. Combine multiple colors for even more dimension.

First lightly pencil each letter with straight lines. Notice that anywhere two lines overlap, the line extends a bit farther, as in the A, E, F, K and Y. With a fine-tip pen, scribble over the pencil lines in any fashion you choose—circles, swirls, straight lines, zigzags or jagged lines. It just doesn't get easier.

Make matching borders or try different materials such as wire, raffia or twine to create these deliberately sloppy letters. Whatever you do, have fun, and scribble away with confidence!

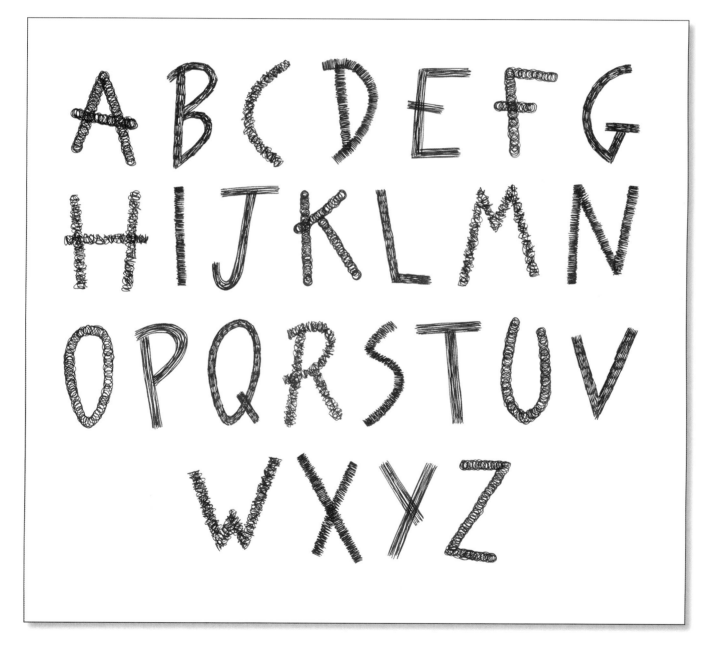

VARIATIONS

Wire letters are a natural variation for this dimensional, tactile lettering. To make the coiled letters F and L, on the *Fall* page at right, wrap thin black craft wire around a narrow rod. Then cut pieces of coil to create each line. Cut and layer various lengths of wire to create the letters A and L.

PLAYFUL

Remember the fun of Silly Putty? One popular use was to pencil a picture and press the peach-colored plastic onto it. When you removed it, the image was transferred to the Silly Putty. Now imagine doing the same thing with standard printed letters and then playing with it. Stretch the Silly Putty for the wide letters like A, E and M. Squeeze for C, D and G. And squash for the quaint O and Q. Now you have Playful lettering.

This style is particularly easy because it's a single set of all-purpose characters. The letter A, which is essentially a short fat triangle, determines the height of most letters, the width of the wide characters and the position of the middle lines in E, F and H.

Because Playful is composed of single lines, the pen size determines the weight of the letters. Use a fine-tip pen for captions but increase the pen size for titles. With the exception of O and Q, the letters line up along the same bottom and top lines. However, the casual style of this lettering invites you to raise or lower characters and extend lines above or below the guidelines. If you like, pick one element of this style that you really like, such as the long, skinny S or short and squashed O. Then incorporate that one element into your journaling to give it a playful look too.

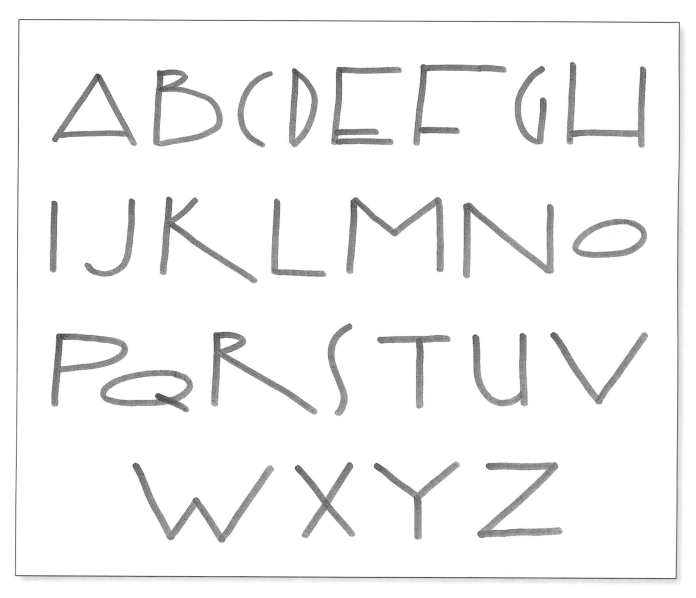

HE IS RISEN... HE IS NOT HERE... FOR... IS RISEN... HE IS... HE IS... OT HER... RISEN... AS... N... W... 2... RI... HE IS

RESURRECTION DAY!
EASTER 2000.
WE CELEBRATED HOLY
WEEK ACTIVITIES ALL WEEK;
THE MEN'S MINISTRY PUT ON
A RE-ENACTMENT OF
THE LAST SUPPER. DAN
PLAYED THE PART OF PETER.
ON SUNDAY MORNING WE
DID A GREAT CHOIR CANTATA
THREE DIFFERENT BACKDROPS
WERE PAINTED BY JANET PON-
TIOUS, ONE DEPICTING THE
TEMPLE, ONE DEPICTING THE
CRUCIFIXION SCENE, AND ONE
DEPICTING THE EMPTY TOMB.
WE HAD GUEST MUSICIANS
AND THE STERNS FAMILY
CAME FROM HOUSTON TO
PARTICIPATE. SADIE DID SOME
BEAUTIFUL INTERPRETIVE
WORSHIP BALLET. IT WAS A
GREAT CELEBRATION!!

A DAY AT THE PARK

ADVENTURE
EXPLORE FUN
CLIMB
HAPPY
THAT IS WHAT
ALEXA IS MADE
OF

VARIATIONS

Playful can double as both a background texture and title. Its simplicity makes it easy to re-create words out of unconventional materials. The jute letters in the park page subtly suggest both the climbing ropes and the playground slide.

FUN AND FUNKY

Ever get the jaggies when you write? Maybe it's fatigue, maybe it's a bad pen, or maybe it's just that you're feeling a little rough around the edges. Whatever the reason, sometimes a title ends up looking like it's been chiseled in stone by a beginning sculptor. But this isn't necessarily bad. In fact, it's Fun and Funky.

The basic idea is to start with a fancy font and purposefully roughen every line. First pencil each character with single lines for placement. Notice that letters such as A, N and S have cute curls. Others turn into outright swirls, as in J, Y and the dramatic O. Most lines that meet also cross over, as in B, F and H. Refer to the lettering guide for the nuances of each character.

Now get jaggy on purpose. Draw around each letter with rough, crooked lines that randomly zig and zag. To finish, color in each jagged line, curl and swirl. You really cannot make a mistake, unless you're too smooth, of course.

VARIATIONS

The irregular effect of Fun and Funky lettering combines well with the crazy-quilt theme of *Guess Who?* As shown in *Yabba Dabba Doo*, a super fast way to create these rough-hewn letters is to draw them with an embossing pen and heat emboss with sparkled embossing powder. No sketching required! As an alternative to solid letters, outline them with tiny dots as in the title above, *Springtime*. Then color with pencils.

"Bedrock", South Dakota
July, 1999

abcdefghijklmno
pqrstuvwxyz

0123456789
!?

GUESS WHO?

when Katie was 7, her favorite movie was THE NIGHTMARE BEFORE CHRISTMAS so she dressed up as SALLY for Halloween.

ILLUMINATED

The art of illuminated letters has its roots in the Middle Ages, when sacred manuscripts were elaborately decorated with ornate borders and illustrations. You can mimic the beauty of this craft without the painstaking labor by designing your own enlarged and embellished characters using modern tools and supplies. It might be just what you need to spice up a plain block of text.

Start by selecting the letter to illuminate. The characters shown below and on the facing page were created using the Times New Roman Bold font, but you can use any hand-drawn, stamped or computer-generated style that is simple and unadorned. Draw or print the character and cut it out. (When using letter stickers, just trim the backing paper.) Place the letter on the background and lightly trace around it to indicate the area the letter will occupy.

Lay the letter aside and decorate the background using any of the techniques listed below and illustrated on the facing page.

- Stencil the background using small stencils or embossing templates (letters A through D).

- Arrange stickers on the background to complement the theme (letters E through H).

- Trim a photo scrap to fit the letter (letters I through L).

- Use pencils and pens to embellish freehand or with a template (letters M through P).

- Stamp on the letter or background (letters Q through T).

- Use punches for the background or letter embellishments (letters U through Y).

These techniques are by no means exhaustive. You can combine them, vary them or use your own techniques for a multitude of different effects. When you're finished, simply adhere the letter to the background and incorporate the character into your title or caption.

VARIATION

A single illuminated letter at the beginning of a caption or story helps draw readers into the journaling. This *Estes Park* page uses four corner designs made by matting cut-out gold leaves with printed and solid papers. One of these designs serves as the backdrop for the letter E, which is mounted with self-adhesive foam spacers to make it further stand out.

stes Park, Colorado

Jacque and I took a road trip up to Estes Park just before Christmas with our friends Amy and Joan. We had been there so many times in the summer months and wanted to see what life was like there during the winter. We stayed in a cozy cabin and visited the lake and the historic Stanley Hotel. One thing that stood out the most was that on this particular weekend there were fewer people and far more animals. The Elk were so close that I could almost reach out and touch one. The view of the mountains from the park took my breath away and reminded me how lucky we are to live in such a beautiful place.   2002

ADVENTURE

It's the Middle Ages, and by the light of a flickering candle, a hooded monk carefully inks a feathered quill and continues his labor of devotion—scribing highly decorative biblical texts using a writing style known as Gothic script. Fast forward 500 years, and by the light of a modern fluorescent bulb, you carefully trace these Gothic-inspired letters with an archival, pigment journaling pen to embellish your own highly decorative labor of love.

Times have changed, but classic lettering never goes out of style. This lettering makes it easy to add a classical element to pages of European travels, academic studies or any topic that evokes a sense of romance or tradition.

While you can learn to freehand these letters, unless you'll be using them frequently, it's best to just trace them using any of the methods described in the front of this book. Use a pencil to draw guidelines and outline each letter. Then trace the outlines with a dark pen and color as desired.

Traditional design elements such as fleurs-de-lis, flowers, vines, hearts and swirls combine well with Adventure lettering. Think of the types of embellishments that would appear in an old Latin Bible and you've got the picture. These letters are also ideal as decorative first letters for a title or caption. Whatever the purpose, put them to good use. After all, many monks worked hard so you could be inspired.

VARIATIONS

Gothic-inspired Adventure lettering complements these pages of European travels and academic achievement. For added emphasis, enlarge the first letter of a word and place it in a separate text block. Turn a title into a graphic element by superimposing a second word on top of the larger letters.

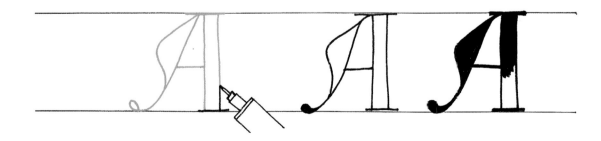

MENAGERIE

Let the fur, wrinkles, scales, fins, shells, stripes and spots creep, crawl and hop their way onto your scrapbook pages. What better way to remember trips to the zoo, nature centers, wildlife refuges or even African safaris? Not to mention pages of your favorite family pet.

Yes, it's a veritable Menagerie of interesting characters that almost leap off the page. Yet their creation is surprisingly easy. First pencil the basic letters with single lines. Use a guideline if necessary and leave plenty of space between characters. Then outline each letter with curved lines to create the smooth and rounded fill-in characters.

Now choose how to transform each character into an animal or animal part. You can copy the lettering guide exactly or simply use the designs as inspiration for your own letters. Sometimes the letter itself suggests an animal, as in the pig tail for the letter Q or the elephant trunk for the letter L. You might want to match the textures in each letter to the scales, feathers and fur of your photos. You can even cut extra animal photos into letter shapes.

Whatever your designs, make each character come alive with vivid color and texture, whether using colored pens, colored pencils, chalk, watercolors or even printed paper. When you're finished, just make sure they don't wriggle away!

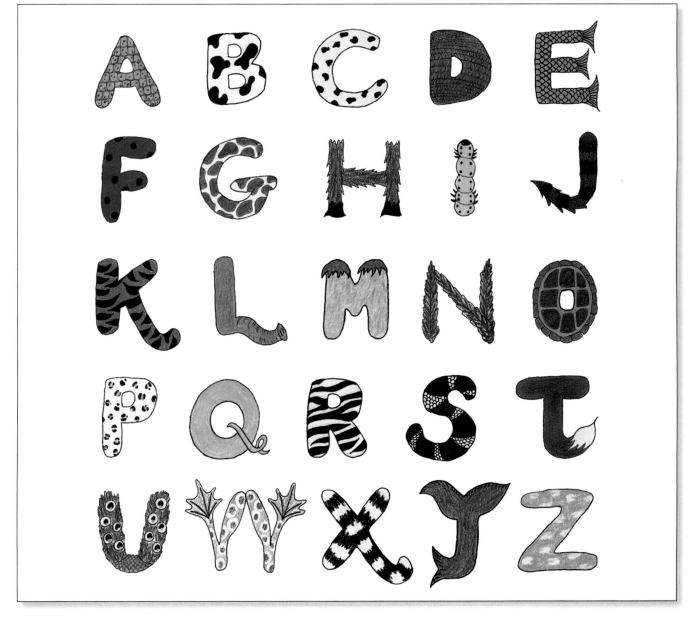

VARIATIONS

Menagerie lettering combines well with patterned papers and animal-theme embellishments such as the giraffe shown in *Riverbanks Zoo*. Stretch the idea even further by turning it into a frame or border idea. Wrap a striped and slithering snake around an entire layout.

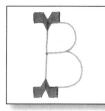

BRANDING IRON

Round up your pony-riding, boot-stompin' and horse-shoe-slingin' snapshots 'cause it's time to lasso your western layouts with some sweetly sizzlin' letters. Inspired by cattle brands, this style is a cinch to re-create with fine-tip and chisel pens.

Start by drawing each letter with a pencil, omitting the V-shaped embellishments. Then trace each letter with a fine-tip pen. For the V shapes at the tops of the uppercase letters, hold a calligraphy or chisel pen so that its wide side is vertical relative to the baseline of the letters. Draw the V from left to right in one continuous motion—draw a short line, slope

down to touch the top of the letter, slope up and finish with another short line. Draw the V shapes at the bottom points in the same manner except upside-down.

To create the daintier embellishments on the lowercase letters, draw with only part of the pen tip so that the lines are narrower. For added decoration, shadow some or all of the letters with dashed "stitch" lines as shown on the facing page.

Complete the western theme with additional embellishments such as bandannas, cowboy hats, cowboy boots, belts, buckles, denims, plaids, leather, saddles, ropes, wagons, hay, fences...or whatever spurs your creativity.

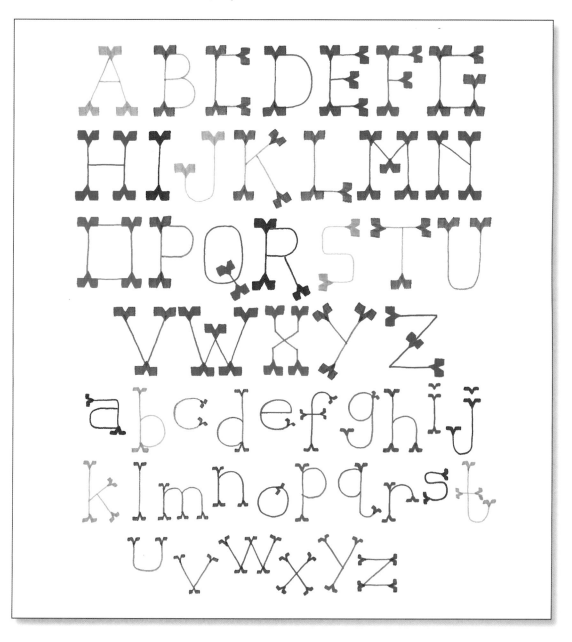

VARIATIONS

"Tie up" a western theme with a zigzag border. Use a chisel pen to draw ½" dashed lines, leaving ¼" spaces between each dash. Connect the dashes with V shapes, turning the tip so that the lines are the same width. Accent with small diamond shapes and thin dashed lines.

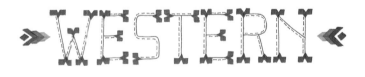

SPRING FORWARD

This lettering caters to those creative souls who love to play with color and pattern. Dots, dashes, plaids, stripes, squares, diamonds, swirls, flowers, leaves—doodle with these basic elements to fill in characters that literally "spring forward" off the page.

Starting with penciled guidelines, draw the basic shape of each letter with single lines. Next, use a ruler to transform the appropriate vertical or diagonal component of each letter into a fill-in space. Some of these spaces are rectangular boxes with straight, angled or curved ends, as in the letters F, A and J, while some have one straight side and one curved side, as in the letter C.

Follow the lettering guide to sketch each fill-in space, keeping the fill-in widths consistent. To finish each character, add the short lines, curves and swirls. When you're satisfied, color over the pencil lines with black pen.

Choose from endless combinations to fill each letter with pattern and texture. Finding inspiration in the colors, textures and theme of your layout, doodle and color to your heart's content. This lettering style is also ideal for alternative fill materials such as scraps of patterned paper, fabric, beads, buttons, eyelets, lace and ribbon. You can't have too much pattern!

VARIATIONS

Give a new "twist" to your titles using wire and sparkling beads. Form each letter and flower from thin craft wire, mount them to the page, and glue small beads inside. To protect these letters, mount a title frame with self-adhesive foam spacers.

THROUGH THE AGES

It has been said that spoken words echo only across the room, but written words echo through the ages. And so, messages left on stone tablets long ago are read today, throwing open doors to time travel. With our eyes, we understand what those who lived long ago felt in their hearts—what they feared, what they desired, what they believed. Just as telling as the scribed message is the *method* in which the missive has been set down. Throughout generations people have written down thoughts in unique ways that speak volumes about their lives. From the inception of crude prehistoric petroglyphs, through the bare, stream-lined lettering style prevalent during the Great Depression, to the bright, hippie-inspired alphabet of the 60s, writing styles are both defined by, and become a symbol of the times.

PRE 1900s

What images pop to mind when you think of the Victorian Era? Antique lace, horse-drawn carriages, candlelit living rooms and quill-and-ink pen sets? Now you can capture the same old-fashioned feel with this delicate, swirling penmanship. It is easiest to replicate this lettering style by photocopying the alphabet, or tracing it using a light box. If you wish, however, to draw it freehand, begin by pencil-sketching each letter, using guidelines to assure consistent letter height. Draw the swooping letters slanting slightly to the right. Many letters, such as C, D and O, can be created without lifting your pencil from the paper, while other letters, including B and H will require two separate strokes. Strive to keep looped-shapes open, exaggerate the curled serifs and make the angles at the tops of letters such as F, H, J, K, M and N pencil-sharp. When you've finished, carefully trace over your penciled words with a fine-tipped pen. Like a perfumed hankie, this alphabet evokes ladylike charm that will weather time just like your scrapbook pages.

1900-1919

The early 1900s were a time of great change for the United States: While the country was emerging as a world leader, serious issues such as immigration, poverty, and child labor plagued the populous. World War I—the "War to End All Wars"—raged. In spite of, or perhaps because of, the turmoil, a deep-seated strength bloomed within Americans. This bold can-do, will-do attitude is evident in the shapely, defiant lettering style found in newspaper and magazine advertisements of the time. This challenging alphabet is most easily replicated by tracing. If you choose to try it freehand, note that the letters have thick vertical lines that may narrow as they enter curves, such as in C, F and G. They sit on broad bases and many have triangular serif "feet." Variations on the triangular shape appear in the mid-strokes of letters such as E and F and at the top of letters such as A, H and I. Many of these characters include curly tails that require a medium-tipped pen to draw. When creating smooth, rounded shapes, such as the letters C, D or G, try rotating your paper so you are consistently pushing, rather than pulling your pen. Add your own embellishments to make this style as homemade as apple pie.

RAY'S RETURN

"Ray's return"

"Ray's Return." Two simple words that say so much. The year was 1918. Ray had spent a year fighting in the trenches of Europe. I can imagine Ruth waiting on her father's farm in Sterling, Colorado without any news of her beloved. Information was hard to come by because telegrams were only sent to families who had lost a loved one. After the war had ended, Ruth would not have known when Ray would return or if he would return at all. In total, the First World War claimed eight and a half million soldiers. I picture Ruth looking out her front window waiting for Ray to walk down the dirt road. Ruth must have shouted with joy when she saw him. Someone followed her outside with a camera to photograph the kiss Ray and Ruth exchanged. They were married a few months later. This photo is very sentimental to me because Ruth and Ray were my great grandparents, and I wouldn't be here if Ray hadn't returned.

VARIATION

A bold lettering style can hold its own, even when coupled with a tiny clock, suspended charms and decorative metallic corners, or 3-D stickers. To create the *Cherished Times* title, letter on patterned paper and cover with a loosely woven web of fabric. Embellish with clock and mount on torn mulberry. Create the *Grandma's* title by lettering on mulberry paper. Double mat the title. Add sticker embellishments.

1920-1929

If there was ever an age of great prosperity in American history, the "Roaring Twenties" was it. From the great boom in consumer goods (one Model T car was produced every ten seconds) to the explosion in popular entertainment (100 million cinema tickets were sold annually), the economy seemed to be on an uphill spiral that wouldn't quit. Clearly, this tall, stylish alphabet is symbolic of a nation that was confident in its future and a bit cocky about its present. Use a medium-tip pen to draw boxy, upright letters, exaggerating the thickness, and flaring the ends of each stroke. Crossbars on most letters, including H and N, begin above the figures' waistline and are slanted upward, as though reaching for the sky. Characters such as A, R, and Y seem to be extending a foot forward, dancing the Charleston with the best of them.

ABCDEFGHIJKLMNOPQR
STUVWXYZ1234567890

CAROL STAUFFER

1930-1939

The 1930s were defined by the Great Depression, the most severe economic crises experienced by the Western world. As a result of the massive stock market crash, nearly 30 percent of Americans lost their jobs. Consumerism dropped and life was streamlined. This bare-bones lettering style, seen on many product packages at the time, reflects the austerity of the era. Create this alphabet with a ruler and a small circle template. Begin by drawing the vertical, rectangular body of the letter, using your ruler to make perfectly straight, parallel and perpendicular lines. Using the same ruler, draw in the thinner lines and then add the tiny triangles at the bottom of letters such as E, L, M and S. Use your circle template to create the curves on letters such as C, D and O. Color in hollow spaces with a medium-tipped pen. With attention to precision, your 1930s lettering will speak loudly about the unshakable fortitude of those who weathered the worst of times.

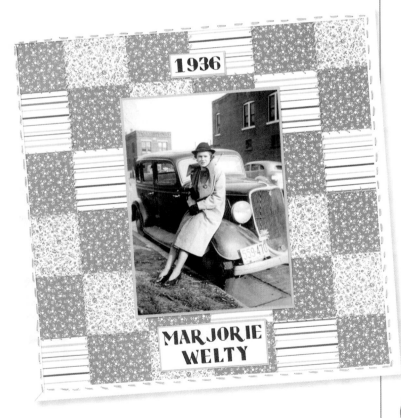

1936

MARJORIE WELTY

ABCD
EFGH
IJKL
MNO
PQRS
TUVW
XYZ
12345
67890

1940-1949

The 40s were dominated by World War II, which pulled America out of the Great Depression by reclassifying more than 50 percent of all job vacancies left by the men who were drafted. The positions were filled by women and African Americans, changing the face of America's workforce forever. The fancy script lettering so popular on consumer goods of the time speaks to the strong feminine influence that emerged as society embraced women in new careers. These free-flowing letters can be created using a fine-tip pen. Begin by penciling in the loopy forms so each sways slightly to the right. The flowing shapes end in curled serifs, and tails on letters such as G and Y are more hooked. Note that O and Q are open as are the lower loops of D and B. Make the point of having *no* points, just gentle slopes and curves, and you'll bring home the bacon for sure.

1944 & Marjorie Susan

DECEMBER 1947

Jane 6 • Nancy 4 • David 1

1950-1959

At the end of World War II, thousands of young servicemen flocked back to the United States, eager to rebuild their shattered lives by starting new families, new jobs and new homes. With an energy never before experienced, the American economy exploded: Television sets, single-family homes and automobiles were snapped up by the thousands. A baby boom was under way. To re-create the thin-thick cursive popular during this booming period of progress, use a fine-tip pen to freehand draw letters. Add width at the top and bottom of each. While all of the letters lean slightly to the right, that's where the rule list ends. Some of the forms are open such as O and Q, some have serifs including R, T and X. M appears to melt, S is in chest-butting mode, U, V and W are only half-grown and crossbars on F and T float just above their bodies. In the post-war world in which the future was waiting to be defined, there was room to flex the muscles of individuality. This alphabet shows how it's done.

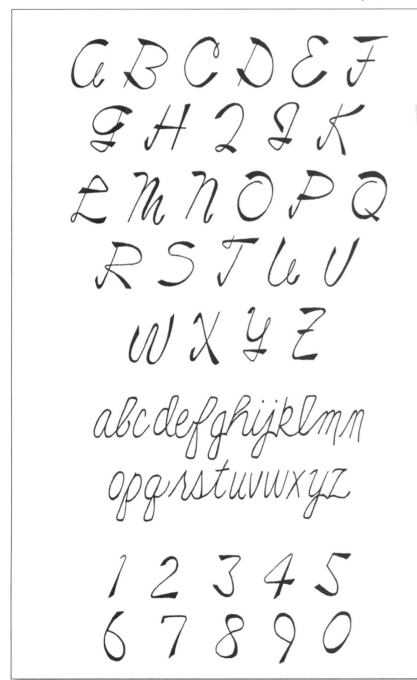

Featherstone Cty. M.N.
Family Farm 1954
Martin, Kathy, Annette,
Carol and Elinor

Bill Krum 18 yrs old
Spending a day at
Devils Lake. 1953

1960-1969

Bell-bottoms. Go-go boots. Love beads. Flowers woven into waist-length, hippy hair. With more than 76 million Baby Boomers beginning to come of age, it's no wonder the 60s—with all of their bright, boisterous fads and fashions—were dubbed "The Age of Youth." To re-create this fun, energetic alphabet, freehand draw straight line letters using a thick-tip pen. In place of serifs, draw smiley faces, peace signs, flowers or other hippie-inspired designs. For variety, use stickers, stamps or punches to embellish the letters. Don't panic if your letters are not perfectly straight. Part of this design's charm is the do-your-own-thing attitude of the individual letters. Add an extra element of funk by drawing each letter with a different color pen. Psychedelic! Peace!

1970-1979

If the 1960s were the decade of youth, the 70s were the era of *you*—as in, do your own thing. Evident by the sexual revolution, wild fashions, and pervasive, rebellious attitude of the time (ABC news anchor Sam Donaldson appeared on TV sporting long side-burns!), individuality ran rampart. This funky bubble-alphabet fits into the theme perfectly with letters that scream, "unique." While they share a few common characteristics, such as their chunkiness and ascending, graduated shading, that is where the similarities end. Want to put a pointed, curled-tailed "hook" in the middle of your I? How about leaving the curl of the O open, while making the Q appear more traditional? Who's got it? YOU!

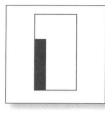

1980-1989

The1980s, the Shop-'Til-You-Drop decade, was a period of self-fulfillment. Reach for your dream and achieve it. Let nothing stand in your way. Binge-buying, credit, designer labels, Nintendo, exercise videos, minivans and camcorders became an integral part of everyday lives. Modern technology found its toehold, influencing everything in society...including this space-age alphabet. To create, freehand draw boxy, sans serif letters with a fine-tip pen. Add rectangular boxes to the vertical lines of each letter (with the exception of V). Then add extra rectangles just for good measure on letters such as N and R. Use the rectangular blocks to create "negative space" in letters W and M. Note that this alphabet is void of curved lines and letters such as C, D, O, P and Q are formed with right angles. Color in the thick, vertical rectangles to coordinate with your page design.

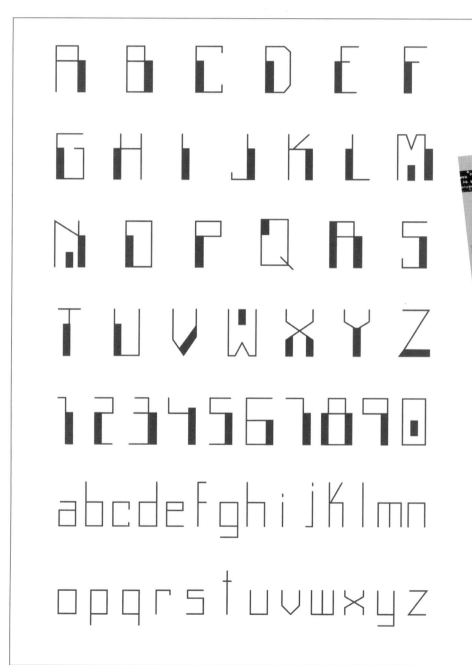

VARIATION

Freehand draw the outline of each letter. With a thick-tip black pen, color in the center space of each outlined character. Using a hole punch, remove black spaces to achieve a "Pac Man" alphabet.

1990-1999

With the birth of the World Wide Web in 1992, the 90s exploded into the electronic age, seemingly overnight. Suddenly, everything about our lives changed, from the way we communicated (e-mail), to the way we spent money (online auctions and stores), to the way we chose to do business (e-commerce). By 1998, an estimated 100 million people were online. Internet lingo like LOL (laughing out loud) and BTW (by the way) had become vocabulary standards. The computer age is reflected in the megabyte alphabet shown on the facing page. Create this techno-script using a medium tip black pen. Freehand draw thick, angular sans serif capital letters, only slightly rounding corners. With a green pen, loosely trace around the edges of each letter, extending your marks visibly beyond the edges. All green lines should be straight, even when extending across the slightly rounded portions of the black letters.

LETS EAT

CINDY AND SARAH SHARING A "MOM AND DAUGHTER" MOMENT.

JENNIFER, CAROL AND SARAH LOOK OVER THE BURGERS.

bottomless pit

always hungry

never stops eating

VARIATION

For a *More* playful version of this lettering style open up the letters by extending border lines around their perimeters rather than cutting into them. This creates letters with wide open fill spaces which can be easily chalked. Triple mat in primary colors and embellish the page with darling buttons.

ABCDEFG

HIJKLMNOP

QRSTUV

WXYZ

1234567890

Lettering Artists

Debra Beagle, Milton, Tennessee
Whimsical Block Page
Simple Stretch Page
Curved Classic Page
Debbie Davis, Spokane, Washington
Roman Holiday Page
Florence Davis, Winter Haven, Florida
Sampler/Inspired Page
Cindy Edwards, Highland, Michigan
Chicken Scratch/Inspired Page
Sarah Fishburn, Fort Collins, Colorado
Contempo Page
Pamela Frye, Denver, Colorado
Fun and Funky Page
Mary Conley Holladay, Jacksonville, Florida
Hearts Entwined Page
Lisa Jackson, San Antonio, Texas
Juliann Page
Fishbone Page
Fleas Page
Jan March, Hilton, Iowa
1980s/Pac Man Page
Lindsay Ostrum, Colfax, California
Shaker Page
1980s Pac Man/Inspiration Page
Allison Pavelek, Salem, Oregon
Adventure/Inspired Page
Michelle Pesce, Arvada, Colorado
Slant Page
Elegance Page
Charity Ball Page
Grace Page
Worldwide Page
Narda Poe, Midland, Texas
Architecture Page
Holly Page
Sunburst Page
Swirl Page
In Bloom Page
Playful Page
Tammy Prueitt, Westminster, Colorado
Bow Tie Page
Carol Snyder, Alpine, Utah
Branding Iron Page
Emily Tucker, Matthews, North Carolina
Puttin' On The Ritz/Inspiration Page
Menagerie Page
JoAngela Vassey, Cherry Hill, New Jersey
Grin Page
Sande Womack, Littleton, Colorado
Fluffy Page

Elementary Page
Signature Page
Pinstripe Page
All For One Page

Memory Makers Lettering By

Pamela Frye
Erikia Ghumm
Pam Klassen
Sampler Page
Puttin' On the Ritz Page
Cross Stitch Page
Color Block Page
Collegiate Page
Worldwide/Inspiration
Chicken Scratch Page
Illuminated Page
Spring Forward Page
Thru The Ages Lettering Pages
(except 1980s/Pac Man)

Art

Art that appears in this book and is not credited on these pages was created by *Memory Makers* artists.

Bow Tie
Border/Inspiration
By **Jodie Bushman** Welches, Oregon

Fluffy
Coincidental Cousins, Mom and Perry Como & Debbie and Sande
By **Sande Womack** Littleton, Colorado

Elementary
Young Ameritowne
By **Sande Womack** Littleton, Colorado
Titles
By **Brandi Ginn** 2003 MM Master, Lafayette, Colorado

Signature
When in Rome & Falling for Fall
By **Sande Womack** Littleton, Colorado

Pinstripe
China Business Trip, Annual Christmas Card, They Say It's Your Birthday, Unwrap Smiles
By **Sande Womack** Littleton, Colorado

Sampler
A Mother's Love & Titles
By **Brandi Ginn** 2003 MM Master,

Lafayette, Colorado

Shaker
Hangin' Out With Miss Jeannie, Out of Our Gourd & Titles
By **Lindsay Ostrum** Colfax, California

Slant
Christmastime
By **Michelle Pesce** Arvada, Colorado
My Girls
By **Brandi Ginn** 2003 MM Master, Lafayette, Colorado

All For One
Hemet High, Lucy Lu Bigglesworth & Columbine Wildcats
By **Sande Womack** Littleton, Colorado

Contempo
Titles
By **Brandi Ginn** 2003 MM Master, Lafayette, Colorado
(Photos by Lorna Dee Christensen, Covallis, Oregon)

Elegance
Spring, Honour of Your Presence & Titles
Michelle Pesce Arvada, Colorado

Whimsical Block
Nuts Over Acorns, Jet Skiing Fun & Fire Chief
By **Debra Beagle** Milton, Tennessee

Juliann
Laura's Graduation & My New Ornament
By **Lisa Jackson** San Antonio, Texas
Titles
By **Brandi Ginn** 2003 MM Master, Lafayette, Colorado

Charity Ball
Faces of Tigger, Auntie's Shower & Titles
By **Michelle Pesce** Arvada, Colorado

Architecture
Little Shaver, Wild Blue Yonder & Vacation
By **Narda Poe** Midland, Texas

Simple Stretch
Ballet Class, Artist Eggs-traodinaire & The Huntress
By **Debra Beagle** Milton, Tennessee

Curved Classic
Mi Abuela & Reading Rocks
By **Debra Beagle** Milton, Tennessee

Grace
Dunsmuir House & Titles
By **Michelle Pesce** Arvada, Colorado

Puttin' on The Ritz
Tub Time, Billie 1926 & Titles
By Pamela Frye Denver, Colorado
(Photos for *Tub Time*, Sally Scamfer,
Be lvue, Nebraska)

Holly
Boy Scout Party
By Narda Poe Midland, Texas
Titles
By Michele Pesce Arvada, Colorado

Cross Stitch
A Gift From Above
By Brandi Ginn 2003 MM Master,
Lafayette, Colorado

Hearts Entwined
Noel, Stanton Senior Prom & Titles
By Mary Conley Holladay

Sunburst
Heritage Square
By Narda Poe Midland, Texas
Lake Mead
By Brandi Ginn 2003 MM Master,
Lafayette, Colorado

Swirl
Cowboy
By Narda Poe Midland, Texas
Titles
By Brandi Ginn 2003 MM Master
Lafayette, Colorado

Color Block
(Photo for *Scuba* by Charlotte Wilhite, Fort
Worth, Texas)

Roman Holiday
Roman Holiday & Titles
Debbie Davis Spokane, Washington

Collegiate
(Photos for *Manteca* by Sandra Escobedo)
Border
By Debra Champlin and **Kari Murpy,**
Olympia, Washington

Worldwide
Aloha, Titles & Borders
By Michelle Pesce Arvada, Colorado

In Bloom
*You Are My Sunshine, For Garden's Sake &
Titles*
By Narda Poe Midland, Texas

Fishbone
Jake
By Lisa Jackson San Antonio, Texas
Titles
By Brandi Ginn 2003 MM Master,
Lafayette, Colorado

Fleas
A Baker's Dozen & Memorial Day Picnic
By Brandi Ginn 2003 MM Master
Lafayette, Colorado

Grin
(Photo for *Sam in the Snow* by Adrienne
Marko, Evergreen, Colorado)

Page 78-79 Chicken Scratch
(Photos for *Hay Ride* by Lora Mason,
Orlando, Florida)
(Photos for *Pick of the Patch* by Chrissie
Tepe, Lancaster, California)
(Photos for *Wigged Out* by Sally Scamfer,
Bellvue, Nebraska)
Fall
By Brandi Ginn 2003 MM Master,
Lafayette, Colorado

Playful
He Is Risen
By Narda Poe Midland, Texas
A Day at the Park
By Brandi Ginn 2003 MM Master,
Lafayette, Colorado

Fun and Funky
Guess Who?, Yabba Dabba Doo! & Titles
By Pamela Frye Denver, Colorado
(Photos by Tracy Johnson, Thornton,
Colorado)

Illuminated
Estes Park
By Nicole La Cour Aurora, Colorado

Adventure
Europe & Logan
By Brandi Ginn 2003 MM Master,
Lafayette, Colorado

Menagerie
RiverBanks Zoo
By Emily Tucker Bristol, Tennessee
Nature Center
By Amy Moxley Mt. Airy, Maryland

Branding Iron
Howdy Pardner
By Brandi Ginn 2003 MM Master,
Lafayette, Colorado

(Photos for *Howdy Pardner* by **Amy
Brasier**, Erie, Colorado)
Border
By Carol Snyder Alpine, Utah

Spring Forward
Eyes of a Child & Brinley
By Brandi Ginn 2003 MM Master,
Lafayette, Colorado

Pre-1900s
Calloway
By Torrey Miller 2003 MM Master,
Westminster, Colorado

900-1919
Ray's Return & Titles
Kelli Noto: 2003 MM Master, Centennial,
Colorado

1920-1929
(Photo for *Carol Stauffer* by Debra Fee,
Broomfield, Colorado)

1940-1949
(Photos for *Marjorie and Susan, Irv 1947,*
by Lydia Rueger, *Arvada, Colorado*
(Photo for *December 1947* by Jane Beck,
Normal, Ilinois)

1950-1959
(Photo for *Kathleen Pattisan* by Jennifer
Robinson, *San Diego, California*)
(Photo for *Bill Krum* by Debbie Streicher
and Judy Mowery, *Delaware, Ohio*)
(Photo for *Featherstone City* by Debbie
Mock, Denver, Colorado)

1960-1969
Go-Go Girls 1968
By Torrey Miller: 2003 MM Master,
Westminster, Colorado

1970-1979
(Photos for *Like Threads* by Sarah
Fishburn, *Fort Collins, Colorado*)

1980-1989
(Photos for *Hands Across America &
Florida* by Joyce Schweitzer, Greensboro,
North Carolina)

1990-1999
More
By Valerie Barton 2003 MM Master,
Flowood, Mississippi
(Photos for *Let's Eat* by Martha Vogt,
Mesa, Arizona)

American Girl

Sarah in summer - bold, beautiful, brilliant and beaming - picking berries.

The material in this compilation appeared in the following previously published Memory Makers Books, and appears here by permission of the authors. (The initial page numbers given refer to pages in the original work; page numbers in parentheses refer to pages in this book.)

Editors of Memory Makers	Creative Paper Techniques for Scrapbooks c. 2002	Pages 1, 3–127 (5–131)
Editors of Memory Makers	Getting the Most From Your Scrapbook Tools c. 2003	Pages 1, 4–95 (132–225)
Editors of Memory Makers	Scrapbook Borders, Corners and Titles c. 2003	Pages 1, 4–95 (226–319)
Editors of Memory Makers	Scrapbook Lettering c. 2002	Pages 1, 4–111 (320–429)

Other fine Memory Makers books are available from your local bookstore, craft store or direct from the publisher.

09 08 07 06 05 5 4 3 2 1

Scrapbook Tips & Techniques: Over 100 quick & easy ideas! / edited by Memory Makers Books—1st ed.
      p. cm.
      ISBN 1-892127-68-7 (hc.: alk. paper)

Cover designer: Leigh Ann Lentz
Production Editor: Jennifer Ziegler
Production Coordinator: Kristen Heller